STUDIES IN LINGUISTICS

Edited by
Lawrence Horn
Yale University

A ROUTLEDGE SERIES

Studies in Linguistics

Lawrence Horn, *General Editor*

STRUCTURAL MARKEDNESS AND SYNTACTIC STRUCTURE
A Study of Word Order and the Left Periphery in Mexican Spanish

Rodrigo Gutiérrez-Bravo

Routledge
New York & London

Published in 2006 by
Routledge
Taylor & Francis Group
711 Third Avenue
New York, NY 10017

Published in Great Britain by
Routledge
Taylor & Francis Group
2 Park Square
Milton Park, Abingdon
Oxon OX14 4RN

First issued in paperback 2013

© 2006 by Taylor & Francis Group, LLC

Routledge is an imprint of the Taylor & Francis Group, an informa business

International Standard Book Number-10: 0-415-97607-3 (Hardcover)
International Standard Book Number-13: 978-0-415-97607-7 (Hardcover)
International Standard Book Number-13: 978-0-415-85088-9 (Paperback)

Library of Congress Cataloging-in-Publication Data

Catalog record is available from the Library of Congress

Taylor & Francis Group
is the Academic Division of Informa plc.

Visit the Taylor & Francis Web site at
http://www.taylorandfrancis.com

and the Routledge Web site at
http://www.routledge-ny.com

Contents

Abbreviations

1	First person
2	Second person
3	Third person
ACC	Accusative preposition
ACC-CL	Accusative (direct object) clitic
Ag	Agent
CL	Clitic
DAT-CL	Dative (indirect object) clitic
Ex	Experiencer
exp	expletive
Loc	Location
p	Plural
s	Singular
Temp	Temporal adverb
Th	Theme

Acknowledgments

This book is a minimally modified and updated version of my 2002 Ph.D. dissertation from the University of California, Santa Cruz. A lot of people have contributed in one way or another to the completion of this work, but thanks go first and foremost to my dissertation supervisor Judith Aissen. Without her continuous support in pretty much every area related to graduate school, this dissertation might not have come into being. Needless to say, this dissertation has benefited enormously from Judith's detailed comments on both form and content. Many thanks also to Jim McCloskey and Donka Farkas with whom I had the opportunity to discuss the issues and proposals developed here, and who were always willing to listen to my half-baked ideas and to motivate me to pursue them further. I would also like to thank Sandra Chung, Jaye Padgett, Peter Sells, James Isaacs and the audience at the Second Joint Stanford-UCSC Workshop on Optimal Typology (12/08/2000) for their comments and feedback on different parts of the analysis presented here.

The linguistics department at UCSC is undoubtedly a unique place for doing scholarly work, and I would like to thank all the other faculty members with whom I've had the opportunity to interact in the last five years. Special thanks to Junko Itô: this dissertation owes a great deal to her expertise in phonology, and, needless to say, to her support throughout graduate school. Also to Jorge Hankamer, Armin Mester, and Geoff Pullum. In one way or another, they have all contributed greatly to my formation and so to the work presented here.

Many thanks are also due to all the people who made this dissertation possible by providing the relevant data from Mexican Spanish (colleagues, friends and family alike): Heriberto Avelino, Yazmín Escoto, Elisa Gutiérrez-Bravo, Mauricio Gutiérrez-Bravo, Gilberto Jiménez, Sofía Jiménez, Paulette Levy, Rebeca Mejía, Verónica Vásquez and all the consultants interviewed indirectly with Verónica's help.

A great many people from the UCSC linguistics community have been a very important part of my life in Santa Cruz, and my gratitude extends beyond the good times we had together. Special thanks to Anne Sturgeon, Dylan Herrick, Kazutaka Kurisu, Christine Gunlogson, and James Isaacs, who have been great friends all along and always succeeded in getting me out of my shell, despite my habitual resistance. Many thanks also to my other peers and to the visiting faculty with whom I shared many enjoyable moments during graduate school: Davina Ramírez, Rachel Walker, Jason Merchant, Ryan Bush, Sacha Arnold, Dan Karvonen, Adam Ussishkin, Andy Wedel, Line Mikkelsen, Brian Lindsey, Klaus von Heusinger, Genoveva Puskás, Edit Doron and Caro Struijke.

Many friends outside of linguistics never failed to provide support and encouragement, along with many hours of fun and delightful interaction. Special thanks go in this respect to Laura Christian, Hiroyuki Matsubara, David Raymond, Conal Ho, Angelina Chin, Christine Takacs, Itzel Cardoso, Rebeca Mejía, and Anke Goebel.

Financially, support for the research reported here was provided by NSF grant SBR-9818177, and by the National Council of Science and Technology of Mexico (CONACYT), scholarship No. 117325.

Finally, I would like to express my deepest gratitude, love, and admiration to my siblings, Mauricio, Elisa and Juan Carlos. We managed to weather the storm together, and few things could make me more joyful than this.

Chapter One
Introduction

The purpose of this work is to investigate some of the grammatical properties that lead to word order variation in Spanish, and to argue that these
properties are inherently related to markedness restrictions on syntactic
structure. In this first chapter I introduce the problems that will be addressed
in the chapters that follow and the theoretical assumptions that I will adopt
for their analysis. I first present an overview of recent analyses of word order
and the data from Mexican Spanish that renders these analyses problematic.
Then I discuss the OT framework that I adopt throughout this work. I conclude by laying out some of my general assumptions about the syntax of
Spanish and by characterizing the variety of Mexican Spanish that provides
the data for this work.

1.1 THE STUDY OF WORD ORDER

1.1.1 General overview

Costa (1998), one of the most influential works on word order variation
developed in recent years, summarizes the fundamental issue that needs to be
addressed when studying word order phenomena. As noted by Costa, the
study of word order variation provides two different, but presumably closely
related areas of investigation. The first one is cross-linguistic word order variation, the study of why constructions with the same interpretive properties
and discourse status can differ with respect to word order across different
languages. The second one is language-internal word order variation, that is,
the study of why, in any particular language, constructions with different
interpretive and discourse properties can show differences with respect to
word order. Although most of the research that follows will concentrate on
the latter issue, it is worth noting that the proposal that I will develop here

stems from what I believe are two serious limitations of most cross-linguistic analyses of word order.

In order to characterize what these two problems are, consider the analysis in Alexiadou & Anagnostopoulou (1998), another very influential work on word order variation. Simplifying somewhat, this analysis takes as its starting point the observation that there are strict SVO languages, strict VSO languages, and languages that show an SVO/VSO alternation with respect to unmarked word order. English would correspond to the first group, Welsh to the second, and Greek and some varieties of Spanish to the third group.

(1)   ENGLISH
      John bought the newspaper.   SVO

(2)   WELSH
      Gwelodd   y   bechgyn   y   draig   VSO
      saw   *the*   *boys*   *the*   *dragon*

      'The boys saw the dragon.'   (Costa 1998: 1)

(3)   GREEK
      a.   O Petros pandrefitke tin Ilektra.   SVO
           Peter   married   Ilektra

      b.   pandrefitke o Petros tin Ilektra.   VSO
           married   Peter   Ilektra

                                    (Alexiadou & Anagnostopoulou 1998: 492[1])

On a first approximation it looks like these word order differences can be accounted for by appealing to the interaction of a number of different parameters, set to different values in the languages under consideration. This is precisely the proposal developed in Alexiadou & Anagnostopoulou (1998). The first parameter they propose has to do with the satisfaction of the Extended Projection Principle (EPP) of Chomsky (1981, 1982). Alexiadou & Anagnostopoulou argue that VSO and SVO/VSO languages without expletives satisfy the EPP via verb raising because they have verbal agreement morphology with the categorial status of a pronominal element.[2] From this it follows that (i) preverbal subjects in SVO/VSO languages are not in an A-position, and (ii) VSO orders never involve a covert expletive. Concretely, Alexiadou & Anagnostopolou propose, following work by Rizzi (1982) and Contreras (1991), that in these languages verbal morphology agreement includes a nominal element

([+D, +interpretable phi-features, potentially +Case], so V-raising in these languages checks the EPP feature in the same way that XP-movement does in non-*pro*-drop languages. Consequently, it is not necessary for the subject DP to move to satisfy the EPP in null subject languages and the VSO order that these languages can display follows automatically. On the other hand, this parameter is set to the opposite value in languages like English. Accordingly, in the absence of expletive insertion, movement of the subject XP to [Spec, AgrS] is the only option available to satisfy the EPP. This explains the strict SVO order attested in these languages.

The second parameter has to do with whether or not [Spec, T], TP being the phrase immediately subjacent to AgrSP, is projected for Case-theoretic reasons. Alexiadou & Anagnostopolou propose that [Spec, T] is projected in Welsh and other Celtic languages. Following the analysis of Irish in McCloskey (1996), the VSO order in these languages is then derived by movement of V through T, ultimately to land in AgrS, and by movement of the subject DP to [Spec,T] to satisfy Case requirements. Consequently, the subject has a fixed position in these languages (the strict VSO order). In comparison, this parameter is set to a negative value in Greek and Spanish: [Spec, T] is not projected in this case, and so the subject does not need to move from its VP-internal position to satisfy Case requirements. Given verb raising, it does not need to move to satisfy the EPP either, and so the SVO/VSO alternation can now be understood as an instance of optionality, presumably related to discourse considerations. The essentials of Alexiadou & Anagnostopoulou's proposal can be summarized as follows:

(4) a. ENGLISH: No verb raising: EPP satisfied by XP movement.

$[_{AgrSP} \ [_{DP} \ Subj \ ]_i \ldots [_{VP} \ t_i \ V \ ]]$ **Strict SVO**

b. WELSH: Verb raising satisfies the EPP, subject DP moves to [Spec, T] for Case-theoretic reasons.

$[_{AgrSP} \ V_i \ [_{TP} \ [_{DP} \ Subj \ ]_i \ t_i \ [_{VP} \ t_i \ t_i \ ]]]$ **Strict VSO**

c. GREEK/SPANISH: Verb raising satisfies the EPP, [Spec, T] is not projected. Subject DP can remain in [Spec, V] or move to [Spec, AgrS].

$[_{AgrSP} \ V_i \ [\ldots [_{VP} \ t_i \ ]]]$ **SVO/VSO**

Impressive as this proposal is, it faces two major challenges that result from broader empirical considerations. On a first approximation it is not evident why a parametrical account of word order variation should be inherently problematic. But this is the result of the fact that too narrow a set of phenomena is being considered in the first place, namely, active clauses with transitive predicates. When we expand this narrowly defined set, a completely different picture emerges. This is because it is not unusual that in any particular language, the relative order of the arguments of a predicate may be different depending on the specific class of verbs to which the predicate belongs.[3] The relevant facts are well-known from the descriptive literature on word order (see for example Arnaiz (1998) for Romance languages and Holmberg & Rijkhoff (1998) for Germanic languages), and Spanish is precisely a case in point. Following the standard assumption that unmarked word order is displayed by sentences that can be felicitous answers to questions like *what's happening?*, in (5) a clear asymmetry can be observed when transitive, psych, and unaccusative predicates are all taken into account.[4]

(5) MEXICAN SPANISH:
    Qué pasa/pasó?
    what happens/happened
    'What's been happening/what happened?'

    Unmarked word order
    a. Una muchacha compró los discos.   S V O
       a   girl   bought   the records
       'A girl bought the records.'

    b. A Juan le gustan   los chocolates.   IO V S
       to Juan DAT-CL *like*.3P *the chocolates*
       'Juan likes chocolates.'

    c. Llegó   tu   hermano.   VS
       arrived your brother
       'Your brother arrived.'

Clearly, any analysis of word order that takes into account only transitive clauses and derives the movement of the subject to a preverbal position as a consequence of a property that the subject must satisfy there, will not derive the right result, since the subject DP does not occupy the same position in different classes of predicates. Whatever condition is met by fronting the subject to a preverbal position in transitive constructions is clearly not being met in unaccusative constructions like (5c), where the subject remains in a post-verbal position and the preverbal position remains empty. Similar complications arise with Psych predicates. Even if we assume that the preverbal oblique *experiencer*[5] of a construction like (5b) satisfies the same condition that the transitive subject does in (5a), it is not clear why it is the oblique *experiencer,* and not the grammatical subject, that is fronted to this position.

This observation is particularly troublesome for analyses of word order in transitive constructions where the subject undergoes movement to the preverbal position in order to satisfy a condition specifically defined with respect to the argument of the verb that bears the subject grammatical relation, such as transformational analyses of Spanish where Case is assigned in the preverbal position. It also represents a serious problem for Optimality-theoretic analyses where the subject moves to this position to satisfy a structural subject condition (typically the SUBJECT constraint of Grimshaw 1997) as in Samek-Lodovici (1996), Grimshaw & Samek-Lodovici (1998), and/or a structural Case requirement (Costa 1998).[6]

It is not immediately evident how this criticism applies to the proposal in Alexiadou & Anagnostopolou (1998), though, where fronting of the subject in transitive constructions is an optional operation. It could be argued that this option is taken in (5a), but not in (5b) or (5c). In either case, no syntactic condition is satisfied by fronting of the subject, so it comes as no surprise that the absence of this fronting operation has no effect on the grammaticality of the relevant examples.

Although Alexiadou & Anagnostopolou's analysis fares better than Subject-condition analyses (either transformational or Optimality-theoretic), it still raises two important issues. First, if fronting is entirely optional in Spanish, it is not obvious why speakers have such clear intuitions about unmarked word order (i.e. IO V S for Psych predicates instead of S V IO, for example). And second, if fronting is entirely optional, this means that for every sentence in Spanish where a constituent is fronted there should be an alternative option, where the preverbal position is empty.

This second issue leads us to the second problem faced by parametrical accounts. Such accounts are based on the assumption that once some parameter is set for a given language, the language will show a fairly uniform set of grammatical properties that are related to the parameter in question. For example, a language is either *pro*-drop or it is not, and a number of (sometimes mutually exclusive) properties follow from this setting of the parameter. In other words, parameters represent an all-or-nothing approach to the characterization of grammar and grammatical constraints. However, as research in Optimality-theoretic syntax has pointed out since its earliest days (see for example Costa 1998; Sells et.al. 1996; Grimshaw 1997; Samek-Lodovici 1996; Grimshaw & Samek-Lodovici 1998) there is considerable empirical evidence that the all-or-nothing approach to word order cannot be entirely correct.

In relation to the parametrical analysis of the satisfaction of the EPP in Alexiadou & Anagnostopolou (1998), Mexican Spanish is particularly illuminating. Mexican Spanish, like any other variety of Spanish, displays all characteristics of languages where the EPP is satisfied through verb raising; null subjects, lack of expletives, lack of definiteness restrictions on post-verbal subjects. Initially, the data in (5) would appear to further provide evidence in favor of this analysis: since the EPP has been satisfied through verb raising, it is not surprising that the presence or absence of a preverbal XP in the examples in (5) has no effect on grammaticality. But, once again, an entirely different picture emerges as soon as we expand the range of constructions in which we expect to find these same effects. In particular, all the examples from Mexican Spanish below, where the preverbal position is empty, are extremely marked, if not downright ungrammatical:[7]

(6) MEXICAN SPANISH

    a. ??Compró Juan el periódico.   V S O
         bought   Juan the newspaper
         'Juan bought the newspaper.'

    b. ??Le regaló Juan un disco a María.   V S O IO
         DAT-CL *gave Juan a record to María*
         'Juan gave a record to Mary.'

    c. ??Le gustan   a Juan   los chocolates.   V IO S
         DAT-CL *like.3p to Juan   the chocolates*
         'Juan likes chocolates (lit. chocolates appeal to Juan).'

Example (6a) is particularly important, since it shows that the SVO/VSO alternation is absent in Mexican Spanish,[8] but all the examples pose the same problem for Alexiadou & Anagnostopolou's proposal. In their analysis, the unacceptability of the data in (6) goes unaccounted for. The verb has raised to I^0 in all cases, carrying the [+D] feature that characterizes verbal agreement morphology in null subject languages, so EPP checking should have taken place successfully. By contrast, all the examples in (7), where the subject appears in preverbal position, are fine[9]:

(7) a. Juan compró el periódico.   S V O
         Juan bought   the newspaper
         'Juan bought the newspaper.'

b. Juan le   regaló   un disco a María.   S V O IO
   Juan DAT-CL *gave a record to María*
   'Juan gave a record to María.'

c. Los chocolates   le   gustan   a Juan.   S V IO
   the chocolates   DAT-CL *like*.3p *to Juan*
   'Juan likes chocolates.'

Interestingly, the relevant fact in (7) is *not* that the subject appears in preverbal position. As shown in (8), what improves the examples in (6) is that there is *some* maximal projection in the preverbal position. It can be an adverbial, as in (8a), the direct object, as in (8b), or the indirect object, as in (8c-d). In this respect Mexican Spanish displays a pattern strikingly similar to the verb-second behavior described for Yiddish in Diesing (1990).

(8) a. Ayer   compró Juan el periódico.   Adv V S O
      yesterday bought Juan the newspaper
      'Yesterday Juan bought the newspaper.'

   b. El periódico lo   compró Juan.   O V S
      the newspaper ACC-CL *bought Juan*
      'John bought the newspaper.'

   c. A Juan le   gustan los chocolates.   IO V S
      to Juan DAT-CL *like*.3p *the chocolates*
      'Juan likes chocolates.'

   d. A María le regaló   Juan   un   disco.   IO V S O
      to María DAT-CL *gave Juan   a   record*
      'Juan gave a record to Mary.'

These data point to the conclusion that Mexican Spanish has an active EPP requirement that is independent of: (i) the *pro*-drop character of this language and: (ii) the requirement that the subject occupy the pre-verbal position.[10] It is crucial to note at this point that the contrasts observed above cannot be analyzed as the result of Mexican Spanish being set to a strict parameter that requires satisfaction of the EPP through XP movement. This is because Mexican Spanish, like any other dialect of Spanish, ordinarily tolerates certain constructions with an empty preverbal position. We have already seen that this is what is observed in unaccusative constructions like (5c), repeated here as (9a). Other constructions that follow this pattern are *pro*-dropped constructions (9b) and impersonal passives (9c):

(9) a. Llegó   tu   hermano.
      arrived   your   brother
      'Your brother arrived.'

   b. Compraron   el periódico.
      bought.3p   *the newspaper*
      '(They) bought the newspaper.'

   c. Se vendió la casa.
      CL *sold*.3s   *the house*
      'The house was sold.'

Intuitively, Mexican Spanish appears to have an active EPP requirement, which has to be satisfied by XP movement, and that can be overridden in cases like (9), but not in cases like (6). Clearly enough, this state of affairs is problematic for parametrical accounts, where grammaticality is related to the satisfaction of some condition, and ungrammaticality to the failure to satisfy it. This is the fundamental observation that will later justify an Optimality-theoretic account of these facts.

To summarize the discussion so far, I have argued for the following two points: (i) any analysis of word order must take into consideration the fact that in some languages, the relative order of the verb with respect to its arguments can be different for different classes of verbs, and; (ii) there is empirical evidence that the fundamental well-formedness conditions that govern word order and word order variation are not all-or-nothing conditions. With these two considerations in mind, I turn now to the second major issue concerning the study of word order, namely, language-internal word order variation.

1.1.2 Language-internal word order variation

As described in detail in Costa (1998), language-internal word order variation corresponds to those instances where the canonical word order attested in a language is perturbed by some syntactic operation. Fronting operations, for example, can change the word order observed in the unmarked case. *Wh*-movement and topicalization in Spanish and many other languages are such operations. Some examples are provided below.

(10) [Los discos]$_{\text{Top}}$ los   compró una muchacha.   O V S
     the records   ACC-CL   *bought   a   girl*
     'The records, a girl bought them.'[11]

(11) Qué   compró Juan?
     what   bought Juan
     'What did Juan buy?'

When considered in isolation, the word order facts in (10) and (11) do not appear to be particularly problematic (or even interesting). Fronting of interrogative *wh*-operators and topicalization can be straightforwardly analyzed as operations that displace constituents from the position where they are generated in order to comply with some principle or parameter of the language in question (the *Wh*-Criterion of Rizzi (1996), for example). From this perspective, the importance of the resulting word order issues is understandably much less than the importance of defining such principles or parameters, on the one hand, and of characterizing the conditions under which displacement operations can take place (island contexts, accessibility, the ECP, etc.), on the other.

However, since the late 1980's it has become increasingly clear that the language-internal word order facts resulting from displacement operations are not only much more complex than previously thought, but they can actually provide fundamental insights for understanding the nature of the principles that trigger such displacements in the first place. Consider, for instance, the impact that object shift has had on the theoretical architecture of the Minimalist Program. It is easy to lose sight of the complexity of language-internal word order variation when looking at a single displacement operation. But when several displacement operations are taking place simultaneously in the same sentence, and when the behavior of these operations is compared across different types of sentences, the enormous complexity of word order variation becomes evident.

Consider in this respect the analysis of Italian in Rizzi (1997), arguably the most influential work on left-peripheral word order facts. Rizzi argues that the relative word order of fronted XPs and of different types of complementizers on the left periphery in Italian is not amenable to an analysis where there is a single functional projection (i.e. CP) above IP. His observations are based on an extensive amount of data, of which I reproduce just an illustrative sample here. In Italian, fronted topics necessarily precede fronted *wh*-operators, as shown in (12).

(12) a. [Il premio Nobel, [a chi lo daranno]]?
          'The Nobel prize, to whom will they give it?'

      b. *[A chi, [il premio Nobel, lo daranno]]?

Fronted topics, however, do not seem to be located in Spec-CP (in the traditional sense), since they follow *che,* the complementizer that introduces finite subordinate clauses.

(13) a. Credo [che [il tuo libro, loro lo apprezzerebbero molto]].
          'I believe that your book, they would appreciate it a lot.'

      b. *Credo [il tuo libro, [che loro lo apprezzerebbero molto]].

Furthermore, the relative order of topics and *wh*-operators in embedded interrogatives can be reversed, resulting in sentences like (14b), where the *wh*-operator precedes the topic.

(14) a. Mi domando, [il premio Nobel, [a chi lo pottrebbero dare]].
          'I wonder, the Nobel Prize, to whom they could give it.'

      b. ?Mi domando [a chi, [il premio Nobel, lo pottrebbero dare]].

Finally, relative clauses are something like the mirror image of matrix interrogatives. In this case, the relative operator must precede a fronted topic.

(15) a. Un uomo [a cui, [il premio Nobel, lo daranno senz'altro]].
          'A man to whom, the Nobel Prize, they will give it undoubtedly.'

      b. *Un uomo [il premio Nobel, [a cui lo daranno senz'altro]].

To account for these and other facts, Rizzi (1997) proposes the exploded-CP structure reproduced in (16).

Under this proposal, the word order facts presented in (12–15) are accounted for roughly as follows. Interrogative operators move to the specifier of a unique Focus Phrase (FocP). They can be preceded by topics, as in (12a), because a Topic Phrase (TopP), which hosts topics in its specifier, is the phrase that immediately dominates FocP. However, there is the possibility of also having a TopP below FocP.[12] This accommodates those cases where the interrogative operator precedes a fronted topic, i.e., example (14b).

(16)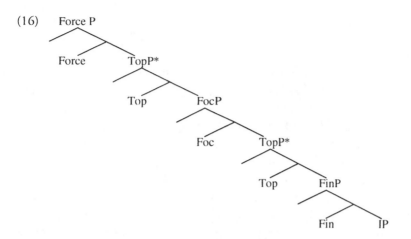

Complementizers that take a finite IP (*che*), are generated in the head of the Force Phrase, the highest phrase in the structure. This is why they always precede fronted topics. Finally, relative pronouns move to [Spec, Force], and this explains why they always precede fronted topics as well.

In a proposal like Rizzi's, the complexity of word order variation is accounted for by suggesting that the set of functional projections of a clause is much more complex than would appear at first sight, an idea that originates in Pollock's (1989) work on the structure of IP. To account for the word order facts, this kind of analysis capitalizes on the larger number of head and specifier positions which it provides.

It seems fair to point out that this kind of proposal comes at a high price, though. The proliferation of functional phrases in the C-system is unappealing in any theoretical framework, for no other reason than Economy of Structure. But additionally, it seems to me that the specific form of Rizzi's (1997) proposal is almost determined *a priori* by the assumptions that Rizzi starts out with. If we assume, as Rizzi does, that different types of clauses have essentially the same template of functional projections, that movement of interrogative and relative operators is *necessarily* movement to a position in the CP system, and if we further assume that fronting of these elements and others, such as topics and fronted foci, *necessarily* involves movement into a specifier position, then it is hard to see how any account of the Italian facts above would not end up looking a lot like Rizzi's.

The crucial point, however, is that none of these assumptions has a strong empirical backup to begin with. The first assumption is a theory-specific assumption characteristic of most transformational frameworks, but one that is not shared by other theories like LFG or OT-syntax. The second assumption, in contrast, is more standard, but may not be as well-founded as it appears to be. A fair number of recent analyses of *wh*-movement in Spanish, for instance, have concluded that [Spec, I] plays a crucial role in this phenomenon, either because the *wh*-operator moves through this specifier position on the way to its ultimate landing site (Goodall 1991a, 1991b) or because it corresponds to its ultimate landing site (Fontana 1994, Zubizarreta 1998). Diesing (1990) also argues that [Spec, I] is the ultimate landing site of *wh*-operators in Yiddish, and even in those languages like English where the correlation between *wh*-movement and the CP system is solidly founded, issues remain. Consider for instance the debate as to whether or not there is movement of the *wh*-operator to [Spec, C] when the operator corresponds to the subject (Grimshaw 1997, *inter alia*). The third assumption, that all fronting operations necessarily involve movement into a specifier position, is even more controversial. At the very least, there is considerable evidence pointing to the conclusion that topicalization can involve adjunction, as discussed in Baltin (1982), Rochemont (1989), Saito (1989), Lasnik & Saito (1992), McCloskey (1992) and Vallduví (1992). Similarly, *wh*-movement has been argued to involve adjunction in some cases, as in Déprez (1991) and Rudin (1988).

If we start out with a different set of assumptions, a very different picture emerges. For example, in her work on the nature of sentential structure (the Extended Projection analysis), Grimshaw (1994, 1997, 2000) argues that sentential projections and many of the operations that take place in them are subject to well-formedness conditions that are defined in relation to the structure of the sentence as a whole and *not* in relation to some particular specifier or head position. Well-formedness conditions defined in this way can be satisfied in different ways in sentences with different structures. For the sake of illustration, assume that topicalization is triggered by a well-formedness condition that requires topics to appear in the sentence-initial position. Costa (1998, 2001), following work in the functionalist tradition, provides an informal definition of such a well-formedness condition, reproduced here in (17).

(17) TOPIC-FIRST: Topics are sentence-initial.

Crucially, topicalization satisfies this condition in all the structures in (18), even if the topic XP is in a different position in each case. In any given language, other considerations might ultimately rule out some of these options over the others,[13] but, in principle, they could all be attested in one and the same language.

(18) a.

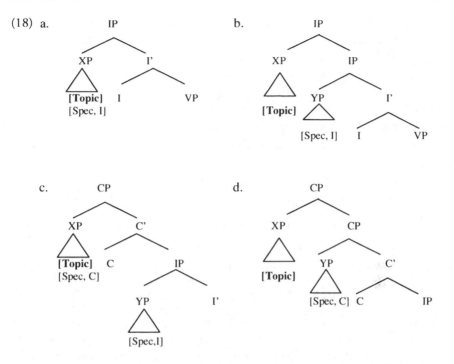

However, it is clear enough that postulating simple well-formedness conditions like TOPIC-FIRST is problematic, since they are almost always trivially falsified by the data. In the Italian examples (14b) and (15) the topic is not the clause-initial constituent, for example. In order to keep simple well-formedness conditions like (17), we require a theoretical framework that can specify with precision the conditions under which they can be overridden. Optimality Theory offers such a possibility.

1.2 OPTIMALITY THEORY

1.2.1 The architecture of OT

Optimality Theory (Prince & Smolensky 2004) is a theory of constraint interaction in generative grammar. In OT, Universal Grammar (UG) is conceived as a set of constraints on linguistic representation, CON, that is present in every language. Crucially, these constraints are interpreted as violable, and the architecture of OT is such that every grammatical construction in a language will still violate a considerable number of constraints. The postulation of violable constraints comes from the observation that many of the well-formedness requirements in any given language seem to be in conflict with one another, but: a) different languages prioritize the satisfaction of different well-formedness requirements, and: b) given a conflict between well-formedness requirements *A* and *B,* prioritizing the satisfaction of *A* over *B* does not necessarily result in a state of affairs such that the effects of *B* are no longer observed elsewhere in the language.

OT accounts for this fact by postulating that constraints are violable, but also that they are hierarchically ranked with respect to one another. This amounts to saying that languages differ with respect to how constraints are prioritized when there is such a potential conflict. Accordingly, in OT the grammar of a particular language is a particular ranking of universal constraints. Constraint rankings are represented as in (19). The connective »
means *dominates* (or *outranks*).

(19) LANGUAGE A: C_α » C_β » C_γ . . .
     LANGUAGE B: C_α » C_γ » C_β . . .
     LANGUAGE C: C_β » C_γ » C_α . . .

In this way, OT provides a simple mechanism for accounting for cross-linguistic diversity while still deriving it from a universal set of well-formedness conditions. Here it is worth clarifying an important point. As such, Optimality Theory is not a theory about natural language, but rather a theory about constraint interaction. The theoretical constructs about linguistic structure that are adopted in an OT analysis are expressed solely in the constraints in CON, and, strictly speaking, nothing about the architecture of the OT framework needs to be reflected in the characterization of these constraints. In this respect OT can be conceived as a framework under which different theories about natural language can be understood.

Returning to the architecture of OT, in this framework the grammar of a particular language is a function that maps a linguistic *input* into its "surface" structural description or *output*. The precise characterization of the input (especially in syntax) depends on what linguistic theory we adopt for our OT analysis. For the time being we can think of it as an abstract representation of the lexical, interpretive and feature specifications that correspond to the (non-structural) properties of the surface representation.[14] The "surface" form of an input (i.e. its output) is arrived at through two different processes. In the first process, a universal function GEN (for Generator) takes the input and generates a set of possible outputs or parses (the *candidate set*) for that input. Once again the precise characterization of the candidates generated by GEN depends on the linguistic theory we adopt, but for the time being we can think of them as some form of surface structure.[15]

(20)

< INPUT >	C_α	C_β	C_γ	C_δ
☞ CANDIDATE A			*	*
CANDIDATE B		*!		*
CANDIDATE C	*!			

In the second process, one of the candidates in the candidate set is selected as the optimal output for the input under consideration by evaluating how it fares with respect to the ranking of constraints that constitutes the grammar of the language. The winning candidate is the candidate that is most harmonic with respect to the constraint ranking. This selection process is carried out by the function EVAL, which takes the candidate set and returns it as a partial order, with its most harmonic member at the top (McCarthy 2002). EVAL does not select the most harmonic candidate based on the number of constraints that it violates, but rather on the relative ranking of the constraints it violates. Given a specific ranking, an optimal candidate is the candidate that satisfies the highest ranked constraint on which competing candidates conflict (Grimshaw 1997). It is of no importance if the optimal candidate fares worse than losing candidates with respect to lower-ranked constraints, as long as it abides by the highest ranked constraint that other candidates fail to satisfy.

The mapping of an input into an output can be represented in a tableau like (20). The input is typically represented in the top left-hand corner of the tableau. The constraint ranking of the language is represented to the right of the input. Solid lines dividing the columns for each constraint symbolize a strict ranking, dotted lines symbolize an undetermined ranking.[16] The candidates generated by GEN are represented in the cells in the column below the input. When a candidate incurs a violation of a constraint, the violation is represented by an asterisk in the cell where the row that corresponds to the candidate intersects with the column that corresponds to the constraint.

Informally, evaluation of the candidates in the candidate set proceeds as follows.[17] First, all candidates are evaluated with respect to C_α, the highest-ranked constraint. Candidates A and B satisfy this constraint, but candidate C violates it. Since this is the highest ranked constraint, candidate C is immediately ruled out of the competition: it incurs a fatal violation (represented as *!) which necessarily makes it sub-optimal (i.e. less harmonious) vis-a-vis the other two candidates, which do satisfy C_a. Notice that in fact candidate C violates less constraints than either of the two other candidates, but this is inconsequential, since satisfaction of constraints is evaluated hierarchically and not quantitatively. The candidate set is now reduced to candidates A and B, and they are evaluated against the next highest ranked constraint, C_β. Since candidate B violates C_β but candidate A does not, candidate B's violation of C_β is fatal and it is dropped out of the competition. With this we have exhausted the candidate set, and so candidate A is selected as the winner, which is represented by the symbol ☞. The procedure outlined here helps to clarify what is meant in OT when we say that an attested surface representation (i.e., the output) is simply optimal. In a state of affairs where every potential output is going to violate a certain number of constraints, the attested output corresponds to the one possibility that best satisfies the hierarchical ranking of constraints that corresponds to the grammar.

OT considers two basic types of constraints, faithfulness constraints and markedness constraints. Faithfulness constraints govern the identity relations between the input and the candidates generated by GEN. In contrast, markedness constraints evaluate the form (i.e. the structural configuration) of these candidates. An important note on terminology is necessary here. Markedness as a technical term for grouping certain kinds of constraints in OT is *not* equivalent to the descriptive or typological definition of markedness (see McCarthy (2002: 13–17) for discussion). It is important to keep this distinction in mind throughout this work because my proposal concerns both markedness in the descriptive sense (i.e. clause *A* is more marked than clause *B*) and markedness constraints, most of which (but not all) are directly related to markedness as understood descriptively. To avoid this terminological confusion as much as possible, in what follows I use the term *structural markedness* to refer to markedness in the descriptive sense, and *markedness constraint* to refer only to those constraints directly related to *structural markedness*.

Before laying out the more specific assumptions that I adopt in the OT analysis to be developed here, it is worth discussing a number of fairly widespread misconceptions that have given raise to criticism of this framework. One of the most common misconceptions about OT is that it is simply a mechanism of interpreting constraints that allows us to account for patterns that do not conform to these constraints. Yet this is far from the case. First, as noted in Grimshaw (1997), the fact that conditions on representation are understood as "soft" constraints in OT allows very simple definitions of these conditions. In other words, OT is a theory where the constraints on linguistic structure are very simple, and the vast complexity of attested linguistic structures is accounted for instead by the interaction between these constraints. This stands in sharp contrast with all-or-nothing representational models like GB, where the definition of conditions on representation has to be, in comparison, fairly complex. Otherwise, the range of empirical facts accounted for by these conditions would be minimal.

Furthermore, the predictive power of these simple, violable constraints is considerable indeed. Even though OT allows for the possibility of constraints to be violated, it is crucial to remember that in OT the grammar of a particular language is considered to be a particular ranking of universal constraints. As a result, for every constraint postulated to be part of UG, in principle it should be the case that such a constraint appears at the top of the constraint ranking in some particular language. This means that in such a language, the conditions determined by the constraint are met without exception, because the constraint is undominated. In other words, we still expect "soft" constraints to display the behavior of "strong" principles or parameters in some cases. This is a powerful and concrete prediction that results from the specific architecture of OT, and it is also a fundamental guideline when trying to determine the nature and form of the constraints in UG. Concretely, the violable nature of constraints in OT does not allow us to simply postulate any kind of constraint on linguistic structure, since in principle there will be languages where this constraint will never be violated. Summing up, interpreting a constraint on linguistic structure as a violable constraint in OT does not make this constraint empirically vacuous.

1.2.2 Optimality Theoretic Syntax

As previously mentioned, OT is not a linguistic theory, but rather a theory of constraint interaction. Accordingly, research in Optimality-theoretic syntax has been undertaken in a variety of theoretical frameworks, including functional-typological syntax (Legendre et. al. 1993; Aissen 1999a, 2003), Lexical-Functional Grammar (Bresnan 2000a, 2000b; Choi 1999; Sells 2001, *inter alia*) and Minimalist-derivational syntax (Pesetsky 1998; Broekhuis 2000; Heck & Müller 2000). The analysis in this work is developed in the OT representational framework that has stemmed from the work in Grimshaw (1997), Legendre et. al. (1995, 1998), Samek-Lodovici (1996), Costa (1998, 2001), Grimshaw & Samek-Lodovici (1998), among many others. The theoretical constructs of this framework share some assumptions with Government and Binding Theory, but strictly speaking they constitute as a whole a very different linguistic theory, whose characteristics have been shaped to a considerable extent by the specific architecture of OT.

The basic assumptions that I adopt from this framework are outlined below.

With respect to the characterization of inputs, I follow Grimshaw (1997), Legendre et. al (1995, 1998), Samek-Lodovici (1996), Grimshaw & Samek-Lodovici (1998) and others in assuming that inputs are predicate-argument structures, which consist of a lexical head and its argument structure, an assignment of lexical heads to its arguments, and also tense and aspect specifications. I assume that adjuncts are also specified in the input (Legendre et. al. 1998, Choi 1999). Following the notation in Legendre et. al. (1998), arguments are kept apart from adjuncts by a semi-colon ";". I further assume, following Legendre et. al. (1998), that arguments and adjuncts in the input are specified with syntactically-relevant features like [wh], [+/- referential], etc.[18] Accordingly, a sentence like (21a) would have the input illustrated in (21b).

(21) a. John bought the newspaper in Brussels.

　　　b. <buy (x, y; z), Past, x=John, y=the newspaper; z=in Brussels>

Following Legendre et. al. (1998), I also assume that the scope of certain operators and other scope-taking elements is specified in the input. The input of a sentence showing sentential negation, for example, would be represented as in (22b).

(22) a. John didn't sleep.

　　　b. < ¬ (sleep (x)), Past, x=John >

However, in contrast with Legendre et. al. (1998) I do not assume that the scope of topics and *wh*-operators is specified in the input. This is an issue that will be addressed in detail in Chapters Four and Five.

I further assume that elements in the input are specified with features relevant to information structure, such as [topic] and [focus] (see Samek-Lodovici 1996, Costa 1998, 2001, Grimshaw & Samek-Lodovici 1998, Choi 1999). An instance of subject focus like (23a) would have (23b) as its input.

(23) a. JOHN bought the newspaper.

　　　b. <buy (x, y), Past, x=John, x=[focus], y=the newspaper>

Lastly, I assume that the semantic role of the arguments of a predicate is specified in the argument structure that is part of the input, as illustrated by (24).[19] In this I depart from the characterization of argument structure in Grimshaw (1990), where arguments are represented by variables that do not bear any semantic role labels.

(24) a. John bought the newspaper.

  b. <buy (x, y), Past, x=John, x=*agent,* y=the newspaper, y=*theme*>

Including semantic role labels as in (24) is in a sense redundant, since such information is already part of the lexical entry of a predicate. However, since reference to such semantic roles will be crucial in the analysis that follows, it will be useful to specify them in each tableau for expository purposes.

My assumptions with respect to GEN are the following. I assume that the candidates generated by GEN are annotated S-structures which, roughly, combine both surface syntax and LF information (see Williams 1986, Brody 1995, Legendre et. al. 1995, 1998), and the prosodic structure of the sentences in question (Truckenbrodt 1999, Gutiérrez-Bravo 2002a, Büring & Gutiérrez-Bravo 2001, Szendröi 2001). Since this work does not concentrate on the interpretive or prosodic properties of the annotated S-structures generated by GEN, I will only lay out my assumptions with respect to their syntax.

I adopt the following assumptions about the syntactic trees generated by GEN. I will assume throughout that GEN generates all and only those structures that conform to X-bar theory (Grimshaw 1997). In other words, a minimal X-bar theory is part of GEN, such that structures like those in (25) are never elements of the candidate set.

(25) a. $[_{x^0}$ $[_{x^0}$ X] $[_{YP}$ Y]]].

  b. $[_{YP} [_{XP}$ X]].

Example (25a) is a structure where a maximal projection is a sister to a head, but where the node dominating both constituents is a zero-level node. Example (25b) is a structure where a maximal projection without a head node is projected on top of another projection. Likewise, I assume that GEN does not generate tree structures that violate other formal restrictions on trees such as the Single Root Condition, the Exclusivity Condition and the Nontangling Condition (see Partee et. al. (1987) for relevant definitions). On the other hand, I assume that directionality (the relative order of a head with respect to its complements and its specifier) and the possibility of having multiple specifiers (Chomsky 1995) are regulated by independent violable constraints, whose precise formulation will not be dealt with here. However, I do assume that the constraints that require complements to be generated to the right of their head and specifiers to the left are undominated in Spanish, and so is the constraint that militates against multiple specifiers. For the sake of simplicity I also assume that a constraint requiring strict binary branching is undominated in Spanish, although this assumption will not be crucial for the analysis in any way. Accordingly, the only candidates considered in what follows are those whose maximal projections correspond to the schema in (26) below, which can be further modified by either left or right-adjunction.

Lastly, I assume that the annotated S-structures that constitute the candidate set can be different from the input in their feature content and interpretive properties (i.e. that they can be unfaithful to the input with respect to these properties). There is considerable debate in OT-syntax as to whether GEN can generate candidates whose interpretive properties and feature content is different from the one specified in the input. Kuhn (2001, 2003) rejects this possibility, based on arguments from efficiency of computation. However, as noted in McCarthy (2002), OT shares with most other generative frameworks a commitment to *well-definition* and not to *efficiency of computation.* As in other generative frameworks, *efficiency of computation* is an issue of performance, not of linguistic competence. In this respect, allowing candidates to be unfaithful to the input is crucial for *well-definition.* Legendre et. al. (1998) and McCarthy (2002) note that serious problems arise if this possibility is not allowed, such as ineffability and problems with characterizing ungrammaticality in any meaningful way.[20]

(26)

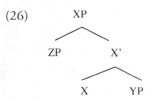

With respect to Thematic Theory, I assume that the locality of θ-marking is regulated by the constraint in (27), from Grimshaw (1997: 374).

(27) LOCAL θ-MARKING   (θ-MARK)
Lexical heads θ-mark within their lexical projections.

I assume that this constraint is undominated in Spanish, which amounts to saying that all of the arguments of a verb must be θ-marked within the VP. In relation to this, I also assume that candidates that omit any of the arguments specified in the input are ruled out by PARSE constraint (Prince & Smolensky 2004, Grimshaw & Samek-Lodovici 1998), which requires all elements specified in the input to be realized in the output.

When an argument surfaces in a position outside the VP, θ-MARK is satisfied by establishing a chain between an argument displaced outside the VP and a VP-internal trace, as in (28).

(28) John$_i$ might [$_{VP}$ t_i buy the newspaper].

This does not imply that the chain <John$_i$, t_i> in (28) is derived by movement. In the OT-syntax framework adopted here it is taken to be a purely representational chain in the sense of Brody (1995). This means that chains are syntactic objects inserted as such in phrase markers in order to express relations between discontinuous positions (see Grimshaw 1997; Legendre et. al. 1995, 1998; Costa 1998). In Optimality-theoretic terms this means that GEN can generate S-structures like (28) directly.[21] Chain formation, however is penalized by the constraint STAY (Grimshaw 1997:374; see also Legendre et. al. 1995, 1998), which is violated once for every trace that is part of the chain.

(29) STAY
Trace is not allowed.

The precise interpretation of this constraint depends on whether one adopts a representational or a derivational model for the OT analysis as a whole. In a derivational model, STAY is violated once for every movement operation. In a representational model, STAY is instead an Economy condition on chains; a chain with a head and one trace violates STAY once, a chain with two traces violates STAY twice, etc. The important point is that there is no movement in this case. GEN can generate chains of any size to represent syntactic displacement, and strictly speaking, every constituent is generated in the same position where it appears in the annotated S-structure that corresponds to the output. Since both my analysis and the OT analyses under discussion here are strictly representational, I henceforth adopt the latter interpretation of this constraint.[22]

The STAY constraint guarantees that displacement will only take place when required to satisfy a higher ranking constraint. In other words, candidates displaying gratuitous displacement chains will lose to candidates that do not because of their unjustified violations of STAY. In this respect, STAY is the OT equivalent of Economy of Movement in transformational frameworks. For the most part, STAY does not play a crucial role in my analysis, though, and for simplicity I will mostly leave it out of the tableaux and the evaluation of candidates in the following chapters.

With respect to surface grammatical relations, I assume that they are determined by constraints that map the thematic properties of the arguments of a verb into such relations, as in Aissen (1999a) and Asudeh (2001). However, my analysis is equally compatible with frameworks where grammatical relations are instead primitives, as in Relational Grammar.

A final issue concerns ungrammaticality. In a framework like Principles and Parameters, violation of a principle or value setting of a parameter leads to ungrammaticality. Clearly enough, this is not possible in OT, since every optimal output will still violate a considerable number of constraints. The solution that is often offered to solve this problem is that ungrammatical constructions are losing candidates (given a specific input) and that grammaticality is a property solely of the winning candidate (see for example Samek-Lodovici (1996) and Müller (1999) for discussion). This is, however, a somewhat problematic solution. In OT syntax, any given set of candidates will include a number of losing candidates that will correspond to ungrammatical constructions (in the traditional sense), but there will also be a number of losing candidates which we can clearly identify as grammatical sentences. These losing candidates, while still grammatical, do not have the interpretive or information structure properties that make the winning candidate the optimal one.

To accommodate this situation, it has been suggested (in Grimshaw & Samek-Lodovici 1998, for example), that grammaticality is context-dependent (and accordingly input-dependent, to the extent that the discourse context can define some of the features of the elements in the input). For example, a sentence that can be pragmatically infelicitous in some instances is taken to be ungrammatical in those contexts where it is perceived to be ill-formed by native speakers, but grammatical otherwise.

Still, one cannot help but have the strong intuition that there is a fundamental difference between sentences that have been labeled "ungrammatical" in traditional terms and sentences that just happen to be semantically ill-formed or infelicitous under certain pragmatic conditions. Accordingly, throughout this work I adopt the characterization of ungrammaticality proposed in Gutiérrez-Bravo (2000), where an ungrammatical sentence is a sentence that, given a specific ranking of constraints, will never surface as an optimal candidate, no matter what the input is. In other words, an ungrammatical sentence is a candidate that is suboptimal for every input.[23] An unfelicitous sentence, in contrast, is a sentence that for a certain number of inputs may not emerge as the optimal candidate, but there will be at least one input for which this sentence will be the optimal output (and thus correspond to a felicitous utterance). This distinction will be further clarified and discussed in the chapters that follow, and plays a crucial part in the analysis in Chapter Four.

1.3 SPANISH

1.3.1 Basic Assumptions

My basic assumptions about Spanish sentential structure are fairly standard, and are mostly based on the analysis in Suñer (1994). I assume that all arguments and adjuncts of a verb are generated in a VP shell, such that adjuncts and adverbials are the most deeply embedded constituents of the VP (Larson 1988), and that the external argument is generated in [Spec, V]. I also assume that V raises to I in all tensed clauses (Pollock 1989, Contreras 1991, Suñer 1994, *inter alia*). Following these assumptions, the SVO order results from movement of the subject to [Spec, I], whereas in the VSO order the subject remains in its base position (Suñer 1994). Following Suñer (1988), I further assume that accusative and dative clitics in Spanish are instances of morphological agreement. More detailed assumptions about sentential structure in Spanish will be introduced as they become relevant for the discussion.

As mentioned in the previous section, I assume following Dowty (1991) and much previous and subsequent work (especially Aissen 1999a and Asudeh 2001), that the grammatical relations of the arguments of a predicate are determined by the semantic properties of the predicate and not by the structural position that these arguments occupy at some level of representation. In this respect, I assume that Case and subject-verb agreement in Spanish are governed by well-formedness conditions that target the subject as defined by these semantic properties or entailments, instead of being associated with specific structural positions. The reason for adopting these assumptions will become clear in the chapters that follow.

1.3.2 A note about the data

Unless otherwise noted, the data used throughout this work corresponds to Mexican Spanish, the variety of Spanish with the largest number of speakers (approximately 100 million, 10 million of whom live in the US). The literature on Spanish syntax usually makes reference to "standard Spanish," under the assumption that this corresponds to some dialect or register of Spanish that is mostly homogeneous across different Spanish speaking countries. I depart altogether from this assumption, and will make reference to different varieties of Spanish according to the geographical area where they are spoken. To the best of my knowledge, the differences between Mexican Spanish and other varieties of Spanish with respect to the word order phenomena that will be the focus of this work have not been previously reported.

The speakers of Mexican Spanish consulted are all from several states in central and western Mexico (Mexico City, Tlaxcala, Jalisco, and Nayarit). No claim is made that the syntax of this variety of Mexican Spanish is different from varieties spoken in northern, southern and south-east Mexico. These other varieties, however, are clearly perceived as distinct by native speakers of the "central-west" variety, and so only speakers from this geographical area were consulted, in order to prevent any interference from potential dialectal variation. Most of the speakers consulted were professionals with college education interviewed in a non-colloquial register, so perhaps the best way to characterize the variety of Spanish under study in this work would be "Standard Mexican Spanish." Again no claim is made at this point as to whether or not the syntax of the colloquial register in this geographical area is any different.

Chapter Two
The EPP and the Notion of the Pole

In this chapter, I develop the infrastructure that will allow us to address the issues on word order in Mexican Spanish that were introduced in the previous chapter. Following the discussion in §1.1, I argue that the EPP plays a fundamental role in explaining language-internal word order variation. Based on data from Spanish, however, I argue that the EPP is not defined with respect to a specific specifier position (say, [Spec, I]), but rather that it should be defined relationally. In the analysis I develop the EPP is satisfied in the specifier of the highest inflectional projection, whatever the specific category of this projection may happen to be, regardless of the grammatical relation (or Case) associated with the phrase that functions as its specifier. The result is that the EPP is defined with respect to the highest inflectional specifier irrespective of whether it corresponds to an A or an A-Bar position. To reflect this fact, and to disassociate this specifier from any specific grammatical relation, I propose that it be referred to as the Pole of the clause.

In section §2.1 I introduce and define the notion of the Pole. Building crucially on the notion of Extended Projection (Grimshaw 1994, 1997), I depart from Grimshaw by suggesting that the minimal Extended Projection allowable in matrix clauses is IP and not VP, and that CP in turn constitutes a functional layer distinct from IP, as in Rizzi (1997). The purpose of establishing these distinctions will be to develop constraints that specifically target different layers of the Extended Projection. I then discuss a number of issues of clause structure in Spanish and I provide evidence from ellipsis that suggests that the EPP is not always satisfied in Spec-IP.

In section §2.2 I introduce the distinction between Pole and grammatical subject. First, I present evidence from ellipsis to show that subjects, topics, and interrogative *wh*-operators all occupy the same position in Spanish, and that this position corresponds to the highest inflectional specifier. At this point, the precise characterization of the notion of the Pole is presented. I go on to discuss some of the advantages of having a notion of Pole that is distinct from the notion of subject. I conclude this chapter by presenting evidence from ellipsis and from the distribution of negative XPs that there are grammatical properties in Spanish that implicate the Pole and not the subject grammatical relation.

2.1 POLE VS. [SPEC, I]

In this section I introduce the notion of the Pole and its relation to the EPP. First I discuss the characterization of Extended Projections that my analysis assumes. I then provide evidence from the syntax of Spanish that supports a relational definition of the EPP. Since the notion of Extended Projection might be unfamiliar for some readers, I provide some detailed discussion of it in §2.1.1. The reader familiar with Grimshaw's proposal can proceed directly to §2.1.2.

2.1.1 Extended Projections

An influential proposal developed in optimality-theoretic syntax is the notion of *Extended Projection* (Grimshaw 1994, 1997, 2000). The core idea is that even though nominal and sentential expressions can contain more than one projection (say $[_{CP} [_{IP} [_{VP} V]]]$ for a clause) all these projections together can constitute a single extended projection, unified by the fact that all its layers share the same categorial feature as the head of the lexical projection that is subjacent to all the other projections. In other words, CP, IP and VP form an extended projection by sharing the categorial feature [verbal]. What distinguishes the lexical projection from the functional projections that dominate it is what Grimshaw (2000) refers to as the *functional status* of each projection. The functional status of a projection is encoded as a value for the functional feature {F}, which is part of the feature content of every head. In this system, lexical categories are {F0}, the functional projection that immediately dominates the lexical projection is {F1}, the next functional projection is {F2} and so on. A category label can now be characterized as a pair that consists of a categorial specification and a functional specification:[1]

(1) a. V   [verbal]   {F0}
     b. I   [verbal]   {F1}
     c. C   [verbal]   {F2}   Grimshaw (2000: 117)

A central idea is that the head of the lexical XP in an extended projection functions as the head of the whole extended projection. So in the structure [$_{CP}$ [$_{IP}$ [$_{VP}$ V]]], the lexical item under V is the head of the extended projection [$_{CP}$ [$_{IP}$ [$_{VP}$]]]. This is defined as follows:

(2) EXTENDED PROJECTION (Grimshaw 2000: 117)
   X is a *head* of YP, and YP is a projection of X iff:

   a. YP dominates X.

   b. YP and X share all categorial features.

   c. All nodes intervening between X and Y share all categorial features,
      (where a node N *intervenes* between X and YP if YP dominates X and N,
      N dominates X, and N does not dominate YP).

   d. No node intervening between X and YP is lexical.

As an example, consider the following structure, from Grimshaw (2000). In (3), IP is an extended projection of V. This is because, given the definition in (2), IP dominates V, IP and V share the same categorial features, in this case the feature [verbal], and the only node that intervenes between IP and V, in this case VP's, also has the feature [verbal] and it is not a lexical node distinct from V.[2] Similarly, CP is an extended projection of V; CP dominates V, they share the same categorial feature, the nodes that intervene between CP and V (i.e. IP and VP) are also [verbal] and there is no lexical node distinct from V that intervenes between CP and V. Crucially, though, VP is not an extended projection of the N that heads the DP complement of V. This is because VP and N do not share the same categorial features: the former is [verbal], the

(3)

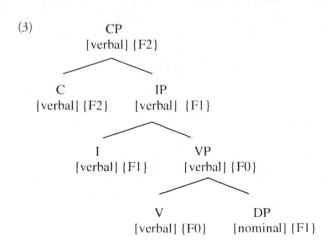

latter is [nominal]. Grimshaw also notes that this system can be readily expanded to more complex analyses of clause structure such as those that include a Polarity or Negation Phrase (Laka 1990, Zanuttini 1997a, 1997b) and exploded versions of IP (as in Pollock 1989).

There is a further requirement governing the well-formedness of extended projections, namely that YP in the definition in (2) has an {F} value higher than the {F} value of X.[3] This condition is met by both CP and IP in (3), which have the {F} values {F2} and {F1}, respectively, while V is {F0}. When V takes an IP (or a CP) complement, however, the projections of V will not form an extended projection with the IP complement of V. This is because the {F} value of V and its immediate projection, {F0}, is lower than the {F} value of I, {F1}.

In Grimshaw's proposal it is still possible to distinguish between the extended projection and the standard notion of a projection and its head, which Grimshaw refers to as a *perfect head/projection,* defined as follows (Grimshaw 2000: 117).

(4) PERFECT PROJECTION

X is a *perfect head* of YP, and YP is a *perfect projection* of X iff:
X is a head of YP and the {F} value of YP is the same as the {F} value of X.

The core of Grimshaw's proposal is that while a number of syntactic conditions clearly need the notion of perfect projection to define locality requirements, others are better understood if locality is defined with respect to the Extended Projection.

The notion of Extended Projection has been successfully used in a number of works, both optimality-theoretic (see Sells *et. al* 1996, Samek-Lodovici 1996, Bakovic 1988, *inter alia*) and transformational (Haegeman 1995, Rizzi 1997). One of the most salient characteristics of Grimshaw's proposal is that it adheres fully to the principle of Economy of Structure, in contrast with characterizations of clause structure that resort to a fixed template of functional and lexical projections. In the latter kind of analysis, a sentence is always a CP (or an exploded CP), which in turn dominates a fixed number of functional projections that in turn dominate a number of lexical projections. In the extended projection analysis, the different layers that constitute an extended projection are only projected to the extent that they are needed in order to satisfy the lexical requirements of functional heads, and/or to meet selection, subcategorization and syntactic requirements independent of the lexical properties of these heads. Accordingly, Grimshaw (1997) suggests that a matrix clause with no auxiliary or modal involves only a VP, as in (5a), and a matrix clause with a modal or an auxiliary is just an IP, as in (5b). CP in matrix clauses is only projected when the presence of this projection is required to meet some extra well-formedness condition, such as fronting of a *wh*-operator to a left-peripheral specifier position.

(5) a. [$_{VP}$ John bought the newspaper].
  b. [$_{IP}$ John will [$_{VP}$ buy the newspaper]].
  c. [$_{CP}$ What will [$_{IP}$ John [$_{VP}$ buy]]]?

2.1.2 Minimal Extended Projections

Throughout this work I adopt the Extended Projection analysis and with it the proposal that phrases are only projected when their presence is necessary to satisfy lexical or syntactic requirements. Still, Grimshaw's proposal raises two separate questions which are independent of the issue of Economy of Structure, and which, to the best of my knowledge, have not received any significant attention in the OT literature.[4]

The first issue has to do with the possibility of having a sentential projection without an inflectional layer. As seen in (5a), where the matrix clause is just a VP, this is indeed a possibility in Grimshaw's proposal. Yet, I believe that there is considerable cross-linguistic evidence that this analysis of matrix clauses is not adequate. First of all, a representation like (5a) as a matrix clause would never be attested in languages where the verb always moves out of VP, such as Spanish and other Romance languages. Spanish, clearly enough, has surface strings identical to English (5a). However, following a classic argument made in Pollock (1989) for French, the position of adverbial elements indicates that even in these cases the verb has moved out of VP. Consider the following examples:

(6) a. Juan envolvió   los chocolates.
    Juan wrapped-up the chocolates
    'Juan wrapped up the chocolates.'

  b. Juan envolvió   cuidadosamente los chocolates.
    Juan wrapped-up carefully   the chocolates
    'Juan carefully wrapped up the chocolates.'

The position of the adverb between the verb and its DP complement is the unmarked position of a whole class of adverbial elements. This can be seen in the fact that if the adverb instead follows the DP complement of the verb, the corresponding reading is one where the adverb is interpreted as a narrow focus.

(7) Juan envolvió   los chocolates   cuidadosamente.
     Juan wrapped-up   the chocolates   carefully
     'Juan wrapped up the chocolates CAREFULLY.'

To the extent that we wish to maintain that the verb and the direct object are in a sisterhood relation at some level of representation, an analysis where the verb moves to a head position outside the VP is called for. In such an analysis, accounting for the word order facts in (6b) is unproblematic, since the position of the adverbial element can be taken to be a position in the left edge of VP, as illustrated in (8).[5]

(8) $[_{IP}$ Juan envolvió$_i$ $[_{VP}$ cuidadosamente [t$_i$ los chocolates]]].
     Juan wrapped-up   carefully   the chocolates
     'Juan carefully wrapped up the chocolates.'

Secondly, English shows a similar contrast that again points to the conclusion that even in cases like (5a) an IP is projected, even when English does not display the kind of verb movement observed in Spanish. Following an argument in Radford (1997), the examples in (9) receive a straightforward analysis if the adverbial is in a position outside (the minimal projection) of VP, and the subject DP is the specifier of an I^0, which in (9a) happens to be null. In contrast, it is not evident how to analyze (9a) if this example is just a VP.

(9) a. John usually reads a book every week.

     b. John can usually read a book every week.

Perhaps the strongest argument against an analysis where matrix clauses can be just VPs comes from verb second phenomena in languages like Dutch and German. Consider the following contrast (from Holmberg & Rijkhoff 1998: 78), amply documented in the literature on V2 languages, where the main verb occupies the verb-second position in the absence of an auxiliary, but appears in the clause final position when an auxiliary is present.

(10) DUTCH

   a. Jan zag een vogel.   SVO
       Jan saw a   bird

   b. Jan heeft een vogel gezien.   SOV
       Jan has   a   bird   seen

In principle, we could analyze (10a) as a VP, just like English (5a). But then (10b) becomes immediately problematic, because now it is not clear why the main verb appears to the right of its complement and not to the left, as in the case where there is no auxiliary. In other words, if SVO is the basic (or underlying) order in (10a), then it is not clear why this order is not preserved when an auxiliary is present. In contrast, the standard analysis of Dutch as underlyingly SOV is straightforward. When there is an auxiliary, it occupies the verb-second position (a head position outside VP) and the subject (or some other XP) moves into the specifier of this head position to satisfy the V2 requirement. The main verb, in turn, remains in its base position. When there is no auxiliary, the main verb moves to the head position that would otherwise be occupied by the auxiliary, as in (11), which results in a derived SVO order. But, crucially for the point under discussion, this clearly implies that at the very least there is one more projection above the VP where the verb and its arguments are base-generated.

(11) Jan zag$_i$ [$_{VP}$ een vogel t$_i$].
     Jan saw   a   bird

The same reasoning holds if we adopt the analysis in Zwart (1997), where Dutch is taken to be underlyingly SVO and where the OV order of (10b) is derived through object shift.[6] If object shift is a surface requirement in Dutch, then in order to derive the SVO order in (10a) we must conclude that verb *and* both its arguments have moved out of VP.

In conclusion, there is enough evidence to safely assume that in the most widely studied European languages a matrix clause consists minimally of a lexical projection and at least one functional projection above it. I will not take a stand on the issue of whether this can and should be characterized as a property of UG, or rather if it is the result of some specific property (or a specific constraint ranking, in an OT analysis) characteristic of these languages. For our purposes, based on the discussion above I assume that every matrix clause in Spanish and the other European languages to be discussed below has a functional shell that dominates the lexical layer. In this I also depart from the analysis of Spanish in Bakovic (1998).

The second question raised by the Extended Projection analysis has to do with the nature of the functional shell itself. Turning back to the schema in (3), notice that Grimshaw's proposal does not contemplate any specific distinction between the phrases that constitute the functional shell, other than the specific category (i.e., C vs. I, for example) of the head of each projection. In relation to this issue, Grimshaw (2000) notes that in some Germanic languages like West Flemish, C inflects for the number of the subject DP.[7] This fact, argued by Grimshaw to provide further evidence for the notion of extended projection, is shown in the examples in (12), from Haegeman (1991), cited in Grimshaw (2000). In these examples *da* corresponds to the [-plural] C and *dan* to the [+plural] C.

(12) WEST FLEMISH

| a ... | da | Jan | noa | Gent | goat. |
| | *that* | *Jan* | *to* | *Ghent* | *goes* |

| b ... | dan | Jan | en | Pol | noa | Gent | goan. |
| | *that* | *Jan* | *and* | *Pol* | *to* | *Ghent* | *go* | (Haegeman 1991:530)

While this phenomenon does provide evidence that VP, IP and CP form an extended projection, a different issue altogether is whether or not there is a fundamental distinction between the different kinds of projections that constitute the functional shell. In his analysis of the left periphery, Rizzi (1997) argues that such a distinction should be made, and that the C system is fundamentally distinct from the inflectional layer of the functional shell. He notes that:

"Whatever "inflectional" properties C reflects, they are not encoded in the form of verbal morphology, in the general case: they are expressed on free functional morphemes (*that, que,* etc.) which, if anything, look nominal more than verb-like, as they often resemble demonstrative pronouns, *wh*-elements, certain kinds of nouns ("fact," etc.), etc."[8]

In Rizzi (1997) the C-system is composed of projections related to illocutionary force and discourse considerations (Topic Phrase, Focus Phrase), and the I-system is composed of projections that license agreement, Case, and the like. The proposal that I develop in this work is considerably different[9], but I adopt from the start Rizzi's idea that there is a fundamental distinction between the functional projections that dominate VP. In this I depart from Grimshaw (1997, 2000). The reasons for adopting this assumption will become clearer as we proceed. For our immediate purposes, I will use the following terminological distinction between the projections that constitute the functional shell.

(13) a. Π-Projections: IP, PolP (a polarity phrase), or exploded versions of these projections (TP, AgrSP, etc.).

b. K-Projections: CP, and recursions of CP.

This proposal does not exclude the possibility of having exploded versions of CP, such as the Force and Finiteness Phrases of Rizzi (1997), or the Mood Phrase of Terzi (1999). However, this is an issue that will not be dealt with here, since throughout I will argue (following Zubizarreta 1998), that the fronting operations that Rizzi (1997) associates with the C-system are related in Spanish to the inflectional layer (the I-system) instead. In the spirit of Grimshaw's original proposal, though, I do assume that CP (in contrast with IP) is only projected when its presence is required to satisfy some specific well-formedness condition. I further assume throughout that matrix clauses in Spanish involve only Π-Projections, and that K-Projections are found only in subordinate clauses (see also Doherty 1993 and Grimshaw 1997).

Summarizing the discussion so far, I adopt here the fundamental notions of the Extended Projection, but with two departures from Grimshaw's original proposal: a) matrix clauses always involve a functional shell, consisting minimally of an IP, and; b) within the functional shell, there is a fundamental distinction between the projections of the inflectional layer and those of the C-system, which I classify under the labels Π-Projections and K-Projections, respectively.

2.1.3 A redefinition of the EPP

In the introduction I argued for the following points: a) the EPP is a crucial factor in determining word order in Mexican Spanish; b) the evidence from Mexican Spanish indicates that the EPP has to be satisfied through XP movement and not through verb raising, *contra* Alexiadou & Anagnostopoulou (1998), and; c) constituents other than the subject DP can satisfy the EPP. These three points are illustrated in the mini-paradigm in (14), which reproduces examples from Chapter One.

(14) MEXICAN SPANISH

    a. ??Compró Juan el periódico.   V S O
        bought   Juan the newspaper

    b. Juan compró el periódico.   S V O
       Juan bought   the newspaper
       'Juan bought the newspaper.'

c. Ayer   compró Juan el periódico.   Adv V S O
    yesterday bought   Juan the newspaper
    'Yesterday Juan bought the newspaper.'

The question now has to do with the precise position referenced by the EPP. As previously mentioned, my proposal is that the EPP is satisfied in the highest inflectional projection of the extended projection, independently of the specific category of the head of this projection. In terms of the definition in (13), this means that the EPP is satisfied in the highest Π-Projection. The reason for adopting a relational definition of the position where the EPP is satisfied is best illustrated by a number of facts of Spanish clausal structure, which I now address.

First, consider a simple transitive clause. The standard analysis of these clauses that derives their SVO order consists of postulating that; (i) the subject is generated in a VP internal position; (ii) the verb moves to the head position of the highest inflectional phrase (IP or TP); and (iii) the VP-internal subject moves to the specifier position of this phrase (see Suñer 1994, Zubizarreta 1998, *inter alia*). This analysis is illustrated in (15).

(15) $[_{IP}$ Juan$_i$ compró$_j$ $[_{VP}$ t_i t_j el periódico]].   S V O
           Juan   bought   the newspaper
      'Juan bought the newspaper.'

Establishing what exactly triggers fronting of the subject has been a more controversial issue.[10] Two different hypotheses have been proposed. In one, fronting of the subject is the result of the need to satisfy syntactic requirements, such as the EPP, and/or Case and agreement licensing (see Fernández-Soriano 1999 and Goodall 2001 for recent developments). In the other, fronting of the subject is the result of information structure considerations; topics are fronted in Spanish, as in many other languages, and the subject in (15) undergoes fronting because it is the default topic of the sentence (Meyer 1972; see also Contreras 1976 and Alexiadou & Anagnostopoulou 1998).[11] Based on the evidence presented in §1 that the EPP is an active requirement in Spanish, I adopt the former hypothesis. I present evidence against the latter hypothesis in Chapter Four.

Consider now clauses where the sentential negation *no* appears. As shown in (16), the word order is the same irrespective of the presence of sentential negation.[12]

(16) Juan   no   compró   el periódico.   S V O
      Juan   not   bought   the newspaper
      'Juan did not buy the newspaper.'

(17)

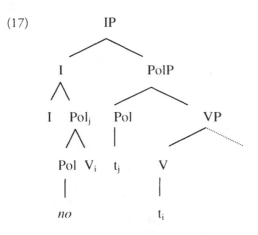

The crucial issue now is determining what exactly the structure of sentences like (16) is. The literature on Spanish and closely related languages like Italian basically considers two alternatives. In the first, *no* is the head of a Polarity Phrase (PolP) that is sandwiched between the projection whose head will be the ultimate landing site for verb movement and the rest of the inflectional layer (Haegeman 1995, Suñer 1995, Zubizarreta 1998). In these analyses, the verb is argued to adjoin to the negation as it moves through Pol^0 on its way to its final landing site in I^0. This is illustrated in above (17):

In the other alternative, PolP is the highest projection of the inflectional layer, but the final landing site of the verb is still I^0, so there is no adjunction or

(18)

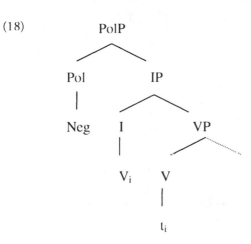

incorporation between the negation and the verb (Laka 1990[13], Contreras 1991; see Zanuttini (1997a) for Italian). This is illustrated in (18) above.

In this latter analysis the fronted subject in (16) would correspond to [Spec, Pol], as opposed to the fronted subject in (15). The consequences of each of these two hypotheses for syntactic phenomena outside negation have not received much attention in the literature (except in Zubizarreta 1998), but their differences surface immediately when we consider subject fronting and word order. In the analysis where PolP (or NegP) is sandwiched between the highest inflectional projection and the rest of the clause, accounting for the word order facts in the negative transitive clause (16) is unproblematic. Whether the subject DP moves to Spec-IP for Case-theoretic reasons, or simply to satisfy the EPP (defined as either a well-formedness condition or as a feature-checking requirement), the landing site is always the same, independently of the presence of the negation. Consequently, it is not problematic to claim that nominative Case is assigned in Spec-IP, or that the EPP is a requirement defined specifically for this specifier position.[14]

In contrast, the word order facts represent a challenge for those analyses where PolP is argued to be the highest inflectional projection because the fronted subject is in a different specifier position in (15) and (16). Accordingly, whatever syntactic requirement triggers the fronting of the subject DP, it cannot be defined with respect to a unique structural position. On the basis of this alone, it would seem that the analysis of Spanish sentential structure in (17) should be preferred. However, data from phrasal ellipsis renders this head-adjunction analysis extremely problematic.

It is a well-known fact about phrasal ellipsis in Spanish that it generally involves a polarity head preceded by the remnant of the elided construction (Brucart 1987, 1999; López 1999; López & Winkler 2000). This is shown in the examples in (19), where the elided phrase is shown in strikethrough.[15]

(19) a. Juan consiguió las   artesanías en   Guadalajara, pero
       Juan got   the handcrafts in   Guadalajara   but

       Luisa no ~~consiguió las artesanías en Guadalajara~~.
       Luisa not
       'Juan got the handcrafts in Guadalajara but Luisa didn't.'

    b. Juan no consiguió las artesanías en Guadalajara, pero
       Juan not got   the handcrafts in Guadalajara but

       Luisa sí ~~consiguió las artesanías en Guardalajara~~.
       Luisa yes
       'Juan did not get the handcrafts in Guadalajara but Luisa did.'

As is also well-known, phrasal ellipsis in Spanish differs from English in that the highest inflectional head cannot appear with, or substitute for the polarity word.[16] This is shown in the examples in (21), adapted from López (1999).

(20) a. Susan had read War and Peace, but Mary hadn't.'

     b. Susan had not read War and Peace, but Mary had.'

(21) a. *Susana había leído   La Guerra   y   la   Paz,   pero María no   había.
         Susana had   read   The   War   and the Peace but María not had

     b. *Susana no había leído La   Guerra   y   la   Paz,   pero María había
         Susana not had   read   The   War   and the Peace but   María had

It has also been widely argued that the constructions in (19) are true examples of phrasal ellipsis, analogous in many respects to English VP ellipsis. For example, they can appear in embedded contexts, as shown in (22):

(22) Susana leyó La Guerra y   la   Paz,   pero creo   [que María no ___].
    Susana read The   War and the Peace but I-think that María not
    'Susana read War and Peace, but I think that María did not.'

Furthermore, they exhibit the strict or sloppy identity pattern observed in English VP ellipsis.

(23) María   no sacó   dinero   de   su   cuenta pero [yo sí   ___].
    María   not took.out money from her account but   I   yes

    STRICT: 'María did not take money out of her account but I did [~~take money out of her account~~].'

    SLOPPY: 'María did not take money out of her account but I did [~~take money out of my account~~].'

The ellipsis facts do not pose a problem for the analysis of sentential structure in (18), where the negation *no* heads a projection that dominates IP. As argued by Laka (1990), under this analysis constructions like (19) and (23–24) can be uniformly analyzed as cases of IP ellipsis.[17] From this perspective, the broader phenomenon under consideration can be characterized as phrasal ellipsis (VP ellipsis in English, IP ellipsis in Spanish). Accordingly, we expect to see some properties shared by these constructions, such as their possibility to appear in embedded contexts, even if their specific instantiation differs from one language to another.[18]

In contrast, in the head-adjunction analysis it is unclear why the polarity head, but not the verb or auxiliary to which it has adjoined, can appear in elliptical constructions. Furthermore, even if an analysis were developed to account for this fact, it would necessarily result in a loss of generalization: since V plus everything that follows it does not form a constituent in the analysis where the verb adjoins to the negation, this elision phenomenon could not be characterized as phrasal ellipsis, and its similarities with English VP ellipsis would go unaccounted for.

At this point, we have reached something of a stalemate. On the one hand, the hypothesis that PolP is sandwiched in the middle of the inflectional layer, which straightforwardly accounts for subject fronting in (15) and (16), is disconfirmed by the data from phrasal ellipsis.[19] On the other hand, the hypothesis that postulates that PolP dominates all other inflectional projections provides a direct account for the ellipsis facts, but it does not account for subject fronting.

However, a solution to this problem is arrived at if we adopt a relational definition of the EPP (like the SUBJECT constraint of Grimshaw 1997), such as the one in (24).

(24) EPP (Preliminary definition)
      The specifier of the highest Π-Projection must be filled.

Crucially, this specifier is not defined in absolute categorial terms, but rather in strictly relative terms (i.e. with respect to the projections that it c-commands, and the projections that dominate it, in the case of subordinate clauses). In other words, if IP is the highest Π-Projection in an clause, then [Spec, I] must be filled. This is what is observed in the standard analysis of (15). But when there is a different Π-Projection above IP, then the EPP is not satisfied in [Spec, I], but rather in the specifier of the projection above IP. With this definition we can adopt the hypothesis that PolP, when present, is the highest inflectional phrase in the Extended Projection in Spanish, which is compatible with the evidence from ellipsis. Fronting of the subject is no longer a problem, since the EPP must now be satisfied in Spec-PolP, not in Spec-IP, because PolP is the highest Π-projection. Accordingly, we can analyze (16) as in (25).

(25) [$_{PolP}$ Juan$_i$ no   [$_{IP}$ compró$_j$ [$_{VP}$ t_i t_j el periódico]]].
        Juan   not   bought   the newspaper
        'Juan did not buy the newspaper.'

The syntactic condition that triggers fronting of the subject is the same for clauses with and without sentential negation. We thus account for the word order facts in (15–16) in a uniform manner, but without claiming that the EPP is satisfied in the exact same position in both cases.

It is here that the importance of assuming a fundamental division in the projections that constitute the functional shell above VP begins to emerge, since it does not seem adequate to claim instead that the EPP is satisfied in the highest phrase of the Extended Projection. This is because the same word order facts in (15–16) are observed in subordinate declarative clauses introduced by a complementizer. In these cases, CP is the highest phrase of the Extended Projection, but the subject is obviously not located in [Spec, C].

The definition of the EPP in (24) is thus conceptually related to the definition of the SUBJECT constraint of Grimshaw (1997). This constraint requires the highest A-specifier of the extended projection to be filled, which in Grimshaw's analysis is sometimes [Spec, V] and sometimes [Spec, I]. In other words, this well-formedness condition is not defined with respect to a unique structural position. The SUBJECT constraint and my definition of the EPP differ in a number of important aspects, which I address in Chapter Three. For the time being, the issue to keep in mind is that the definition of the EPP in (24) is so far neutral to whether the specifier of the highest Π-Projection corresponds to an A or an A-Bar position. I adopt this definition of the EPP because there is evidence that the specifier of the highest Π-Projection in Spanish can be occupied by constituents other than the subject. In the next section, I illustrate this with further data from ellipsis.

2.2 POLE VS. SUBJECT

In the previous section I argued that ellipsis provides evidence that a polarity phrase can be the highest projection of the inflectional layer in Spanish. I now argue that ellipsis also provides evidence in favor of an analysis where different kinds of fronted constituents (fronted subjects, topicalized XPs and *wh*-operators) all compete for the same "left peripheral" position in Spanish. This provides our initial justification for a distinction between the notion of the Pole and the notion of grammatical subject.

2.2.1 Topicalization and wh-fronting in ellipsis.

The idea that constituents other than the subject can occupy what has been referred to traditionally as the canonical subject position has a fairly long tradition in Spanish. In essence, there are two versions of this proposal. In one version, whose origins can be traced back to Meyer (1972), there are two left-peripheral positions, one for fronted topics, and a lower position for *wh*-phrases. In some variants of this version the subject position corresponds to the higher topic position, and the lower position corresponds to [Spec, I] (Vallduví 1992, Fontana 1994) or to the specifier of some other functional projection (Ordóñez & Treviño 1999). In another variant (Groos & Bok-Benema 1986, Jiménez 1994), the position occupied by fronted subjects corresponds instead to the lower position (Spec-IP), and the higher position (Spec-CP) corresponds to the position occupied by fronted topics. In other words, one variant of this analysis claims that fronted subjects have the same distribution as topics (see also Zagona 2002), and the other one claims that they have the same distribution as *wh*-operators.

In the second proposal all fronted constituents compete for the "canonical" subject position, [Spec, I] or [Spec, T], depending on the analysis. This is either because these constituents must move through this position on their way to their ultimate landing site (as in the analysis of *wh*-movement in Goodall 1991a, 1991b) or because this position is in effect the ultimate landing site of all these constituents, as in the Generalized TP analysis of Zubizarreta (1998).[20]

Space considerations do not allow me to discuss the details and merits of each of these analyses. In what follows, I simply follow Zubizarreta's (1998) proposal that all kinds of fronted constituents compete for the same landing site in Spanish. However, my analysis is different from Zubizarreta's in that this position does not necessarily correspond to [Spec, T], as discussed in the previous section for fronted subjects. Now, the crucial descriptive observations about ellipsis that lead us to the conclusion that a variety of fronted constituents have the same landing site are the following.

First, it is a well-known fact that the remnant of ellipsis in Spanish need not be the subject, as in the examples in §2.1, but rather it can be any argument or adjunct of the elided predicate (see Brucart 1999, López 1999). This is shown in the examples in (26). In (26a), the remnant of the elided construction is the subject, in (26b) it is the dative experiencer of a Psych predicate, and in (26c) it is a topical locative PP:

(26) a. Luis   reprobó   a   Ernesto, pero   [Juan no___]
         Luis   failed   ACC   *Ernesto but*   *Juan   not*
         'Luis failed Ernesto, but Juan didn't.'

    b. A Luis le   gusta el café,   pero [a Juan no ___].
            to Luis DAT-CL *likes   the coffee* *but   to Juan not*
            'Luis likes coffee, but Juan doesn't.'

    c. En ese café   cobran   carísimo,   pero [en el otro no___].
            in that coffee.shop they.charge very.expensive but   in the other not
            'In that coffee shop they charge a lot, but in the other one they don't.'

The fact that subjects and fronted topics show the same distribution with respect to ellipsis suggests that they occupy the same structural position.[21] This argument was first developed in Ordóñez & Treviño (1999) in relation to fronted subjects and left dislocated DOs and IOs. These authors suggest that the relevant position is the specifier of a Topic Phrase, and these ellipsis facts are presented by them in support of an analysis of preverbal subjects in Spanish as left-dislocated topics.

But consider now a second descriptive observation that has not received very much attention in the literature, namely, that fronted *wh*-operators can also be the remnants of phrasal ellipsis in Spanish (Sánchez-López 1999). Just as in the cases examined above, the remnant *wh*-operator can be the subject DP, the dative experiencer of a Psych predicate, or some other argument or adjunct of the predicate in the elided phrase. Also, again analogous to what is observed in the phrasal ellipsis constructions previously discussed, the remnant can appear with either a negative or a positive polarity head. Some examples are presented below:[22]

(27) a. Luis   apoya   al   candidato, pero [quién no]?
         Luis   supports   ACC-*the candidate   but   who   not*
         'Luis supports the candidate, but (then again) who doesn't?'

    b. A Luis no le   gusta ir al   doctor,   pero [a quién sí]?
            to Luis not DAT-CL *like go   to-the   doctor   but   to whom yes*
            'Luis doesn't like to go to the doctor, but who does?'

    c. No sé   que   libros ya   compré   y   [cuáles   no].
            *not I-know which   books   already I-bought and which-one-*PL *not*
            'I don't know which books I have already bought and which ones I haven't.'

d. No sé   a   quiénes no les   pidieron   identificación
   not I-know to   whom-PL *not* DAT-CL-PL *they-asked-for ID*

   y   [a quiénes sí].
   and to whom-PL *yes*

   'I don't know to whom they didn't ask for ID and to whom they did.'
   (=I don't know who wasn't asked for ID and who was.)

e. En ese café   cobran   carísimo,   pero   [en dónde no]?
   in that coffee.shop they-charge very.expensive but   in where not
   'In that coffee shop they charge a lot, but where don't they?'
   (=That coffee shop is very expensive, but (then again) which one isn't?)

These constructions behave just like other instances of phrasal ellipsis. For example, they can also appear in embedded contexts, as shown in (28).

(28) a. Sé   que muchos colegas   apoyan al   candidato, pero Juan
     I-know that many   colleagues support ACC-*the candidate, but Juan*

     todavía   no me   ha   dicho [quiénes   no ___].
     still   not to-me has   said   who-PL   *not*
     'I know that many colleagues support the candidate, but Juan still hasn't told me which (of them) don't.'

   b. Sé   que Juan quería   comprar algunos de estos libros,
     I-know that Juan wanted   buy   some   of these books

     pero no sé   [cuáles no ___].
     but   not I-know which-PL *not*
     'I know that Juan wanted to buy some of these books, but I don't know which ones he didn't.'

   c. Aquí, en casi todos los bares te   piden identificación,
     here   in   all   the bars to-you ask.for ID

     pero Juan ya   me   dijo [en cuáles   no ___].
     but Juan already to-me said   in which-ones not
     'Here, in almost every bar they ask you for ID, but Juan has already told me in which ones they don't.'

Furthermore, just like other phrasal ellipsis constructions, they display both a strict and a sloppy reading, as shown in (29).

(29) Luis apoya   a   sus estudiantes, pero [quién no __]?
     Luis supports ACC *his students   but   who   not*

   STRICT: 'Luis supports his students, but who doesn't [~~support his~~ (=Luis')
           ~~students~~]?'
   SLOPPY: 'Luis supports his students, but who doesn't [~~support his~~
           (own) ~~students~~]?'

We have seen that the examples in (26) have been used in Ordóñez & Treviño (1999) as evidence for an analysis where subjects and fronted topics occupy the same position. Once we consider (27–29), parity of reasoning suggests that this position is also occupied by fronted *wh*-operators. Crucially though, this also shows that the relevant position is not the specifier of a Topic Phrase, since it is not usually assumed that *wh*-phrases can occupy such a position. These examples also show that the highest inflectional specifier in Spanish is not necessarily an A-position, and so defining it in terms of the A/A-Bar distinction is not adequate either.

Summarizing the discussion so far, the data from ellipsis points to the conclusion that subjects, topics, and *wh*-operators all occupy the same position and that this position is not [Spec, Top]. Clearly, the simplest analysis is one where all these constituents correspond to the specifier of the polarity head. Recall now that Spec-Pol further is the position where the EPP is satisfied, since PolP is the highest projection in the inflectional layer in (26–29). What we need to do now is to reconcile these facts with the definition of the EPP in (24).

2.2.2 Characterizing the Pole

The definition of the EPP in (24) targets the specifier of the highest Π-Projection. With respect to this, notice now that the specifier of the highest Π-Projection is not just any specifier. All else being equal, in matrix clauses the constituent functioning as the specifier of this projection c-commands the whole of the extended projection.[23] In other words, the XP in this specifier position is more prominent than any other constituent in the extended projection. In my view, this is why the specifier of the highest Π-Projection has a special structural status, and why there exist well-formedness constraints and conditions on representation that specifically target it. I further propose that the specifier of the highest Π-Projection has this special structural status regardless of whether it corresponds to an A-position or to an A-bar position.[24]

Now, one of the core ideas that I pursue here is that the specifier of the highest Π-Projection does *not* correspond to what is referred to as the canonical subject position in the literature on word order. I discuss this in detail in the following chapter, where we will see that Spanish provides strong evidence that there needs to be a crucial distinction between this specifier position and what Grimshaw (1997) and others refer to as the "canonical subject position," even though they overlap in many cases. In order to denote the specifier of the highest Π-Projection without making any reference to subjecthood, from here onwards I refer to this specifier as the **Pole** of the clause. My final version of the EPP is thus defined with respect to the Pole specifier:

(30) EPP
     Clauses must have a Pole.

In claiming that the EPP can be satisfied by constituents other than the subject I follow recent proposals developed both in transformational frameworks and in Optimality-theoretic syntax (Branigan 1992; Jonas & Bobaljik 1993; Babyonyshev 1996; Collins 1997; Zubizarreta 1998; Fernández-Soriano 1999; Chomsky 2000; Holmberg 2000; McCloskey 2001; Holmberg & Nikanne 2002; Grimshaw 1997 and Roberts 2000, *inter alia*) which argue that the EPP is a purely structural condition that requires some specifier position to be filled, independently of the category or grammatical relation of the constituent that fills it.[25] However, the central claim of this work is that the Pole in Spanish is associated with a number of other grammatical properties, and not just the satisfaction of the EPP. Before providing evidence in support of this claim, it is worth examining some further details of what I take the Pole of the clause to be.

As we have seen in our discussion of sentential structure in Spanish, the crucial characteristic of the Pole is that it corresponds to a specifier position that is defined relationally. When the highest inflectional projection of a clause is IP,

(31) a.

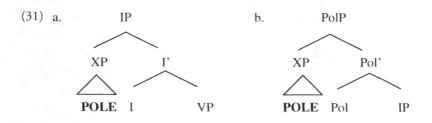

(32) a.

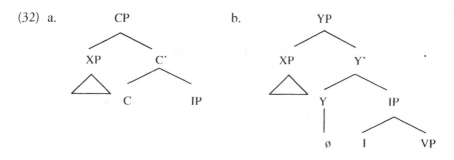

then [Spec, I] is the Pole of the clause. When the highest inflectional projection of a sentence is PolP, then the Pole is [Spec, Pol], as in (31).

There are two crucial cases where I assume that a specifier position in the functional shell above VP *does not* correspond to the Pole of the clause, though. The first one is Spec-CP, the other one is the specifier of an inflectional projection that has the same features as the inflectional projection that it immediately dominates (roughly, IP recursion). These two cases are schematized in (32) above, where, for exposition, IP stands as the highest projection of the inflectional layer (i.e. the highest Π-Projection).

[Spec, C] in (32a) is not the Pole of the clause, since CP is not part of the inflectional layer. Notice, though, that [Spec, C] still is the highest specifier of the extended projection, even when it is not the highest specifier of the inflectional layer. As will become clear in the chapters that follow, there is in fact a need for both notions, since there are properties related to the highest inflectional specifier (the Pole) and properties related instead to the highest specifier of the extended projection.

Case (32b) is somewhat different. Here, I take YP to be indeed part of the inflectional layer, but it is a phrase that is not distinct in its feature content from IP. In a number of Optimality-theoretic analyses (for instance, Grimshaw 1997), structures like (32b) are generated by GEN and can emerge as winners when, for example, it is necessary to move an operator to a specifier position above IP but below CP. From here onwards, I refer to projections like YP in (32b) as *vacuous projections*. This label is not intended to imply that this kind of projection does not play any role in the syntax. Rather, it is meant to characterize the fact that the inherent features[26] of the head of a phrase like YP are identical to inherent features of the head of the functional projection that it immediately dominates (this is why, alternatively, we could characterize YP in (32b) as an instance of IP recursion). Crucially for the analysis that follows, I assume that the specifier of a vacuous projection is never the Pole of the clause. In other words, whatever syntactic constraints target the Pole position (such as the EPP), will target [Spec, I] in (32b), and not the specifier of YP. Nor does an XP adjoined to the highest inflectional projection correspond to the Pole, since the Pole is defined exclusively in terms of a Spec-head relation between an XP and the highest inflectional head.

Ultimately, my suggestion is that the Pole is not a construct specific to Spanish, since facts similar to those that I will analyze in the following chapters have been reported in the literature for other languages. For instance, the unmarked word orders of different kinds of predicates in Spanish (to be analyzed in Chapter Three) are also attested in Italian (Pinto 1994; Arnaiz 1998; see also Belletti & Rizzi 1988), Russian (Moore & Perlmutter 2000), German (Zaenen et. al. 1985, Sigurðsson 2004), Japanese (Perlmutter 1984), Georgian (Harris 1984) and a number of other languages (see Ackerman & Moore 2001 for an overview). Topicalization facts similar to the ones discussed for Spanish in Chapter Four are observed in Tz'utujil (Mayan: Aissen 1999b; Aissen, p.c.). Word order facts similar to those discussed in Chapter Five for Spanish *wh*-interrogatives are reported for Greek in Costa (2001). However, it is beyond the scope of this work to address this issue, which requires detailed and careful investigation for each relevant case. Instead I concentrate on providing a detailed analysis of a number of facts from the syntax of Spanish that support the adoption of the Pole as a relevant grammatical construct. A preliminary OT typology that results from this notion, however, is developed in § 3.4.

Now that we have defined the concept of the Pole, it is necessary to discuss its relation to the concept of grammatical subject. One of the central proposals of this work is that the notion of the Pole is not equivalent to, and needs to be kept separate from, the notion of subject, even though the Pole and the subject overlap in a great many cases. Consider a simple example from English.

(33) Some students are waiting outside the coffee shop.

This is a case where the Pole and the subject overlap. The DP [*some students*] is the Pole since it is the specifier of the highest Π-phrase (IP or TP, depending on the analysis). Under the assumption that agreement with the highest inflectional head and/or nominative Case is a diagnostic for subjecthood (in the traditional sense), this DP is also the subject of the clause.[27] Yet even in a language like English, where the correlation *subject-highest inflectional specifier* is very strong, there are cases where it can be argued that the two notions are clearly differentiated. Existential-*there* constructions are perhaps the most common case.

(34) There are some students waiting outside the coffee shop.

In this case (pre-theoretically, at least) the DP that agrees with the verb is not the specifier of the highest inflectional head and this highlights the distinction between the subject and the Pole. Concretely, [*the students*] in (34) is still the DP that regulates agreement (i.e., the subject in the traditional sense), but in this case the expletive *there* functions as the Pole of the clause. The syntactic conditions that each of the two elements satisfy are also different. The argument DP functions as the *pivot* that regulates agreement with the highest inflectional head, while the expletive is nothing more than a place-filler that satisfies the EPP.[28]

In this respect, the notion of the Pole stems in part from the central assumption of both Government and Binding and the Minimalist Program that the subject grammatical relation should not be considered a primitive of the theory. Instead of postulating a unified notion of subject, these transformational frameworks have claimed that the properties traditionally associated with the subject DP are distributed in different positions in the clause (see McCloskey 1997). For English and other Germanic languages, a good number of the arguments in favor of this idea have in fact been provided by the study of expletive-associate constructions like the one above (see for example Chomsky 1995, 2000).[29]

Existential-*there* constructions are also illustrative in that they show that the distinction I propose between subject and Pole does not correspond to the traditional distinction between *subject* and Brentano and Marty's *logical subject* (see Kuroda 1972 for a contemporary approach) either. Under this distinction, thetic judgements correspond to sentences that have no logical subject, and existential-*there* sentences are typical instances of thetic constructions in English. Yet these constructions still require a place-filler in the highest inflectional specifier. In our terms, they still require a Pole to satisfy the EPP, even when they lack a logical subject altogether. In terms of their function, the Pole and the logical subject are also clearly distinct. As I will argue throughout this book, the *prima facie* function of the Pole is to satisfy the EPP, defined as nothing more than a structural requirement on sentential structure. In contrast, the logical subject identifies an entity of which some property will be later ascribed, i.e., it is the target of predication. Furthermore, recall that the evidence from ellipsis indicates that *wh*-operators can correspond to the Pole (in Chapter Five I present more evidence to this effect). Crucially, this also supports the distinction between Pole and logical subject, since *wh*-operators are not usually assumed to be possible logical subjects.[30]

The need for a notion of the Pole independent from both the subject grammatical relation and the logical subject is most evident when we consider a number of syntactic phenomena in Spanish, though. The bulk of the evidence is presented in the chapters that follow, where I show how the notion of the Pole can account for facts related to unmarked word order, topicalization and *wh*-movement in Spanish in general, and in Mexican Spanish in particular. In the remainder of this chapter, I present some preliminary evidence from ellipsis and the distribution of negative XPs in Spanish which indicate that these phenomena crucially implicate the Pole, and that the Pole cannot be identified with the grammatical subject.

2.3 PRELIMINARY EVIDENCE FOR THE POLE IN SPANISH

2.3.1 The Pole as the remnant of ellipsis

We have seen that there is evidence from ellipsis that suggests that subjects, topics and *wh*-operators all occupy the same position in Spanish. However, clauses that display ellipsis differ from clauses that do not in one important respect. As is well-known, topics in Spanish can freely stack over either another topic or a *wh*-operator. This is attested both in the absence and in the presence of an overt polarity head, as shown in the examples in (35) and (36).[31]

(35) a. Las artesanías, Juan las   consiguió en   Guadalajara.
       the handcrafts Juan ACC-CL *found   in   Guadalajara*
       'The handcrafts, Juan got them in Guadalajara.'

   b. Las artesanías, Juan no las   consiguió en   Guadalajara.
       the handcrafts Juan not ACC-CL *found   in   Guadalajara*
       'The handcrafts, Juan didn't get them in Guadalajara.'

(36) a. La tarea,   quién ya   la   hizo?
       the homework   who   already ACC-CL *did*
       'Who already did the homework?'

   b. La tarea,   quién no la   hizo?
       the homework   who   not ACC-CL *did*
       'Who did not do the homework?'

The detailed analysis of this stacking pattern will be the subject of Chapters Four and Five. For present purposes it is enough to note that in the analysis I will develop I analyze the leftmost fronted XP in (35–36) as adjoined to the highest Π-projection and the one that follows it to be the Pole of the clause ([Spec, I] in the (a) examples, [Spec, Pol] in the (b) examples).

This stacking pattern, however, is not possible in phrasal ellipsis constructions. As noted in López (1999; fn 15), stacking of a fronted topic over a remnant *wh*-operator results in robust ungrammaticality. The examples in (37) are my own.

(37) a. *Ya   sé   quién hizo los ejercicios, pero [la tarea   quién no]?
       already I-know who   did the exercises but the homework who not

     b. *A Juan no le   gusta Oslo, pero [Noruega a quién sí]?
        to Juan not DAT-CL *like Oslo but   Norway to whom yes*

The situation with stacked topics slightly more complex. Speakers of Mexican Spanish mostly reject elliptical constructions with stacked topics. Similar judgments are reported for both Mexican and Peninsular Spanish in Ordóñez & Treviño (1999). Examples are included below.[32]

(38) MEXICAN SPANISH
     a. *Juan consiguió las artesanías en Guadalajara, pero los dulces Luisa no.
        Juan found   the handcrafts in Guadalajara but the sweets Luisa not

     b. *Juan consiguió las artesanías en Guadalajara, pero en Mérida Luisa no.
        Juan found   the handcrafts in Guadalajara but in Mérida Luisa not

     c. ??Juan consiguió las artesanías   en Guadalajara, pero Luisa en Mérida no.
        Juan found   the handcrafts in Guadalajara but Luisa in Mérida not

Brucart (1999) and López (1999), however, report examples like (39a-b), where apparently two topical remnants are allowed, presumably from a different variety of Peninsular Spanish than the one reported in Ordóñez & Treviño (1999). In an informant survey of six speakers of Mexican Spanish, all found (39b) robustly ungrammatical. Half of these six speakers further consider (39a) either ungrammatical or strongly deviant.[33]

(39) a. Yo podría regalarle   los pendientes a mi madre,   pero [el collar
          I could   give-to-her the ear-rings to my mother   but   the necklace

          a mi padre no].
          to my father not

          'I could give the earrings to my mother, but I couldn't give my father
          the necklace'   (López 1999: 285)

      b. Luis no   estaba haciendo crucigramas, pero [Pedro   jeroglíficos sí].
          Luis not   was   making   crosswords   but   Pedro   hieroglyphs yes
          'Luis was not making crossword puzzles, but Pedro was (making) hieroglyphs.'

                                                          (Brucart 1999: 2816, fn. 38)

It is not immediately obvious that the examples in (39) truly constitute instances of topic stacking under ellipsis. Notice that the relative order of the two remnants in these examples is the same as the one in the antecedent clause, i.e. the canonical linear order of the arguments under consideration in non-elided sentences. Although this is indeed a possibility allowed for multiple fronted topics in Spanish, the typical case is that the relative order of multiple fronted topics is different from the one that these constituents show when they remain in-situ.[34] So compare the examples in (35), where the fronted DO precedes the fronted subject with (39b), where the subject precedes the DO. Neither Brucart (1999) nor López (1999) indicate whether both orders are possible in cases like (39), and they do not test these constructions with the diagnostics used to identify true cases of ellipsis (acceptability in embedded contexts, sloppy readings, etc.).

Another possibility is that ultimately this might just be an issue of dialectal variation. In support of this hypothesis, notice that Portuguese (Matos 1994:349; reported in Lopez 1999: 285) shows the same restriction as Mexican Spanish against stacking multiple topics in elliptical constructions.

(40) PORTUGUESE
      a. Esse editor, à Maria pagou os direitos de autor.
          that editor, to Mary paid   the copyright

      b. *O João já   pagou os direitos de autor   ao Pedro e
          John   already   paid   the copyright   to Peter and

[esse editor, à Maria também].
that editor to Mary   too

English, on the other hand, does allow for more than one remnant in VP ellipsis constructions. As noted in Schuyler (2001), one of the remnants corresponds to the subject, and the other one can be an interrogative operator, a relative operator or a fronted topic (see also López & Winkler 2000).

(41) a. I don't know which puppy you SHOULD adopt, but I know [which one you SHOULDN'T ___].

   b. I discovered that my cat had scratched some of the furniture, and then I sold the furniture [that he HADN'T ___].   (Schuyler 2001)

   c. The knife, he put in the cupboard, but [the forks, he didn't ___].
                                                (López & Winkler 2000: 659, fn. 17)

   d. At UCSC we pay our junior faculty a considerable amount of money in their first year, but [at UCM they don't ___].

Pending further investigation of this issue, I will assume that the difference in judgments on the examples in (39) is indeed due to dialectal variation. Consider now how the data from Mexican Spanish in (37–38) suggest that the remnant of phrasal ellipsis has to be the Pole. Assume that some languages like Mexican Spanish and Portuguese are set to a condition that requires the remnant of phrasal ellipsis to be licensed by a Head-Spec relation with the head of the highest phrase in the inflectional layer (in these cases the polarity head of PolP).[35] Now, in the analysis where different kinds of fronted constituents all compete for the same position (the Pole), the facts observed in Mexican Spanish receive a straightforward explanation. The remnant of phrasal ellipsis can be a subject, the experiencer of a Psych predicate, a fronted topic or a *wh*-Operator, since they all occupy the same position. But since the remnant of ellipsis has to be licensed in a Head-Spec relation with the head of the highest head in the inflectional layer, it follows that only one of these elements can appear as the remnant in phrasal ellipsis constructions. In contrast, in cases where there is no ellipsis multiple topics can be adjoined freely to the highest phrase when the Pole specifier is already occupied.

In contrast, compare this analysis with a multi-phrasal analysis of the left-periphery. Consider a sketch of clausal structure in such an analysis, schematized in (42). Following Rizzi (1997), the multiple Topic Phrases would host multiple fronted topics in their specifiers, and [Spec, Foc] would correspond to the position occupied by fronted *wh*-operators.

(42)

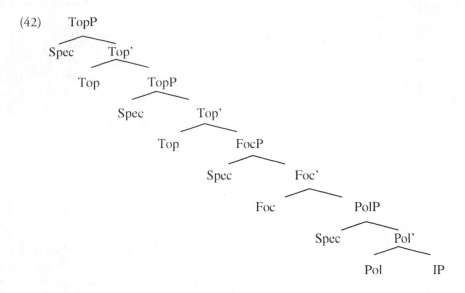

Given the structure in (42), it is not clear why there can only be one fronted remnant in phrasal ellipsis, since the landing sites for subjects, *wh*-operators and topics are still available after IP has been elided. It would not be clear how the condition licensing the single remnant should be stated either, since subjects, *wh*-operators and topics all occupy distinct positions. In the analysis I propose, the remnant is always the Pole, which stands in a Spec-Head configuration with the head of the highest inflectional phrase. In the structure in (42), by contrast, no such relation could arise. Even if we devised a mechanism where, for some reason, only one left peripheral phrase could be projected when ellipsis takes place, if the remnant were a topic or a *wh*-operator, it would still not be in a Spec-Head configuration with the highest inflectional head, and extra machinery would be required to define the licensing condition on the remnant.

2.3.2 Negation and the Pole in Spanish

The Pole is also relevant for determining some of the interpretive properties of a clause, independently of; a) the specific category of the highest inflectional phrase, and; b) the grammatical relation of the constituent that functions as the Pole. The relevant data come from negation, the distribution of negative XPs, and double negation constructions in Spanish.

Spanish is a negative concord language, as is well-known, and its properties in this respect have been widely studied (Bedell-García 1993,

Haegeman 1995, Suñer 1995, Sánchez-López 1999, to cite a few references). Just as in many other negative concord languages, there are two ways of expressing negation in Spanish: either by the negative head *no,* as in (43a), or by a preverbal negative XP,[36] as in (43b).

(43) a. No llegaron los muchachos.
          not arrived the boys
          'The boys didn't arrive.'

      b. Nadie llegó.
          no-one arrived
          'No one arrived.'

In Spanish, the preverbal negative XP that expresses negation does not need to be the subject DP, as shown in (44). In (44a) the preverbal negative XP corresponds to the direct object of the verb, in (44b) to a temporal adjunct.[37]

(44) a. A   nadie   vio   Juan en su viaje a las montañas.
          ACC *no-one   saw   Juan in his trip to the mountains*
          'Juan saw no-one in his trip to the mountains.'

      b. Nunca habíamos viajado   a   París.
          never we-had   traveled to Paris
          'We had never traveled to Paris.'

As is also well-known, a negative XP cannot appear by itself in the post-verbal field. This is shown in the examples in (45).

(45) a. *Llegó   nadie.
          arrived   no-one

      b. *Juan vio a   nadie en su viaje a las montañas.
          Juan saw ACC no-one in his trip to the mountains

      c. *Habíamos viajado nunca a   París.
          we-had   traveled never to Paris

Post-verbal negative XPs can be licensed by either of two mechanisms, by the negative head *no,* as in (46), or by a preverbal negative XP, as in (47).

(46) a. No llegó   nadie.
       not arrived   no-one
       'No one arrived'

   b. Juan no vio a   nadie en su viaje a las montañas.
      Juan not saw ACC *no-one in his trip to the mountains*
      'Juan saw no-one in his trip to the mountains.'

   c. Juan no había viajado nunca a París.
      Juan not had   traveled never to Paris
      'Juan had never traveled to Paris.'

(47) a. Nadie dijo nada.
       no-one said nothing
       'No one said anything'

   b. Aquí nunca viene nadie.
      here never comes no-one
      'No one ever comes here.'

   c. A nadie   le   entregó   nada.
      to no-one DAT-CL *he.handed-in   nothing*
      'He handed in nothing to no one/ He didn't hand in anything to anyone.'

Most sources in the literature agree that there are two crucial characteristics of the Spanish pattern (also seen in closely related languages, such as
Italian[38] and Portuguese; see Zanuttini 1997b for discussion) that need to be
accounted for. The first is the fact that there is more than one way to license
a post-verbal negative XP, as in (46) and (47). The second one relates to the
interpretive properties of the negative concord pattern, namely, the fact that
preverbal negative XPs contribute to the polarity value of the clause (as in
(43a) and (44)) but post-verbal negative XPs do not: in other words, in (46)
and (47) there is more than one negative element, the post-verbal negative
XP and the preverbal negative element that licenses it, but this does not
result in a multiple negation interpretation.

   In what follows I suggest an answer to the second question based on
the notion of the Pole, and this in turn provides an answer to the first question about of the licensing of negative XPs. The first relevant observation
comes from Ladusaw (1992). Ladusaw argues that the interpretive properties
observed in negative concord are best understood as the result of conditions
that specify the structural positions where a feature [NEG] is semantically
potent. In negative concord languages (as opposed to, say, standard English)

the presence of a feature [NEG] in the clause does not by itself guarantee that this feature will have an effect on the polarity value of the clause. There are some structural positions where the presence of a [NEG] feature has an effect on the interpretive properties of the clause and others where it does not. In Ladusaw's analysis, sentential negation is ultimately expressed by the head of a phrase in what would correspond to the Extended Projection in our terms. There are two different ways in which such a head can bear the [NEG] feature. It can be part of its inherent feature content (as in the case of *not* in English) or it can acquire it from a specifier sister or an adjoined sister. In this, I adopt Ladusaw's analysis as a starting point, but I will suggest a number of modifications as we go along.

First, I propose that the expression of negation in Spanish is regulated by two (and only two) separate conditions. One corresponds to Ladusaw's case where an inherently negative head is part of the representation. I define this condition in (48).

(48) NEGATIVE HEAD CONDITION

A feature [NEG] is semantically potent if it is an inherent feature of the head of XP, XP one of the phrases of a clausal Extended Projection.

Simplifying somewhat, the reason for defining this condition as in (48) is related to the observation that a sentential negative polarity head (say *no* in Spanish, *not* in English) has an effect on the polarity value of the sentence irrespective of where its position in the Extended Projection happens to be (see Zanuttini 1997b), both in negative concord and in non-negative concord languages. Example (43a) meets this condition and thus it has a negative interpretation. The second condition I propose relies on the notion of the Pole.

(49) NEGATIVE POLE CONDITION

A feature [NEG] is semantically potent if it is a feature of the Pole.

Conditions (48) and (49) express the fact that in Spanish these are the only two positions where a feature [NEG] is semantically potent. We can now informally state that a clause is negative iff it contains a feature [NEG] that is semantically potent.

Example (43b) corresponds to the case contemplated in (49). For this example I propose the analysis in (50) where there is no Polarity phrase (*contra* the analyses in Laka 1990, Haegemann 1995, Suñer 1995, and Ladusaw 1992) and accordingly no polarity head anywhere in the representation.

Also, in contrast with Ladusaw's (1992) analysis, I propose that ultimately it is the Pole that expresses sentential negation, and not the head that the Pole is the specifier of. In other words, the sentence has its negative polarity value because the negative XP is the Pole of the clause, [Spec, I] in this case. The reason for this will become clear in what follows.

(50) [$_{IP}$ Nadie llegó   [$_{VP}$ *t*]].
      no-one arrived
      'No one arrived.'

Consider now a negative concord example, (46a), repeated here as (51).

(51) [$_{PolP}$ No [$_{IP}$ llegó   [$_{VP}$ nadie].
      not   arrived   no-one
      'No one arrived'

In this case, the [NEG] feature of the post-verbal negative XP *nadie* 'no-one,' does not meet either the NEGATIVE HEAD CONDITION or the NEGATIVE POLE CONDITION. *Nadie* is not the head of a phrase of the [verbal] (i.e. the sentential) extended projection, nor does it correspond to the Pole of the clause. Accordingly its [NEG] feature has no effect on the polarity value of the sentence.

Now the crucial observation that supports this analysis is that these two conditions can operate simultaneously in Spanish. In this language, when a negative XP in the Pole co-occurs with the sentential negation, the result is a double negation (DN) construal.[39] Some examples are presented below. In all these examples, the negative concord reading is not possible.

(52) a. ?Nadie no lo hizo.
       no-one not it did
       'Nobody didn't do it (= everyone did it).'   (Suñer 1995: 234, fn.4)

    b. Hasta ahora, a nadie no le   ha   gustado esa   película.
       until   now   now   not CL-DAT has liked   that movie
       'Up to now, no one hasn't liked that movie (=everyone liked it).'

    c. ?Hasta ahora, en ninguna de las secretarías no   nos han   apoyado.
       until   now   in none   of the ministries not us   they-have supported
       'Up to now, in none of the ministries they haven't supported us.
       (=In every ministry they have supported us).'

This is a fact widely acknowledged in the literature on negation in Spanish (see for example Laka 1990, Suñer 1995, and Sánchez-López 1999), but which, to the best of my knowledge, has not yet been analyzed in any detail.[40]

Crucially, these examples constitute the fundamental piece of evidence that shows that the NEGATIVE POLE CONDITION has to be defined with respect to the Pole and not, say, with respect to [Spec, I] (which is where the [+NEG] feature is located in (50)). If we were to define the properties of negation with respect to [Spec, I], and not relationally (with respect to the Pole), then we would be hard pressed to explain the DN reading of the examples in (52). This is because the preposed negatives XP that add their [+NEG] feature to the interpretation are not in [Spec, I], but rather in [Spec, Pol]. What provides a unified account of (50) and (52) is that the Pole is defined relationally: when IP is the highest phrase in the inflectional layer, [Spec, I] functions as the Pole, as in (50). But when a polarity phrase is present, as in (52), then [Spec, Pol] corresponds to the Pole. In both cases the [NEG] feature in the Pole contributes to the overall polarity value of the clause.

This data further provide evidence in favor of my proposed distinction between the Pole and the highest specifier of the extended projection. Although the [NEG] feature is indeed found in the Pole both in (50) and (52), these are two cases where the Pole coincides with the highest specifier of the extended projection as well (i.e. the highest inflectional specifier also happens to be the highest specifier of the extended projection). This raises the question of whether the NEGATIVE POLE CONDITION should be specified in terms of the highest specifier of the extended projection instead. Embedded contexts show that this would not be the correct definition. In the embedded clause in (53), the highest phrase of the extended projection is CP, but C has no specifier in this case. The negative XP that provides the embedded clause with its polarity value is still found in the highest specifier of the inflectional layer, in this case [Spec, I].[41]

(53)   Creo [$_{CP}$ que [$_{IP}$ nadie   compró   [$_{VP}$ el periódico]].
       I-think   that   no-one bought   the newspaper
       'I think that no one bought the newspaper.'

The double negation facts in (52) also highlight the advantages of my analysis over a potential alternative that relies on the Negative Criterion of Haegeman & Zanuttini (1991). In analyses based on the Negative Criterion, there is always a Negative Phrase (NegP) that is part of the representation of negative clauses. The examples in (43) would be recast as in (54) under such an analysis.[42]

(54) a. [$_{NegP}$ No [llegaron   los muchachos]].
              not   arrived   the boys
              'The boys didn't arrive.'

      b. [$_{NegP}$ Nadie ø [llegó]].
              no-one   arrived
              'No one arrived.'

In (54), it is the head Neg^0, whether overt or not, that ultimately defines the polarity value of the sentence. The [NEG] feature of the pre-verbal negative XP in (54b) is cancelled out for interpretive purposes because it is in a Spec-Head configuration with the head of Neg-P (see Haegeman 1995 for details). This is why (54b) does not have a double negation reading. But this incorrectly predicts that the [NEG] feature of the preverbal negative XPs in the double negation examples in (52) should also be cancelled out, contrary to fact. In contrast, the analysis I propose here is not only simpler (in that it does not need to stipulate the presence of a Polarity Phrase with a null head for cases like (54b)), but it can also account for the attested interpretive properties in a straightfor-ward way.

We can now return to the second issue to be addressed in relation to negative concord, namely, the question of how negative XPs are licensed. With the analysis of sentential negation developed up to here, it is possible to appeal to a fairly simple surface condition on representation for the licensing of negative XPs, like the one proposed in Bedell-García (1993:8).[43]

(55) A negative element must occur in a negative clause.

In our terms, this means that a negative XP must occur in an Extended Projection specified for negative polarity. Consider now how we can analyze previous examples under this licensing condition. When the negative head *no* is present, as in (56a), it is this element that makes the clause a negative clause.

(56) a. [$_{PolP}$ No [$_{IP}$ llegó [$_{VP}$ nadie]]].
              not   arrived   no-one
              'No one arrived'

      b. *[$_{IP}$ Llegó   [$_{VP}$ nadie]].
              arrived   no-one

Since the clause is specified as [NEG], the post-verbal negative XP meets the condition in (55) and so the resulting construction is fine. In contrast, the sentence in (56b) is not specified as [NEG]. It lacks the negative head *no* and the negative XP does not correspond to the Pole, so its [NEG] feature has no effect on the interpretive properties of the clause. Since the clause is not a negative clause in this case, the post-verbal negative XP fails to meet the condition in (55) and is thus ungrammatical.

Consider now an example with a preverbal negative XP, such as (57). In this case the negative XP is the Pole of the sentence, and so its [NEG] feature defines the polarity value of the clause. As a result, the clause as a whole is [NEG] and so the negative XP complies with the licensing condition in (55). This captures the insight in Ladusaw (1992) and Bedell-García (1993) that preverbal negative XPs are "self-licensing."

(57) [$_{IP}$ Nadie llegó [$_{VP}$ *t*]].
    no-one arrived
    'No one arrived'

Finally, consider a case where there are two negative XPs, one in the Pole position and one in the post-verbal field, as in (58). In (58), the negative XP functioning as the Pole provides the [NEG] feature that makes the clause negative, just like in (57). Both the preverbal and the post-verbal negative XP now comply with the licensing condition in (55) and as a result the construction is grammatical. My analysis thus captures the insight in Ladusaw (1992) that it is not strictly speaking the preverbal negative XP that licenses the post-verbal one. Rather, the preverbal negative XP provides the conditions under which *both* negative XPs can be licensed, in a way in which the post-verbal one cannot.

(58) [$_{IP}$ Nadie dijo [$_{VP}$ *t* nada]].
    no-one said   *nothing*
    'No one said anything'

My analysis further predicts that *any* negative XP (not just the subject) occupying the Pole should be able to license itself and a post-verbal negative XP in the same way that *nadie* 'no-one' does in (58). This is because the Pole in Spanish is not a position exclusively of subjects, so the [NEG] feature of preverbal non-subject negative XPs will be semantically potent irrespective of the grammatical relation borne by the XP. As shown in (59), this prediction is correct. In these examples the preverbal negative XP corresponds to the indirect object and a temporal adjunct, respectively.

(59) a. A nadie   le   hemos dicho nada.
         to no-one DAT-CL *we-have said   nothing*
         'We haven't said anything to anyone.'

     b. Nunca   vamos   a   ningún   lado.
        never   we-go   to   none   place
        'We never go anywhere.'

To conclude this section, I show how my analysis makes another correct prediction regarding the distribution of negative XPs in Spanish. My analysis predicts that it should not be possible to front a negative XP to a position other than the Pole. This is because the [NEG] feature of a fronted negative XP outside the Pole is not semantically potent, i.e., in our terms, the resulting clause would not satisfy the NEGATIVE POLE CONDITION. Accordingly, the clause cannot be specified as a negative clause, and so, following the licensing condition in (55), the fronted negative XP would remain unlicensed. This prediction is also correct. As is well-known, fronting of a negative XP in Spanish does not block the fronting of other constituents (either subjects or non-subjects) functioning as topics. The negative XP, however, must appear in the immediate preverbal position, as in the (a) examples in (60–63). Otherwise, the resulting constructions are ungrammatical (Bedell-García 1993, Fontana 1994, Zubizarreta 1998, Ordóñez & Treviño 1999, Sánchez-López 1999).[44] Notice that these examples are particularly telling in that they show that it is descriptively inadequate to simply state that negative XPs in Spanish are "self-licensing" as long as they are located in the preverbal field.

(60) a. Juan, a   nadie quiere ver.
         Juan ACC *no-one wants   see*
         'Juan wants to see no one.'

     b. *A   nadie Juan   quiere ver.
        ACC *no-one Juan   wants   see*   (Sánchez-López 1999: 2568)

(61) a. Los malos   nadie   los   ha comprado
          the bad-ones   no-one   ACC-CL   has bought
          'Nobody has bought the bad ones.'

      b. *Nadie los   malos   los   ha comprado.
          no-one the   bad-ones ACC-CL   has bought   (Fontana 1993: 246[45])

(62) a. Juan   a   nadie   vio   en su viaje   a las montañas.
          Juan   ACC   no-one   saw   in his trip   to the mountains
          'Juan saw no-one in his trip to the mountains.'

      b. ??A   nadie   Juan vio   en su viaje   a las montañas.
          ACC   *no-one Juan saw   in his trip   to the mountains*

(63) a. Juan   nunca había   viajado   a París.
          Juan   never had   traveled   to Paris
          'Juan had never traveled to Paris.'

      b. ??Nunca Juan   había viajado   a   París.
          never Juan   had   traveled   to Paris

Recall our assumption from §2.3.1 that when there is more than one fronted XP in the preverbal field, the leftmost one is adjoined to the highest inflectional phrase. Accordingly, the examples in (60) would be analyzed as in (64).

(64) a. [$_{IP}$ Juan, [$_{IP}$ a nadie   quiere ver]].
          Juan   ACC no-one   wants   see
          'Juan wants to see no one.'

      b. *[$_{IP}$ A   nadie   [$_{IP}$ Juan quiere ver]].
          ACC   *no-one   Juan wants   see*

The crucial difference between (64a) and (64b) is that in the former the negative XP occupies the Pole specifier, whereas in the latter it is adjoined to IP. In (64a) the negative XP is the Pole of the clause; its [+ NEG] feature defines the polarity value of the clause as negative, which in turn licenses the presence of the negative XP, but in (64b), where the fronted negative XP is not the Pole, the relevant conditions are not met.

2.4 CONCLUSIONS

The central issue of this chapter has been the introduction and the definition of the notion of the Pole and its relation to the EPP. I have suggested, in accordance with most transformational conceptions of sentential structure (and departing from Grimshaw 1993,1997), that the notion of Extended Projection requires both a distinction between the lexical and the functional layer, and a further distinction between the phrases in the inflectional layer of the sentence (Π-Phrases) and those in the C-system (K-Phrases). Following this distinction, I have suggested that the specifier of the highest Π-Phrase has a special structural status that is independent of the category of the head that it is the specifer of, and of whether it corresponds to an A or an A-Bar position. It is this position that is referenced by the EPP. Among other things, an EPP that references a relationally defined position explains why clauses where the highest inflectional projection is different still show the same word order in Spanish. I call this specifier the Pole of the clause and the EPP can then be defined as a purely structural condition that requires clauses to have a Pole.

The Pole is a notion distinct from the subject grammatical relation. Drawing on evidence from ellipsis, I have argued that subjects, fronted topics and *wh*-operators in Spanish all occupy the same position, and that there is evidence that this position corresponds to the Pole. In English the distinction can be seen in existential-*there* constructions where the expletive is the Pole and the post-copular DP is the subject. In Spanish, the distinction plays a much more pervasive role in clausal syntax. Specifically, evidence has been presented that only the constituent in the Pole can be the remnant of ellipsis in Spanish, and that the Pole is the position where the polarity feature of negative XPs is made semantically potent in this language.

Chapter Three
Markedness Constraints on Syntactic Structure

In the preceding chapter I introduced the notion of the Pole as a relevant notion for understanding a number of phenomena in Spanish. Building on this proposal, in this chapter I relate this notion to the word order facts observed in Spanish in the unmarked case. To the best of my knowledge, the unmarked word order facts addressed in this chapter are the same across different varieties of Spanish. As will be discussed in detail in Chapters Four and Five, though, this same analysis can accommodate the word order phenomena specific to Mexican Spanish, which are mostly observed in focus, topic and *wh*-constructions. This is one of the reasons why an OT analysis is proposed to account for the unmarked word order of Spanish. We will see in the following chapters how the differences between Mexican Spanish and other varieties of this language can be accounted for by simple constraint re-ranking.

The guiding idea that I develop in this chapter is that syntactic structure in Spanish is subject to markedness considerations in a way that is not unlike the markedness considerations that govern syllable structure in prosodic phonology. I begin by suggesting that, because of Economy of Structure, clauses with a Pole are more marked than those that lack a Pole. Economy of Structure is thus in direct conflict with the EPP as defined in the previous chapter, which requires clauses to have a Pole. However, I will argue that just as in prosodic phonology, markedness is not necessarily simply a contrast between a marked structure and an unmarked one. Rather, different structures can show different degrees of markedness. I then show how Optimality Theory provides an ideal theoretical framework for analyzing this state of affairs.

The crucial idea that I develop is that there exist constraints that target the relative markedness of different constituents in the Pole position. The existence of these constraints allows us to understand why the specifier of the highest inflectional projection must be filled in some cases but not in others. I suggest that Harmonic Alignment (Prince & Smolensky 2004, Aissen 1999a) of a structural scale with a scale of semantic roles can derive a hierarchy of appropriate markedness constraints in a straightforward way. Embedding the EPP constraint in this hierarchy of markedness constraints then provides a direct analysis of unmarked word order in Spanish. Throughout this chapter I discuss alternative analyses (both transformational and Optimality-theoretic), showing that they cannot account for the full range of data considered here.

3.1 UNMARKED WORD ORDER IN SPANISH

In characterizing the unmarked word order for different kinds of clauses in Spanish I follow the standard diagnostic that this is the order that is felicitous in a sentence-focus context, which is the word order attested in sentences that felicitously answer questions such as *'what happened?'* and *'what's been happening?.'*

Let us briefly recapitulate now why the unmarked word order data from Mexican Spanish and other varieties of this language represents a challenge for previous analyses of word order, both transformational and optimality-theoretic. Consider transitive clauses first. As first discussed in Chapter One, transitive clauses show an SVO order in the unmarked case.[1] I also noted there that the main reason to suspect that the EPP is a crucial factor for deriving the unmarked word order is that transitive (and also psych clauses) with an empty preverbal position are very strongly degraded in Mexican Spanish. The relevant contrast is shown in (1) and (2).

(1)   UNMARKED WORD ORDER

    Juan compró   el   periódico.
    Juan bought   the   newspaper
    'Juan bought the newspaper.'   SVO

(2)   MEXICAN SPANISH

    ??Compró Juan el   periódico.   VSO
    bought   Juan the newspaper

As mentioned in Chapter One, the fact that the SVO/VSO alternation is absent in Mexican Spanish represents strong counter-evidence to the proposal in Alexiadou & Anagnostopoulou (1998) that the EPP is satisfied by

verb raising in null subject languages.[2] In their analysis, the unacceptability of (2) goes unaccounted for, because the verb has risen to I^0, carrying
the [+D] feature that characterizes verbal agreement morphology in null
subject languages, so EPP checking should have taken place successfully.
More importantly, as I have been suggesting up to this point, the evidence
points to the conclusion that the EPP, although clearly active in Spanish,
cannot be taken to be an all-or-nothing requirement. This is because a
very large number of constructions *do* allow for the preverbal position to
remain empty in the unmarked case. Such is the case of unaccusative
clauses, pro-dropped constructions, and impersonal passives, repeated
here as (3).

(3) a. Llegó   tu   hermano
        arrive.3s your brother
        'Your brother arrived.'

     b. Compraron el   periódico.
        bought.3p   the newspaper
        '(They) bought the newspaper.'

     c. Se vendió la casa.
        CL *sell.3s*   *the house*
        'The house was sold.'

The examples in (3) show that it is not possible to account for the contrast between (1) and (2) by suggesting that Mexican Spanish (as opposed to
other varieties of Spanish) is set to the strict parameter where the EPP has to
be satisfied by XP movement, since in (3) there is no pre-verbal XP that
could potentially satisfy this requirement. I also pointed out in Chapter One
that any analysis of this data needs to be compatible with the fact that Mexican Spanish still displays all the characteristics of languages in which the EPP
is satisfied through verb raising in Alexiadou & Anagnostopoulou's analysis,
namely, null subjects, lack of expletives, and lack of definiteness restrictions
on post-verbal subjects. Furthermore, as will be discussed in this chapter,
Mexican Spanish has the same unmarked word order facts as any other variety of Spanish. These are the crucial observations that motivate an OT analysis of the contrasts in (1–3).

    Consider now OT analyses of word order. The two best-known analy-
ses of word order in OT-GB are Grimshaw & Samek-Lodovici (1998),
which is closely related to Grimshaw (1997), and Costa (1998, 2001). These

analyses have in common the standard GB proposal that fronting of the subject in SVO clauses is the result of a well-formedness condition that the subject can satisfy only in the preverbal field.[3] Costa's analysis is arguably the most influential analysis of word order typology in OT, so I begin the discussion by reviewing it. This analysis relies on the idea that fronting of the subject in the unmarked case in SVO languages is directly related to Case considerations, such that it satisfies the following constraint (Costa 1998, 2001).

(4)   SUBJCASE

Subjects are Case-licensed in Spec-IP.

This constraint crucially interacts with the STAY constraint of Grimshaw (1997), which penalizes the presence of traces in the representation (see §1.2 for discussion).

(5)   STAY

Trace is not allowed.

In a nutshell, Costa's analysis for languages where the subject surfaces in the preverbal position in the unmarked case, such as English, Italian, Portuguese and most varieties of Spanish is as follows. Independently of the ranking of other constraints, these are all languages where SUBJCASE outranks STAY. Consequently it is better to have the subject DP in [Spec-I] with a trace in the representation than to leave the subject in its VP-internal position, where it would not receive Nominative case. This is exemplified for English in the tableau in (6).

Costa (1998) argues convincingly that Case plays a crucial role in determining word order effects in numerous languages, particularly so for

(6) ENGLISH: John will buy the newspaper.

	SUBJCASE	STAY
☞ a.[$_{IP}$ John$_i$ will [$_{VP}$ t$_i$ buy the newspaper]].		*
b.[$_{IP}$ will [$_{VP}$ John buy the newspaper]]	*!	

direct objects. This kind of analysis, however, cannot straightforwardly account for the unmarked word order observed in different kinds of clauses in Spanish. Consider psych clauses with dative *experiencers* first. As shown in (7), in these clauses it is the dative IO *experiencer* and not the subject that occupies the preverbal position in the unmarked case (Fant 1984, Masullo 1993, Arnaiz 1998, *inter alia*). [4] [5]

(7) a. A   Carlos le   gusta Pilar
          to Carlos DAT-CL *likes Pilar*
          'Carlos has a crush on Pilar.'   (Fant 1984:111)

     b. A   Marcos le   interesa la   danza moderna
          to Marcos DAT-CL *interests the dance modern*
          'Marcos is interested in modern dance'   (Masullo 1993:304)

     c. A Juan   le   encantan las películas de David Lynch.
          to Juan DAT-CL *charm-3P the films   of David Lynch*
          'Juan loves movies by David Lynch.'

The SUBJCASE analysis instead predicts that the subject should be the argument that surfaces in the preverbal position. This is shown for example (7a) in the tableau in (8) below, where ✖ signals the candidate wrongly selected as the winner.[6]

This data from Spanish presents a further conceptual complication for an analysis based on SUBJCASE. In both transitive and psych clauses, an argument of the verb appears in the preverbal position. However, if a unified analysis of these two cases is correct, then Case considerations are apparently not involved here at all. Under standard assumptions, the *experiencer* DP in Psych clauses is independently assigned inherent Case by the preposition *a* 'to.' Accordingly, since there is at least one instance where a non-subject argument appears in the preverbal position in the unmarked case, it is much

(8)   SPANISH PSYCH VERBS: UNMARKED WORD ORDER

	SUBJCASE	STAY
☞ a. [a Carlos$_i$ le gusta [$_{VP}$ t$_i$ Pilar]]. **IOVS**	*!	*
✖ b. [Pilar$_i$ le gusta [$_{VP}$ a Carlos t$_i$]]. **SVIO**		*

less obvious that the *agent* DP in transitive clauses undergoes fronting in order to be assigned [NOMINATIVE] Case.[7]

Similar observations hold of the analysis in Grimshaw & Samek-Lodovici (1998), which is similar (but not identical) to Costa's. This analysis relies on the SUBJECT constraint of Grimshaw (1997), which interacts with STAY in the same way as in Costa's analysis. In Grimshaw (1997), there are two alternative formulations of the SUBJECT constraint, listed in (9a) and (9b).

(9)   SUBJECT

      Clauses have subjects.   Grimshaw (1997: 374)

      a. The highest A-specifier in an extended projection must be filled.
      b. The specifier of the highest I-related head must be filled, where I-related includes V, T, Agr, Neg, etc.

                                                            Grimshaw (1997: 390)

Although Grimshaw suggests that SUBJECT corresponds essentially to the EPP of Chomsky (1981), this appears to be true only for the formulation in (9a). Under this formulation, SUBJECT is violated by clauses without a grammatical subject in the canonical position, which is the definition used in Grimshaw & Samek-Lodovici (1998). The second formulation of SUBJECT is more closely related to the numerous works cited in §2.2.2, where the EPP is taken to be a structural condition that requires a given specifier position to be filled by *some* XP, which can, but need not be, the grammatical subject. If my interpretation of Grimshaw (1997) is correct, (9b) is independent of whether the highest I-related specifier is an A or an A-Bar position. Grimshaw further notes that it is conceivable that it can be satisfied by constituents other than the subject, although this does not play a role in her analysis.[8]

With these observations in mind, consider now an analysis of the Spanish data in terms of SUBJECT and STAY. Under the first formulation of SUBJECT, such an analysis faces the same problems as the one that relies on SUBJCASE. This is because this formulation specifically targets an A-specifier and the DP that bears the subject grammatical relation (since the subject is the argument that has one of its A-properties, i.e. Case, licensed in this specifier position; hence the name of the constraint itself). This incorrectly predicts that the subjects of psych clauses should appear in the preverbal position. The second formulation of SUBJECT fares somewhat better, but still cannot

(10)   SPANISH: UNMARKED WORD ORDER

	SUBJECT	STAY
a. [a Carlos₁ le gusta [VP t₁ Pilar]]. **IOVS**		*
b. [Pilar₁ le gusta [VP a Carlos t₁]]. **SVIO**		*

account for the data. In this formulation, fronting to [Spec, I] is not related to the satisfaction of some A-property of the fronted XP, so fronting of the *experiencer* in a psych clause arguably satisfies SUBJECT, as shown in the tableau in (10) above. However, the candidate where the subject *theme* is fronted also satisfies this constraint, as can be seen in the same tableau. Consequently, the unmarked IO-V-S order cannot be derived by these two constraints alone.

What's more, when further constraints are taken into account, this analysis equally selects the incorrect candidate (10b) as the winner. This is because a Case requirement on DP's is also present in the analysis in Grimshaw (1997), in the form of the CASE constraint in (11).

(11) CASE

DPs must be Case marked.   Grimshaw (1997: 374)

In Grimshaw (1997), there are at least two positions where CASE can be satisfied by subject DPs, [spec, V] and [Spec, I], but [spec, V] is only a Case position when no IP is projected. Accordingly, in all of the examples considered here the only Case position for subjects is [Spec, I]. Now notice that as a result of this, even if CASE was a very low ranked constraint in Spanish, it would still get to decide the outcome, wrongly selecting as the winner the candidate where the subject surfaces in the preverbal position because it satisfies CASE. This is shown in tableau (12).

Consider now unaccusative predicates. As previously mentioned, the unmarked word order of unaccusative clauses in Spanish is VS (see H.

(12)   SPANISH: UNMARKED WORD ORDER

	SUBJECT	STAY	CASE
☞ a. [a Carlos₁ le gusta [VP t₁ Pilar]]. **IOVS**		*	*!
✘ b. [Pilar₁ le gusta [VP a Carlos t₁]]. **SVIO**		*	

Kahane & R. Kahane 1950, Hatcher 1956, Contreras 1976, Fant 1984, and Arnaiz 1998). Some examples are presented in (13).[9]

(13) a. Está cayendo granizo.
          is   falling   hail
          'It's hailing.'   (H. Kahane & R. Kahane 1950:239)

      b. Empezó la   resistencia.
          began   the   resistance
          'The resistance began.'   (Contreras 1976:5)

      c. Estallaron dos bombas en la universidad de Navarra.
          exploded   two bombs   in the university   of Navarra
          'Two bombs exploded at the University of Navarra'   (Fant 1984:105)

      d. Llegó   tu   hermano.
          arrived your brother
          'Your brother arrived.'

This data is also problematic for the OT analyses discussed above. In Costa's analysis, the ranking SUBJCASE » STAY again predicts that the subject should surface in the preverbal position.[10] This is shown for (13d) in tableau (14) below.

The analyses in Grimshaw (1997) and Grimshaw & Samek-Lodovici (1998) face the same problem. In this case, as the reader can verify for himself, under either definition of SUBJECT in (9), the ranking SUBJECT » STAY incorrectly predicts that the subject of unaccusative clauses will surface in [Spec, I] in the unmarked case.

Before proceeding to develop an alternative OT proposal of these facts, it is worth highlighting what the more general problem of these two previous OT proposals is. In order to account for word order, these analyses rely on constraints that target either the subject grammatical relation or some property of the subject DP, such as (nominative) Case. Yet the evidence from

(14)   SPANISH: UNMARKED WORD ORDER FOR UNACCUSATIVE VERBS

	SUBJCASE	STAY
☞ a. [IP llegó [VP tu hermano]] **VS**	*!	
✘ b. [IP tu hermanoᵢ llegó [VP tᵢ]] **SV**		*

Spanish suggests that grammatical relations and Case considerations do not play a role in determining the unmarked word order in this language. Taking this observation as a starting point, in the following section I develop an analysis in which the unmarked word order in Spanish is dependent instead on the EPP as defined in Chapter Two, but where the satisfaction of the EPP crucially interacts with the semantic roles of the arguments of the verb and with structural markedness considerations.

3.2 MARKEDNESS AND SYNTACTIC STRUCTURE

As a first step in developing an analysis of unmarked word order in Spanish, I suggest that the notion of markedness, which has been used successfully in many areas of linguistic analysis, also extends to certain aspects of syntactic structure, in particular to the Pole as defined in the previous chapter. Recall that the Pole is defined as the specifier of the highest Π-Projection (i.e. the highest inflectional projection). The Pole is a position defined relationally, so it corresponds to [Spec, I] when IP is the highest Π-Projection, but it corresponds to [Spec, Pol] when PolP is the highest Π-Projection (as is the case in Spanish when a sentential negation is present). For the sake of simplicity in this and subsequent chapters I concentrate on cases where IP is the highest Π-Projection, and so the Pole corresponds to [Spec, I]. However, the conclusions reached below equally extend to cases where the Pole corresponds to a different specifier position.

In terms of markedness, the first relevant observation is that, for reasons of Economy of Structure (Chomsky 1993, 1995), clauses with a Pole are more marked than clauses without a Pole. In other words, the structure in (15a), where [Spec, I] is projected, is more marked with respect to Economy of Structure than the structure without a Pole in (15b).

(15) a.

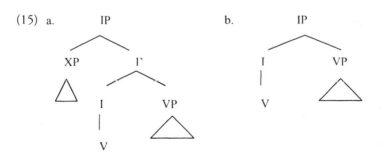

Intuitively, it is fairly straightforward why this should be so: (15a) has an extra layer of structure that (15b) lacks altogether. This is consistent with numerous intuitions on Economy of Structure developed in both transformational and optimality-theoretic research. Broadly, the intuition is that structure is only projected when necessary (i.e., as a "last resort": see specially Grimshaw 1997).[11]

However, the EPP is clearly in direct conflict with Economy of Structure, since the EPP requires clauses to have a Pole. In other words, the EPP favors the structure that is more marked with respect to Economy of Structure. This is another fact that motivates the OT analysis that follows, since Optimality Theory is designed to deal with potentially conflicting grammatical requirements. My proposal, though, is that Spanish provides evidence that the resolution of the conflict between the EPP and Economy of Structure is not just an issue of prioritizing either requirement over the other. Rather, what is crucial for understanding the word order facts discussed in the previous section is the *relative* degree of markedness of the canonical word order for different classes of sentences.

It is a well-known fact that markedness is not necessarily just a contrast between a marked structure and an unmarked one.[12] Amongst marked structures, there are some structures that are more marked than others. In prosodic phonology, for example, syllables with a coda are more marked than syllables without a coda. However, amongst syllables that have a coda, those with a coda segment that is [+sonorant] are less marked than those where the coda segment is [-sonorant] (see for example Vennemann 1972, 1988; Zec 1988, 1994). What I propose is that something similar is observed with respect to the Pole position in clause structure. Although all clauses with a Pole are marked with respect to Economy of Structure when compared to those without one, the relative degree of structural markedness of clauses with a Pole crucially depends on the semantic role of the constituent functioning as the Pole.

3.2.1 The Pole and the thematic hierarchy

The relevant word order contrasts discussed in the previous section are reproduced in (16).

(16) a. Una muchacha compró los discos.   S V O
     a girl   bought   the records
     'A girl bought the records.'

    b. A Juan le   gustan   los chocolates.   IO V S
     to Juan DAT-CL *like*-3P   *the chocolates*
     'Juan likes chocolates.'

c. Llegó   tu   hermano.   VS
   arrived your brother
   'Your brother arrived.'

Recall from the previous chapter that evidence from ellipsis, negation and the licensing of negative XPs indicates that the subject in (16a) and the oblique *experiencer* in (16b) occupy the same structural position, an idea first developed in Masullo (1993).[13] In terms of my proposal, they both correspond to the Pole of the clause, in this case [Spec, I]. Accordingly, I analyze the structural representation of these examples as in (17).[14]

The question that needs to be addressed at this point is why transitive and psych clauses display a constituent functioning as the Pole (and thus comply with the EPP), but unaccusative clauses do not. My proposal is that the Pole is a position that is sensitive to the semantic role of the constituent that occupies it, and that this relates directly to markedness. I previously argued that clauses with a Pole are more marked with respect to Economy of Structure than those without a Pole. However, the word order facts from Spanish in (17) show that markedness is not an all-or-nothing matter: rather, these facts are amenable to an interpretation where there are different degrees of markedness. The reasoning goes as follows. As previously discussed, there is an inherent conflict between the requirements of the EPP, which requires that the specifier of the highest Π-Projection be filled, and Economy of Structure, which requires that the projection of structure be kept to a minimum. The structures in (17a) and (17b), where the Pole of the clause is an

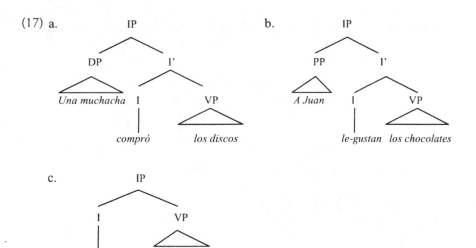

(17) a.

IP
├── DP
│   └── *Una muchacha*
└── I'
    ├── I
    │   └── *compró*
    └── VP
        └── *los discos*

b.

IP
├── PP
│   └── *A Juan*
└── I'
    ├── I
    │   └── *le-gustan*
    └── VP
        └── *los chocolates*

c.

IP
├── I
│   └── *Llegó*
└── VP
    └── *tu hermano*

agent and an *experiencer,* respectively, are both marked with respect to Economy of Structure, since Spec-IP is projected. Their particular degree of markedness, however, is not high enough to warrant a violation of the EPP. In other words, it is better to have a marked syntactic structure than to leave the requirements of the EPP unfulfilled. Here, the EPP overrides structural markedness.

Crucially, in the case of the unaccusative construction in (17c), the exact opposite state of affairs is observed. The unique argument of the verb, the *theme,* stays in its VP-internal position and does not move to Spec-IP. Apparently, a construction with a *theme* as the Pole in Spanish has a degree of markedness high enough that now it is preferable to violate the EPP. In this case, structural markedness overrides the EPP.

These observations correlate directly with much work done on the Thematic Hierarchy. The works that postulate the existence of the Thematic Hierarchy all suggest that what are described traditionally as semantic roles are not only different because of their semantic properties or entailments. Semantic roles are further organized in a hierarchical relation where some roles are more prominent than others, and this hierarchical relation has an effect on numerous grammatical properties (mapping into argument structure, case marking, morphological cross-reference, etc.).

There have been a number of proposals regarding the precise characterization of the Thematic Hierarchy, and I cannot provide a complete overview of them and their differences here. For the purposes of the analysis that follows I assume a characterization of the Thematic Hierarchy based on the proposals in Larson (1988), Speas (1990) and Bakovic (1998), which are shown below (in Bakovic's proposal, ARGUMENT encapsulates *agent* and *theme*).

(18)   a.   Larson (1988: 382)
           AGENT > THEME > GOAL > OBLIQUES (manner, location, time, . . .)

       b.   Speas (1990: 16)
           AGENT > EXPERIENCER > THEME > GOAL/SOURCE/LOCATION > MANNER/TIME

       c.   Bakovic (1998: 37)
           ARGUMENT> LOCATION > MANNER > REASON

The hierarchical relations AGENT > EXPERIENCER and EXPERIENCER > THEME are mostly uncontroversial in the literature on the Thematic Hierarchy (see also Pesetsky 1995). The three proposals in (18) have a further property in common, namely, that they consider a *theme* to be higher in the hierarchy than *locative, temporal, manner* and *reason*. This is a fairly controversial issue, since a number of characterizations of the thematic hierarchy in the literature have the *theme* semantic role at or near the bottom of the hierarchy. Settling this particular issue is a problem that goes beyond the scope of this work, though, and so I simply assume the proposals laid out in (18).[15]

Specifically, I assume the characterization of the thematic hierarchy in (19). This hierarchy brings together different elements from the hierarchies in (18a-c), while respecting the basic hierarchical relations they have in common (I include only those theta-roles that will be relevant in my analysis). For our immediate purposes, the crucial hierarchical relations represented in (19) are: (i) *agents* are more prominent than both *experiencers* and *themes,* and; (ii) *experiencers* are in turn more prominent than *themes.*

(19) AGENT > EXPERIENCER > THEME > LOCATION > MANNER/TIME > REASON

We can now return to the analysis of unmarked word order in Spanish and its relation to markedness. I have suggested that the degree of markedness is the factor that settles the conflicting requirements of the EPP and Economy of Structure. My proposal was that clauses with an *agent* or an *experiencer* as the Pole are not marked enough to warrant a violation of the EPP, but clauses with a *theme* as the Pole are. Accordingly, in the latter case we get a VS and not an SV clause. Simply stated as such, at first sight there is no obvious reason why this should be so. But once we see that this correlates directly to numerous proposals about the structure of the Thematic Hierarchy in the literature, these descriptive observations can be grouped together in a broader generalization, namely, that the degree of structural markedness of the Pole is inversely proportional to its relative prominence in the Thematic Hierarchy. In other words the more prominent the semantic role of the constituent in the Pole, the lower the Pole's structural markedness.[16] The cut-off point at which the degree of markedness is high enough to warrant a violation of the EPP in Spanish is found between the *experiencer* and the *theme* roles in the scale in (19).

It is now necessary to characterize the state of affairs above in a meaningful way that will derive clear, falsifiable predictions and consequences that can be tested in other areas of the syntax of Spanish. Furthermore, given the interpretation of the data proposed above, there are two crucial issues that any analysis of the facts needs to account for. The first one is that the inherent conflict between the EPP and structural markedness is not resolved in such a way that the EPP always overrides markedness or vice versa. The second one is that markedness does not represent an absolute value, but rather, there are different degrees of markedness that appear to correlate with thematic information. In the remainder of this chapter, I argue that Optimality Theory provides an ideal set of theoretical tools for addressing these issues. More specifically, I develop an analysis where the EPP, as defined in the previous chapter, is taken to be a violable constraint. This constraint, as part of the constraint ranking that corresponds to the grammar of Spanish, is embedded in a hierarchy of markedness constraints that target the thematic role of the constituent that corresponds to the Pole. This hierarchy of markedness constraints is derived through Harmonic Alignment of a hierarchy of semantic roles with a binary structural scale.

3.2.2 Harmonic Alignment

The idea developed in the previous section is that Poles that bear a semantic role that ranks high in the Thematic Hierarchy are less marked than Poles whose semantic roles rank low in this same dimension. The question at this point is how to formalize this particular state of affairs. One of the main reasons for developing an Optimality-theoretic account of the data presented so far is that OT provides the ideal mechanism achieving this formalization, namely, Harmonic Alignment (Prince & Smolensky 2004).

Harmonic Alignment is the alignment of two scales that derives a complex pair of relative well-formedness scales (i.e. harmony scales in standard OT terminology), which in turn can be translated into a pair of subhierarchies of markedness constraints.[17] The definition of this mechanism is presented in (20) below, from Prince & Smolensky (2004: 161).

In other words, alignment of the dimensions D_1 and D_2 (where the connective > between the elements of these two dimensions stands for "more prominent than") results in two different well-formedness scales, H_x and H_y

(20)   Alignment. Suppose given a binary dimension D_1 with a scale $X > Y$ on its

elements $\{X, Y\}$, and another dimension D_2 with a scale $a > b \ldots > z$ on its

elements. The *harmonic alignment* of D_1 and D_2 is the pair of Harmony scales:

H_x: $X/a \succ X/b \succ \ldots \succ X/z$

H_y: $Y/z \succ \ldots \succ Y/b \succ Y/a$

The constraint alignment is the pair of constraint hierarchies:

C_x: $*X/z \gg \ldots \gg *X/b \gg *X/a$

C_y: $*Y/a \gg *Y/b \gg \ldots \gg *Y/z$

(where the connective > between the elements of these scales stands for "more harmonic than"). Constraint alignment is the translation of these two scales into two hierarchies of markedness constraints. In the original proposal in Prince & Smolensky (2004), which is designed to formalize a number of universal properties on syllable structure, D_1 is a binary structural scale Peak/Margin (P > M). Peak corresponds to the syllable nucleus and margin to onsets and codas. The hierarchical relation P > M represents the fact that syllable nuclei are more prominent than onsets and codas. D_2 in turn is a prominence scale determined by the sonority of different segments.

It is worth pointing out from the start that Harmonic Alignment is not just a technical mechanism for deriving markedness constraints. Rather, Harmonic Alignment is a formalism that expresses two fundamental properties of markedness/relative well-formedness. The first one is that there are instances of markedness that arise only when elements from two different dimensions are combined into interpretable representations. As noted in Prince & Smolensky in their discussion of prosodic phonology, high sonority (for instance) does not by itself entail high or low markedness. Rather, when a segment occurs in a structural position such as nucleus, onset or coda, its intrinsic sonority in combination with the character of its position results in a given degree of markedness. Secondly, Harmonic Alignment expresses the fact that associating less prominent elements (like *z* in (20)) to the more prominent position and more prominent elements (like *a*) to the less prominent position results in higher degrees of markedness. This also relates to the fact that, for example, even when a less prominent element (like *z*) in the more prominent position constitutes a marked representation, this same element in the less prominent position constitutes an unmarked representation (see also Aissen 1999a). This situation is characterized in the literature on markedness as Markedness Reversal (Aissen 1999a; Battistella 1990, 1996; Croft 1996).

Harmonic Alignment was originally developed to account for phenomena in the domain of prosodic phonology, but has later been expanded into the domain of syntax and morphosyntax in Aissen (1999a, 2003).[18] Here I illustrate Aissen's application of Harmonic Alignment to syntax with her analysis of markedness and subject choice (Aissen 1999a). Aissen's analysis begins with the observation widely attested in the descriptive and the functional literature that different languages are sensitive to different prominence scales when determining which of the arguments of a predicate will be realized as the grammatical subject. Aissen suggests that the formalization of these facts can be achieved by aligning a binary scale of grammatical relations (for example, Subject > Object), with different prominence scales, such as a scale of semantic roles, a scale for different grammatical persons, and a scale of discourse prominence. This results in a number of different hierarchies of markedness constraints, each of which targets the relative markedness of subjects and objects with respect to a specific prominence scale. For example, given the two scales in (21), Harmonic Alignment derives the harmony scales and constraint hierarchies in (22) and (23), respectively.

(21) a. Subject > Object
　　　 b. Agent > Patient

(22) a. Su/Agt > Su/Pat
　　　 b. Obj/Pat > Obj/Agt

(23) a. *Su/Pat » *Su/Agt
　　　 b. *Obj/Agt » *Obj/Pat

The effect of the constraints in (23a), for example, will be the following. When the input of a representation includes both an *agent* and a *patient,* the *agent* is mapped as the subject and the *patient* as the object, all else being equal. This is shown in the tableau in (24).

　　　Following Aissen's fundamental insights about the application of Harmonic Alignment in syntax, and Prince & Smolensky's original idea that the binary dimension (D_1) that undergoes alignment is a structural prominence dimension, I now develop a Harmonic Alignment analysis of the word order facts in Spanish that crucially relies on the notion of the Pole developed in the preceding chapter.

(24) SEMANTIC ROLES AND SUBJECT CHOICE (Aissen 1999a)

INPUT: <V (x, y), x= agent, y=patient>	*Su/Pat	*Su/Agt
☞ a.　Agent/Subject - Patient/Object		*
b.　Patient/Subject - Agent/Object	*!	

3.2.3 The Pole Hierarchy

Returning now to word order in Spanish, the analysis I propose follows the idea developed in §3.2.1 that Poles that bear a semantic role that ranks high in the Thematic Hierarchy are less marked than Poles whose semantic roles rank low in this same dimension. To formalize this state of affairs by Harmonic Alignment, I will make use of the structural prominence scale in (25), where Non-Pole is a term that encapsulates every complement and specifier position in the lexical layer of the extended projection (VP or a VP shell for our purposes).

(25) Pole > Non-Pole

Appealing to a dimension of structural prominence (as opposed to, for example, one of relational prominence) is consistent with the discussion developed so far. Briefly, we have seen in the preceding chapter that there is evidence for the existence of a particular specifier position in the functional layer of the sentence, and that the grammatical properties associated with this position do not depend on the grammatical relation of the constituent that occupies it. Furthermore, I have suggested in this chapter that the presence vs. the absence of this specifier position is closely related to Economy of Structure considerations. Lastly, I have also argued that the word order observed in different kinds of clauses in the unmarked case is directly related to the semantic role of the constituent that occupies this structural position, and not by its grammatical relation. What unifies these observations is a specific structural position, the Pole, and so it is appropriate to postulate a structural prominence dimension based on it.

Following the assumption from the preceding chapter that matrix clauses are minimally constituted by an IP, the scale in (25) is intended to reflect the fact that the Pole is more prominent than any other constituent in the extended projection, all else being equal. Structurally, this is because the Pole c-commands every other constituent of the extended projection except the IP itself (see §2.2.2). Once we have this binary structural scale, it can be aligned with the Thematic Hierarchy assumed here (repeated in 26). The result of the alignment of these two scales is the two harmony scales in (27), which translate into the constraint hierarchies in (28).

(26) AGENT > EXPERIENCER > THEME > LOCATION > MANNER/TIME > REASON

(27) a. Pole/Agent > Pole/Experiencer > Pole/Theme > Pole/Location
          > Pole/Manner-Time > Pole/Reason.
      b. Non-Pole/Reason > Non-Pole/Manner-Time > Non-Pole/Location
          > Non-Pole/Theme > Non-Pole/Experiencer > Non-Pole/Agent

(28) a. *Pole/Reason » *Pole/Manner-Time » *Pole/Location » *Pole/Theme »
          *Pole/Experiencer » *Pole/Agent
      b. *Non-Pole/Agent » *Non-Pole/Experiencer » *Non-Pole/Theme »
          *NonPole/Location » *Non-Pole/Manner-Time » *Non-Pole/Reason

The harmony scale in (27a) expresses the fact that the least marked instance of a Pole is one filled by the *agent*, whereas a Pole filled by a *reason* adverb corresponds to the most marked instance. Inversely, the harmony scale in (27b) expresses the fact that a VP-internal *agent* corresponds to the most marked instance of a VP-internal argument or adjunct, whereas a *reason* adverb corresponds to the least marked instance of a VP-internal argument or adjunct.[19] As mentioned before, these harmony scales are in turn translated into the hierarchies of markedness constraints in (28). The constraints in the hierarchy in (28a) target the relative markedness of a constituent with the specified semantic role when it appears as the Pole of the clause. The most severe violation is incurred when the Pole is filled by a *reason* expression, whereas the least severe violation is incurred in when an *agent* functions as the Pole. The hierarchy in (28b), by contrast, targets the relative markedness of a constituent with the specified semantic role when it surfaces in its VP-internal position. In this case, the most severe violation of the hierarchy in (28b) is incurred when an *agent* occupies a VP-internal position, whereas the least severe violation is incurred in when a *reason* expression occupies a VP-internal position. Crucially, I further assume that adjoined positions (both in the lexical and in the functional layer) are never targeted by the constraints in these hierarchies.

Throughout the remainder of this work, I concentrate on the constraint hierarchy in (28a), which I will refer as the *Pole Hierarchy*. The role that the constraints in (28b) play in the syntax of Spanish and other languages is an issue that I leave for future research.[20]

3.3 AN OT ANALYSIS BASED ON MARKEDNESS

3.3.1. Structural markedness and unmarked word order

At this point we need only one more constraint in order to provide an analysis of unmarked word order in Spanish. Since the EPP is central to our discussion, and since there are languages (and one variety of Spanish) where the EPP is satisfied by expletive insertion, we first need to account for the fact that most varieties of Spanish lack expletives altogether. For this purpose, I incorporate into the analysis the FULL-INTERPRETATION constraint of Grimshaw (1997) and Grimshaw & Samek-Lodovici (1998). This is the OT constraint that penalizes DEPendency violations (McCarthy & Prince 1995) in syntax.

(29) FULL-INTERPRETATION
      Parse lexical conceptual structure.
      Failed by expletives and auxiliary *do*.   Grimshaw & Samek-Lodovici (1998).

This constraint is violated when there is a lexical item in the output that has no corresponding element in the input (in OT-syntax this is the way of understanding the fact that expletives and auxiliary *do* are devoid of meaning). Specifically for the analysis that follows, it is violated by insertion of an expletive, as in Grimshaw & Samek-Lodovici (1998). With these constraints set up, we can now provide an analysis of Spanish. This language is characterized by the constraint ranking in (30), where, crucially, the EPP is interpolated into the Pole Hierarchy between *Pole/Theme and *Pole/Experiencer. Furthermore, undominated FULL-INTERPRETATION prevents an expletive from being inserted in the Pole to satisfy the EPP.

(30) FULL-INT » *Pole/ Reason » *Pole/Manner-Time » *Pole/Location »
      *Pole/Theme » EPP » *Pole/Experiencer » *Pole/Agent[21]

Consider now how the ranking in (30) derives the word orders of different kinds of clauses. The first case, illustrated in (31) below, corresponds to the transitive construction (16a).

Let us go through the losing candidates in (31) one by one. Candidate (31b) leaves the Pole position empty, and thus loses to (31a) because of its

(31) INPUT: <buy (x, y), x=a girl (Ag), y=the records (Th)>

		FULL-INT	*Pole/ Theme	EPP	*Pole/ Agent
☞ a. [IP una muchacha compró [VP los discos]] **SVO**					*
b. [IP compró [VP una muchacha los discos]] **VSO**				*!	
c. [IP los discos los compró [VP una muchacha]] **OVS**			*!		
d. [IP *exp* compró [VP una muchacha los discos]]		*!			

violation of the EPP constraint. Candidate (31c) satisfies EPP because the direct object occupies Spec-IP, but by doing so it incurs in a fatal violation of *Pole/Theme. Finally, the *exp*-VSO candidate (31d) also satisfies EPP by insertion of an expletive (*exp*), but loses because of its fatal violation of FULL-INTERPRETATION. Candidate (31a), which incurs only in a violation of the low ranked markedness constraint *Pole/Agent, thus emerges as the winner. Note that I am not claiming by this analysis that all losing candidates are unattested or ungrammatical sentences in Spanish in general, or in Mexican Spanish in particular. Once the constraints related to information structure are introduced in the following chapter, it will become clear how, for instance, candidate (31c) can emerge as the winner over the candidate that displays the unmarked word order.[22]

In the case of Psych clauses, the ranking in (30) ensures that it is not the subject that emerges in the preverbal position, but rather the IO, since given the Pole Hierarchy in (28a) it is better to have an *experiencer* than a *theme* as the Pole of the clause. The analysis for the psych clause (16b) is presented in table (32) below.

Just as in the case of (31), the candidate that leaves the Pole position empty, candidate (32b), loses because of its violation of EPP, while (32d) loses because of its violation of undominated FULL-INTERPRETATION. However, in this case candidate (32a), where the subject emerges in the preverbal position, loses because of its fatal violation of *Pole/Theme. The most harmonious candidate (32c) is the one that violates the low-ranked *Pole/Experiencer constraint and thus it emerges as the winner.

Lastly, consider unaccusative constructions. What is crucial in this case is that under the ranking in (30), it is better to leave the Pole position empty than to have a *theme* occupying it, because the degree of markedness of a clause with a *theme* as the Pole is higher that the degree of markedness of a clause that lacks a Pole altogether. Consequently, as opposed to the previous two cases, a verb-initial construction emerges as the output. This is shown in tableau (33) for the VS clause (16c).

(32) INPUT: <like (x, y), x=Juan (Ex), y=chocolates (Th)>

	FULL-INT	*Pole/Theme	EPP	*Pole/Exper
a. [IP los chocolates le gustan [VP a Juan]] **S V IO**		*!		
b. [IP le gustan [VP a Juan los chocolates]] **V IO S**			*!	
☞ c. [IP a Juan le gustan [VP los chocolates]] **IO V S**				*
d. [IP *exp* le gustan [VP a Juan los chocolates]]	*!			

(33) INPUT: <arrive (x), x=your brother (Th)>

	FULL-INT	*Pole/ Theme	EPP
a. [$_{IP}$ tu hermano llegó [$_{VP}$]] SV		*!	
☞ b. [$_{IP}$ llegó [$_{VP}$ tu hermano]] VS			*
c. [$_{IP}$ *exp* llegó [$_{VP}$ tu hermano]] exp-VS	*!		

The analysis presented in (31–33) represents the core of my proposal, and it has three crucial properties. First of all, it accounts for the fact that for different verb classes different arguments occupy the preverbal position in the unmarked cases. Secondly, by embedding the EPP constraint in the sub-hierarchy in (28a) we explain why the preverbal position needs to be occupied in some cases but not in others, a result that cannot be achieved straightforwardly in frameworks where satisfaction of the EPP is an all-or-nothing requirement. Lastly, by introducing the notion of Pole it is possible to achieve this result without the need to invoke specific grammatical relations when determining which argument of the verb occupies the preverbal position. This is the core of the analysis, and for Spanish it cannot be replaced by a constraint hierarchy that targets specific grammatical relations instead, as the discussion of previous analyses in §3.1 shows.

3.3.2 Alternative analyses

To end this section, I comment briefly on two alternatives to my proposal, one based on null expletives and the other one based on null locative topics (Pinto 1994, Zubizarreta 1998, Goodall 2001).[23] Consider an analysis where, just as in my analysis, transitive subjects and dative experiencers satisfy the EPP in the unmarked case, but where the VS order of unaccusatives is the result of an inviolable EPP being satisfied by a null expletive in [Spec,I], as in the representation in (34), where (*exp*) represents a null expletive.

(34) [$_{IP}$ (*exp*) llegó [$_{VP}$ tu hermano]]
      arrived your brother

Independently of whether or not this is a viable proposal, (34) is not a possible representation in an OT analysis. The reason for this is as follows. As previously noted, in OT syntax expletive elements are elements that are included in the representation by GEN when it generates the set of candidates, 'but which do not correspond to any element in the input. As such, they necessarily incur a DEPENDENCY (DEP) violation, typically understood as a violation of the FULL-INTERPRETATION constraint previously discussed. Crucially, though, in order to establish whether a DEP violation has indeed occurred one must be able to compare the elements in the candidates with the elements in the input. This comparison cannot be established directly if the expletive elements inserted by GEN are null elements that have no visible effect on the representation, so it is a standard assumption in OT syntax that expletive elements necessarily have phonetic content (Grimshaw & Samek-Lodovici 1998: see also McCarthy & Prince 1995). This is a welcome result, since the resulting theory is very restrictive with respect to the null elements that it allows. Further notice that the null expletive analysis would not explain why the unmarked word order of psych verbs with dative experiencers is IO-VS, whereas in my analysis this word order and the word order of unaccusative clauses are both explained by the ranking *Pole/Theme » EPP.

Independently of this, it is worth underlining that the null expletive analysis has been rejected in a number of works, including Samek-Lodovoci (1996), Alexiadou & Anagnostopoulou (1998) and Goodall (2001). These authors point out that it is very implausible that a null expletive satisfies the EPP in a construction like (34) since the fundamental characteristic of expletives is that they induce a definiteness effect which is not observed in unaccusative or other types of VS clauses in Spanish and other *pro*-drop languages. Now one could consider the possibility that null expletives in some languages do not induce a definiteness effect, and that precisely this would appear to be the case in Spanish. But this carries with it the consequence that the null expletive hypothesis then becomes unfalsifiable. To the extent that we assume the existence of null expletives whose properties are not those of overt expletives, and whose only observable effect on the surface representation is the VS word order attested in a very specific number of cases, it becomes impossible to verify or refute their existence. In other words, if (in contrast with overt expletives), null expletives have no set of properties associated with them other than satisfying the EPP, we cannot test for their presence in any way. Consequently, such an alternative should be abandoned on methodological grounds and does not constitute a viable alternative to my proposal.

Another alternative analysis, proposed in Pinto (1994) for Italian and further developed in Zubizarreta (1998) and Goodall (2001) for Spanish, relies on the idea that in VS clauses the preverbal position is occupied by a null topical locative or temporal adverb. There are two facts that disconfirm this alternative. Fronted topics create islands for extraction, as is well known (see Rochemont 1989, Rizzi 1990, Müller & Sternefeld 1993, *inter alia*) and this is clearly attested for left-peripheral locative and temporal expressions in Spanish, as shown in (35).

(35) a. ??Qué dices   [que ayer   compró Juan]?
          what you-say that yesterday bought Juan
          ('What are you saying that yesterday Juan bought?')

      b. *Cuántas personas decidieron   [que en Mérida van   a entrevistar]?
          *how-many persons   you-*PL-decided that in Mérida you-*PL-*go to interview*
          ('How many people did you decide that in Mérida you are going to interview?)'

Wh-extraction from complement VS clauses, however, is not subject to any such effects, as shown by the extraction of a downstairs adjunct in (36).

(36) Cómo dices   [que llegó   tu hermano *t*]?
      how   you-say that arrived your brother
      'How are you saying that your brother arrived (i.e., by bus, by train, etc.)?'

If, in order to sidestep the contrast between (35) and (36), we suggest that null locatives and temporal adverbs do not have the same properties as overt topics, then once again we face an unfalsifiable hypothesis, since we cannot test for their presence in the representation in any way.

Secondly, the null locative/temporal hypothesis faces a serious problem when transitive clauses are considered. We have seen that VSO and V-IO-S sentences with an empty preverbal position are not tolerated in Mexican Spanish. But if a null locative/temporal can satisfy the EPP in unaccusative VS sentences, then it is unclear why such an option cannot rescue the unacceptable clause VSO sentence in (2), for instance.

3.4 OTHER CONSTRUCTIONS

I now discuss how a number of constructions different from the ones discussed so far fit in the analysis developed here. The constructions I will look at are *pro*-drop constructions, impersonal passives, other kinds of psych clauses and impersonal active constructions.[24] Much work remains to be done in terms of characterizing the precise behavior of some of these constructions, and so for the time being I will only suggest a tentative analysis for them.

Impersonal passives and *pro*-dropped constructions, exemplified in (37a) and (37b) respectively, are straightforwardly analyzed in the proposal developed so far.

(37) a. Se vendió la casa.
         CL *sold*.3s *the house*
         'The house was sold.'

      b. Compraron el periódico.
         bought.3p   *the newspaper*
         '(They) bought the newspaper.'

The subject *theme* of the impersonal passive surfaces in the post-verbal position because of the ranking *Pole/Theme » EPP, so the analysis in this case is essentially the same as the one of unaccusative sentences. A similar situation is found in *pro*-dropped constructions like (37b). Here the only overt argument XP of the predicate is the direct object *theme*. As expected under this proposal, this XP still does not move to the preverbal position to satisfy the EPP.[25]

Consider now other kinds of psych predicates. In their influential analysis of psych verbs in Italian, Belletti & Rizzi (1988) list three basic classes of these verbs. One class, the *piacere* 'please' class, where the *theme* is realized as the nominative subject and the *experiencer* as a dative oblique, corresponds to the psych verbs we have discussed so far. In another class, the *temere* 'fear' class, the *experiencer* is realized as the nominative subject and the *theme* as an accusative argument. This class of psych verbs is also observed in Spanish, and includes verbs like *conocer* 'know,' *admirar* 'admire,' *amar* 'love,' *odiar* 'hate,' *despreciar* 'loathe/despise,' *aceptar* 'accept,' etc. The unmarked word order of clauses with these verbs, where the *experiencer* subject occupies the preverbal position, is illustrated in (38).

(38) Juan ama   a   María.   S   V   O
     Juan loves ACC *María*   \<EXP\> \<THEME\>
     'Juan loves María.'

These word order facts are the ones predicted by my analysis. In terms of semantic roles, these predicates are just like *gustar* 'like,' analyzed in (32), and so we expect them to behave in a similar way, independently of the specific grammatical relations that their arguments display.

The situation is slightly more complex with the third class considered in Belletti & Rizzi (1988), which corresponds to the *preoccupare* 'worry,' class. In this case the *experiencer* is realized as an accusative argument, and the nominative subject occupies the preverbal position, as shown in the Italian example in (39).

(39) ITALIAN (Belletti & Rizzi 1988:291)

     Questo preoccupa Gianni.   S   V   O

     this   *worries*   *Gianni*

Most of the Italian verbs of this class considered in Belletti & Rizzi (1988) actually belong to the *gustar* class in Spanish (i.e. the *experiencer* is a dative that surfaces in the preverbal position in the unmarked case). This is shown for *preocupar* 'to worry' in example (40)

(40) A Juan le   preocupan sus hijos.   IO   V   S

     to Juan DAT-CL *worry-3p*   *his children*   <EXP> <THEME>

     'Juan is worried about his children.'

Spanish does have some psych verbs where the *experiencer* is realized as an accusative object in the post-verbal field, though. Examples are shown in (41).

(41) a. Juan atemoriza a   sus hermanos.   S   V   O

       Juan terrorizes ACC *his siblings*

       'Juan terrorizes his siblings.'

    b. El gobierno   intimida   a   los activistas.

       the government intimidates ACC *the activists*

       'The government intimidates the activists.'

My claim, however, is that in these cases the subject is not really a *theme*, but rather is closer in its thematic properties to an *agent* (see also Pesetsky 1995).[26] The broad semantic role labels we have been using so far are not enough to clarify the state of affairs in (41), but Dowty's (1991) finer distinctions in terms of ProtoRole entailments do shed light on this issue. The subjects in (41), are perhaps not equivalent to transitive *agents*, but these verbs do necessarily entail their *volitional involvement in the event or state*, which is one of the entailments associated with the Agent Proto-Role in Dowty's analysis.[27] This is in contrast with what is observed with respect to the object in (38) and to the subject in (40), where the psych verbs do not entail the *volitionality* of these arguments.

Notice also that, just like the *theme* arguments of the *gustar* 'like' class (see (40)), the subjects in (41) already carry two of Dowty's five possible Proto-Agent entailments, *causing an event or change of state in another participant* and *existing independently of the event named by the verb* (see Dowty 1991). Apparently, the additional *volitionality* entailment of the verbs in (41) is enough for their subjects to qualify as *agents*.[28] With these considerations in mind, the word order in (41) is expected under my analysis. Given the ranking EPP » *Pole/Experiencer » *Pole/Agent (see (30)), whenever there is both an *agent* and an *experiencer* present, the candidate that satisfies the EPP by moving the *agent* into the Pole emerges as the winner.

In support of this proposal, notice that even though Spanish does not appear to have a large class of verbs equivalent to the Italian *preoccupare* class, it does have a large class of psych verbs that show an alternation where the *experiencer* is realized either as a dative or as an accusative argument (Treviño 1992). Verbs in this class include *molestar* 'bother,' *alterar* 'get on one's nerves,' *conmover* 'be moved by,' *asustar* 'frighten,' *excitar* 'turn on,' etc. Crucially, this alternation is correlated to an alternation in unmarked word order, a fact that to the best of my knowledge has previously gone unobserved. Both alternations are shown in (42).[29]

(42) UNMARKED WORD ORDER
　　　a. Los niños　　molestan　a　　Juan.　　　　　　　　　S　V　O
　　　　　the children　bother　　ACC　Juan
　　　　　'The children bother Juan.'

　　　b. A Juan　le　　　molestan　los niños.[30]　　　　　　IO V S
　　　　　to Juan　DAT-CL　bother　　the children
　　　　　'(The) children bother Juan.'

Example (42a) means that the children are intentionally engaged in doing things with the purpose of bothering *Juan*. In contrast, (42b) means that *Juan* finds the children bothersome, i.e., he is irritated by their mere presence or by the normal things that children usually do. This alternation can be straightforwardly accounted for in terms of Proto-Role entailments. In both cases, *the children* is the *cause* of Juan's mental state, but (42a) further has a *volitionality* entailment.

Here we can test for the presence of this *volitionality* entailment with the diagnostics in Ackerman & Moore (1999, 2001), where an analysis is developed of the alternation of the grammatical function of the *experiencer* in (42). Ackerman & Moore (2001) show that the external argument of verbs with the *volitionality* entailment are compatible with adverbials that entail volitionality, whereas verbs that lack this entailment are not. This same behavior is observed with the verbs in (42). Whereas (42a) is compatible with certain adverbs like *a propósito* 'on purpose,' (42b) (with a subject-oriented reading) is not.

(43) a. Los niños   molestan a   Juan a propósito.
     the children   bother   ACC   *Juan to purpose*
     'The children bother Juan on purpose.'

    b. ??A Juan le   molestan los niños   a propósito.
      *to Juan *DAT-CL *bother*   *the children to purpose*
      (The children irritate Juan on purpose.)

Secondly, in testing for the presence of this entailment in data from Polish, Ackerman & Moore (2001) show that external arguments can control into purpose clauses only if the verb has the *volitionality* entailment. Once again, this same behavior is observed in Spanish. As shown in (44), the subject of the verb with an accusative *experiencer* can control into a purpose clause, but the subject of the verb with a dative *experiencer* cannot.

(44) a. Los niños molestan a   Juan [para PRO hacerlo   llorar].
     the children bother   ACC *Juan*   *for*   *to-make-him cry*
     'The children bother Juan in order to make him cry.'

    b. *A Juan le   molestan los niños [para PRO hacerlo   llorar].
      *to Juan *DAT-CL *bother*   *the children for*   *to-make-him cry*
      (The children irritate Juan in order to make him cry.)

Now, in terms of my proposal, the word order facts are explained as follows. When *molestar* 'to bother' entails *volitionality*, its subject has enough Proto-Agent entailments to count as an *agent,* and so it surfaces as the Pole in the unmarked case, as in (42a). In the absence of this entailment, the subject of *molestar* corresponds to a *theme,* and so (42b) displays the *experiencer-*verb-*theme* order observed in the two other major classes of psych verb (the *gustar* 'like' class, and the *amar* 'love' class).[31]

Summarizing the discussion so far, the other classes of psych verbs in Spanish provide further evidence that unmarked word order is regulated by the thematic roles of the arguments of a verb and not by the subject grammatical relation. The observed semantic contrasts are subtle enough that it is not immediately obvious how to capture them with broad semantic role labels like *agent.* However, once more nuanced analytical tools like those of Dowty (1991) and Ackerman & Moore (2001) are introduced into the analysis, the evidence points to the conclusion that the Pole in Spanish in the unmarked case does correspond to the argument of the verb that ranks higher in the Thematic Hierarchy.

To conclude this section I consider a number of active intransitive constructions, labeled *impersonal* constructions in the literature on Spanish, which have been recently analyzed in Fernández-Soriano (1999). These constructions are of two kinds. The first kind involves intransitive stative predicates and meteorological verbs that can appear with a preposed locative XP; some of these predicates (such as *faltar* 'lack') can also alternatively take a dative XP as their preverbal argument. The second class corresponds to intransitive eventive predicates (such as *suceder, ocurrir* 'happen') that can take either a locative or a dative XP as an argument, which can also appear in the preverbal position. The two constructions are exemplified in (45) and (46), respectively.[32]

(45) En Madrid   nieva.
     in Madrid snows
     'It snows in Madrid.'

(46) a. Aquí pasa   algo.
       here happens   something
       'Something's going on here.'

      b. A Juan le   pasa   algo.
       to Juan DAT-CL happens something
       'Something's going on with Juan.'

Fernández-Soriano provides evidence that the locative and dative XPs in (45–46) are arguments of these predicates, since they behave differently from adjuncts in a number of respects, such as extraction from coordinate clauses and interrogative inversion. Also, these arguments are base-generated in a position that is both structurally higher than the base position of the *theme* subject and the base position of the locative and dative (*goal*) arguments of other classes of predicates. These conclusions seem well-motivated and will not be contested here.

However, Fernández-Soriano goes on to propose that these locative and dative XPs are quirky subjects that appear in the preverbal subject position in the unmarked case. Although from the preceding discussion it seems clear that these preverbal obliques are not quirky subjects,[33] the word order facts reported by Fernández-Soriano are potentially problematic for my analysis for two reasons. First, in the proposal I have developed, *agents* and *experiencers* are predicted to appear in the preverbal Pole position in the unmarked case, but it is not immediately clear if the dative arguments of impersonal constructions can be grouped under either of these semantic roles. The second problem is that my analysis predicts that *locative* XPs should not appear in the Pole position in the unmarked case, because the constraint *Pole/Locative, which penalizes locative Poles, outranks the EPP (see (30)). In this respect, Fernández-Soriano's claims about the unmarked word order of these constructions require some clarification.

Consider first the predicates that take a dative argument, like *pasar* 'happen' in (46b). For these constructions I agree with Fernández-Soriano both in that the unmarked word order corresponds to the one in (46b), where the dative appears in the preverbal position, and in that it is fairly clear that these are not psych predicates in the general sense. However, this does not by itself exclude the possibility that the dative XP has the *experiencer* semantic role. In fact, Fernández-Soriano hints at this solution in two different ways. First, she notes that the dative XPs in these constructions do not behave like the *goal* arguments of ditransitive predicates with respect to secondary predication, interrogative inversion and other phenomena. Secondly, she notes that other predicates in this class express a psychological state in relation to some element (call it X) that is not realized as a nominal expression. Instead X is realized as a clause, as in (47a) or it has no (overt) syntactic expression whatsoever, as in (47b):

(47) a.

　　　A Pedro le　　　daba lo mismo [decírmelo o no].
　　　to Pedro DAT-CL *gave the same　　to-tell-me-it or not*
　　b. 'Pedro didn't care about telling me or not.'

　　　A Marta le　　　fue　bien en　Buenos Aires.
　　　to Marta DAT-CL *went　well in　Buenos Aires*
　　　'Marta had a very good time in Buenos Aires.' (Fernández-Soriano 1999: 123)[34]

Based on this observation, it is not unreasonable to suggest that the predicates in (47) simply correspond to a particular kind of Psych predicate. In this class, the *theme* that corresponds to the origin/cause of the psychological state need not be realized as a nominal argument. Similar observations can be made with respect to (46b). In this case, the dative XP can be thought of as an *experiencer* that is affected by the state expressed by verb and the subject *theme*. Still, one has to acknowledge that the *experiencer* status of the datives in other verbs of this class is much less clear than in the examples in (46b) and (47). This is the case of the verb *faltar* 'lack' in (48).

(48) A la   silla le   falta   una   pata.
      to the chair DAT-CL *lacks a   leg*
      'The chair has a leg missing (Lit. "a leg is lacking to the chair").'

The thematic characterization of the arguments of this verb does not seem
to fit in the Thematic Hierarchy assumed up to now. The dative is clearly not an
experiencer, but it is clearly not a *goal* either, since the verb expresses a state.
Rather, *faltar* seems to establish something akin to a whole-part relation between
the *dative* argument and the subject DP, where it is unclear if semantic roles as
understood in §3.2 are of any relevance in defining this relation.[35] However, it
does not necessarily follow from this that the arguments of the verb must be
equally prominent. In light of our discussion of semantic entailments in psych
verbs, it is not unreasonable to think that the Pole may be sensitive to other
prominence hierarchies, one of which could include *whole > part* as a part of the
scale. This would explain why the dative appears in the preverbal position, since
the whole would be more prominent than the part. Investigating this issue in
detail, however, requires a more detailed analysis of the semantics of these predicates than is possible here.
        The case of preposed locative XPs in (45) and (46a) is somewhat
clearer. In this case there is considerable evidence that these preposed locative
XPs are topics, and that, *contra* Fernández-Soriano's analysis, they do not
appear in the preverbal position in the unmarked case. Fernández-Soriano
claims that the word order in (45) and (46a) is felicitous in an out-of-the-
blue (i.e. sentence focus) context, our diagnostic for unmarked word order.
Although I do not share this judgement, it is possible that part of the problem has to do with the fact that (45) and (46a) correspond to the habitual
present, which to my ear is easily amenable to an interpretation where the
referent of the locative has already been introduced in the discourse and/or is
readily identifiable by both speaker and hearer.[36] In contrast, imagine a context where speaker A walks into a room and sees speaker B watching the
news on television; he then utters the question in (49). In this context, the
answers where the locative PP occupies the preverbal position are robustly
infelicitous for all speakers of Mexican Spanish consulted:

(49) Qué   pasa?
      'What's happening?'

(50) a. Está nevando en   Barcelona.
          it-is snowing in   Barecelona
          'It's snowing in Barcelona.'

b. #En Barcelona está nevando.
   in   Barcelona it-is snowing

(51) a. Está lloviendo en Guadalajara.
     it-is raining in Guadalajara
     'It's raining in Guadalajara.'

   b. #En Guadalajara está lloviendo.
      in Guadalajara it-is raining

As further evidence that fronted locatives in these constructions are functioning as topics, notice that for some speakers their acceptability is considerably downgraded in an out-of-the-blue context when they are indefinite, as shown in (52–53).[37] Although this is not the case for all speakers, its worth pointing out that, in contrast, preverbal *agents* and *experiencers* are not subject to this restriction, as shown in (54).

(52) a. Aquí pasa   algo.
     here happens something
     'Something's going on here.'

   b. %En un salón   pasa   algo.
      in a   classroom happens something

(53) a. Aquí falta azucar.
     here lacks sugar
     'There's sugar missing here.'

   b. %En una mesa falta azucar.
      in a   table lacks sugar

(54) a. Una muchacha compró los discos.
     a   girl   bought the records
     'A girl bought the records.'

   b. A un reportero le   gustó tanto   tu   discurso que lo   quiere
      to a journalist DAT-CL liked so-much your speech   that ACC-CL he-wants
      publicar.
      to-publish
      'A journalist liked your speech so much that he wants to publish it.'

Consider also one of the crucial arguments presented by Fernández-Soriano in favor of her analysis of these locative XPs as quirky subjects. In her analysis, these locative XPs must receive quirky case in [Spec, I], which helps explain why they surface in this position in the unmarked case. In support of this proposal, Fernández-Soriano notes that the locative XPs are in complementary distribution with the dative XPs previously discussed, which are also quirky subjects. This is shown in (55)

(55) a. Me   falta   café.
         to-me   misses   coffee
         'I am missing coffee.'

      b. Aquí falta   café.
         here   misses coffee
         'Coffee is missing here.'

      c. ??Aquí me   falta   café.
         here   to-me misses   coffee   (Fernández-Soriano 1999:121)

The argument is that if quirky case is discharged on the dative, then there is no possibility for the locative to receive quirky case in [Spec, I]. Example (55c), however, seems to me to be simply pragmatically anomalous, since one can readily construct other instances where the *locative* and the dative are not in complementary distribution.

(56) a. En Barcelona nos pasó   lo   peor.
         in Barcelona to-us happened the worst
         'The worst happened to us in Barcelona.'

      b. En esta colonia   nos faltan   policias.
         in this neighborhood to-us lack   policemen
         'We do not have enough policemen in this neighborhood.'
         (*When we are in this neighborhood we do not have enough policemen.)

Fernández-Soriano claims that constructions like (55) are only possible when the locative is not an argument of the verb, in which case their interpretation is necessarily that of an adjunct. In other words, (55c) would have to be interpreted as something like 'when I am here, I lack coffee' (Fernández-Soriano 1999: 122). Although this is certainly a possible interpretation for (56a), ('When we were in Barcelona, the worst happened to us'), example (56b) cannot have an interpretation along these lines (i.e. 'When we are in this neighborhood, we don't have enough policemen'). This points to the conclusion that the presence of the locative XP in [Spec, I] is not related to its status as either an argument or an adjunct, but rather to information structure considerations (i.e. topicalization).

Finally, recall from §3.3.2 that fronted topics create islands for extraction. The fronted locative XPs of impersonal verbs behave like topics in this respect, as shown in the examples in (57–58). Notice here that extraction is perfect when the locative XP appears in the post-verbal field. In contrast, preverbal subjects (Goodall 2001) and *experiencers* do not lead to such island effects, as shown in (59) (example (59a) is from Goodall 2001). This contrast holds both when the extracted *wh*-operator is D-Linked (as in (58a) and (59b)) and when it is not (as in (57a) and (59a)).

(57) a. *Qué$_i$ dices [que en Barcelona pasó t_i la semana pasada]?
    what you-say that in Barcelona happened the week past

   b. Qué$_i$ dices [que pasó t_i en Barcelona la semana pasada]?
    what you-say that happened in Barcelona the week past
    'What did you say happened in Barcelona last week?'

(58) a. ??Cuántos días$_i$ dices [que en Barcelona nevó t_i la semana pasada]?
    how-many days you-say that in Barcelona snowed the week past

   b. Cuántos días$_i$ dices [que nevó t_i en Barcelona la semana pasada]?
    how-many days you-say that snowed in Barcelona the week past
    'For how many days did you say that it snowed in Barcelona last week?'

(59) a. A quién crees [que Juan le dio el premio]?
    to whom you-think that Juan DAT-CL gave the prize
    'Who do you think that Juan gave the prize to?'

   b. Qué discurso$_i$ dices [que a Juan le gustó tanto t_i [que
    what speech say that to Juan DAT-CL liked so-much that
    lo quiere publicar]]?
    ACC-CL wants to-publish
    'What speech did you say that Juan liked so much that he wants to publish it?'

Summing up, Spanish impersonal constructions clearly deserve more study, but their behavior does not appear to represent immediate counter-evidence against my proposal. On the one hand, the dative arguments of impersonal verbs can be taken to be either *experiencers* or elements that are semantically more prominent than the subject DP along a scale different from the Thematic Hierarchy. On the other, the *locative* arguments of these verbs do not seem to surface in the Pole position in the unmarked case, and in those cases where they do appear in the preverbal field the evidence indicates that this is the result of topicalization.

3.5 SOME TYPOLOGICAL PREDICTIONS

In this final section I discuss some typological predictions that are derived from the analysis developed here. Many of these predictions are similar to those that result from the subject-oriented analyses of word order in Samek-Lodovici (1996), Costa (1998, 2001) and Grimshaw & Samek-Lodovici (1998), with the added advantage that further distinctions can be made with respect to the semantic roles of the arguments of the verb.

Consider first VSO languages like Irish (McCloskey 1997, 2001). Irish is a strict VSO language where no constituent moves into the highest inflectional specifier in the unmarked case:

(60) Thóg   sí   teach dófa   ar   an   Mhullach Dubh
      raised she house for-them on   the
      'She built a house for them in Mullaghduff.'   (McCloskey 2001: 161)

In the present analysis, the word order of Irish results from the ranking where all of the constraints in the Pole Hierarchy outrank the EPP constraint (i.e. *Pole/Reason » . . . » *Pole/Agent » EPP). Under this ranking, any candidate that moves an argument or adjunct to the highest inflectional specifier (irrespective of its semantic role) loses to the verb-initial candidate that leaves the highest inflectional specifier empty, in violation of the EPP. Observe that this analysis is consistent with McCloskey's arguments that the subject in Irish does move to a position in the inflectional layer below TP where subjects have their nominative Case licensed. Since the Pole is defined as the highest inflectional specifier, movement of the subject in Irish to a specifier position below TP does not bring with it any violations of the constraints in the Pole Hierarchy. Irish can thus be analyzed as a language where clauses do not have a Pole in the unmarked case, without this entailing that there will not be other positions in the inflectional layer that license properties typically associated with subjects, such as nominative Case. Finally, the fact that Irish and similar VSO languages display no expletive insertion results from any ranking where FULL-INTERPRETATION outranks EPP. Consider now a language where the whole of the Pole Hierarchy outranks the EPP, as in Irish, but where EPP in turn outranks FULL-INTER. This corresponds to a VSO language where expletives are inserted in the highest inflectional specifier to satisfy the EPP. Some varieties of Arabic (Huybergts 1996, cited in Alexiadou & Anagnostopoulou (1999), seem to instantiate this kind of language, as shown in (61).

(61) inna-hu fatah-a 1-'awlaad-u 1-baab-a
     that-CL PERF.*open*-3SG.M *the boys*   *the door*   (Huybregts 1996)[38]

Next, consider the effects of having the EPP constraint dominate FULL-INTER and embedding them both in the Pole Hierarchy.[39] This results in a number of possible languages where expletives are inserted in [Spec, I] to satisfy the EPP in some cases but not in others, depending on the semantic roles of the arguments involved.[40] For instance, the ranking in (62) corresponds to a language that inserts expletives in [Spec, I] when the only argument of a verb is a *Theme* (because *Pole/Theme » FULL-INTER), but not when one of the arguments of the verb is an *Agent* (or an *Experiencer*). This is because in any ranking where FULL-INTER dominates *Pole/*Agent,* the candidate that moves the *agent* to [Spec, I] to satisfy the EPP will best the candidate that instead inserts an expletive in this position.

(62) ... *Pole/Theme » EPP » FULL-INTERPRETATION » *Pole/Experiencer » *Pole/Agent

There is in fact one variety of Spanish that instantiates this kind of language, namely, Dominican Spanish. Dominican Spanish is perhaps unique amongst the different dialects of contemporary Spanish in that it is well-known to allow expletive insertion (see Toribio 2000 and references therein).[41] Some examples are shown in (63), where an expletive homophonous with the demonstrative pronoun *ello* 'that,' appears in the preverbal position.

(63) a. Ello llegan guaguas hasta allá.
     expl arrive buses   until   there
     'Buses reach there.'

    b. Ello hay   muchos mangos este año.
     expl be-3pl *many   mangoes this year*
     'There are many mangoes this year'   (Toribio 1994: 422)

Now notice that Dominican Spanish, in contrast with Arabic, does not allow expletive insertion in transitive clauses (i.e., it does not display Transitive Expletive Constructions).

(64)   *Ello   compró   Ramón   un   chivo
        expl   bought   Ramón   a   goat

In the analysis developed here no extra machinery is required to account for the fact that some languages allow transitive clauses with expletives (the variety of Arabic in (61)) whereas others do not (Dominican Spanish). This follows directly from the ranking of FULL-INTER relative to *Pole/*Agent* (*Pole/*Agent* » . . . » FULL-INTER in Arabic, FULL-INTER » . . . » *Pole/*Agent* in Dominican Spanish).

Furthermore, my analysis predicts that there should be no language that allows expletive constructions with transitive verbs but not with unaccusative verbs, a prediction that appears to be correct. Such a language can only be derived by the ranking EPP » *Pole/*Agent* » . . . » FULL-INTER ». . . » *Pole/*Theme*. However, Harmonic Alignment does not allow for a hierarchy of constraints where *Pole/*Agent* outranks *Pole/*Theme*, because *Agent* is more prominent than *Theme* in the Thematic Hierarchy that Harmonic Alignment starts out with. Observe that this prediction is also consistent with what is observed in languages where [Spec, I] strongly correlates with the subject grammatical relation, such as English and French. A possible interpretation of this fact is that in languages like English and French most of the effects that result form the Pole Hierarchy are masked by the high ranking of the SUBJCASE constraint that requires the nominative argument to be assigned Case in [Spec, I]. However, they will still be observed in other areas of the syntax of these languages, such as semantic role restrictions on *there*-existential clauses. Future research should indicate if some of the differences between Spanish, on the one hand, and French and English, on the other, are best accounted for in this way.

The analysis proposed here can also be extended to account for languages that differ with respect to the interaction between [Spec, I] and topicalization. I consider three different patterns here. The first pattern corresponds to English, where the subject occupies the Pole position irrespective of its semantic role and of the fronting of any sentence topic. I take these sentence topics to be left-adjoined to IP (McCloskey 1992).

(65)   [$_{IP}$ Yesterday [$_{IP}$ John bought the newspaper]].

The characteristics of this kind of language relevant for the comparison are: (i) the EPP is always satisfied; (ii) in most cases the EPP is satisfied by the subject, and; (iii) the language tolerates adjunction to IP in order to accommodate a fronted topic, since [Spec, I] is not an available landing site for the topic. As previously mentioned, the fact that the subject occupies the Pole position irrespective of its semantic role is derived with a ranking where the SUBJCASE constraint of Costa (1998, 2000) is very high in the constraint ranking. Concretely, this result is achieved when SUBJCASE outranks all of the constraints in the Pole Hierarchy. Accordingly the priority is that the subject receive nominative Case in [Spec, T]. On the other hand, the fact that a sentence topic is allowed to adjoin to IP follows from any ranking where the TOPICFIRST constraint of Costa (1998, 2000), which requires topics to be leftmost, dominates the constraint that militates against adjunction in general, which I henceforth represent as *ADJUNCTION.[42] A possible ranking that derives these properties is presented in (68).

(66)　TOPICFIRST
　　　Topics are sentence-initial.　　　　　　　　　(Costa 2001: 176)

(67)　*ADJUNCTION
　　　No adjunction: violated by XP or head adjunction structures.

(68)　EPP » SUBJCASE » TOPICFIRST » *ADJUNCTION, *Pole/Reason » . . . » *Pole/Agent

The second pattern corresponds to Spanish. As we have seen, two central properties of Spanish are: (i) the EPP has to be satisfied in some, but not all instances, and (ii) the EPP can be satisfied by non-subjects (including fronted topics, as discussed in Chapter Two), in which case the transitive subject stays in its VP-internal position. Now, Spanish is just like English in that a topic can be adjoined to IP when [Spec, I] is already occupied by some other constituent. This is most clearly observed in cases of multiple topicalization like (69).[43]

(69)　[$_{IP}$ Ayer　[$_{IP}$ el　periódico　lo　compró　[$_{VP}$ Juan]]].
　　　yesterday　　the newspaper CL *bought　　　Juan*
　　　'Yesterday, JUAN bought the newspaper.'

A constraint hierarchy that derives these properties is presented in (70). The ranking of SUBJCASE below the whole of the Pole Hierarchy derives the effect observed in Spanish that any constituent can move into [Spec, I] even if this means that the subject is not assigned nominative Case in this position. On the other hand, just as in English, the ranking of TopicFirst over *Adjunction allows for a topic to be adjoined when [Spec, I] is already occupied by some other constituent.

(70) TopicFirst » *Adjunction » *Pole/Reason » . . . » *Pole/Theme » EPP » *Pole/Experiencer » *Pole/Agent » SubjCase

The third pattern corresponds to a certain kind of verb-second language. V2 languages disallow the pattern in (65) and (69), where two different XPs appear simultaneously in the preverbal field. This is shown in (71) for German.

(71) *Auf dem Weg der Junge wird eine Katze sehen.
       on the   way the boy   will a   cat   see
       (On the way, the boy will see a cat).   (Santorini 1992)

Consider now the V2 languages where the verb remains in I and the XP that precedes it is in [Spec, I], such as Yiddish (Diesing 1990, Santorini 1992, Zwart 1997). In these languages (although perhaps not in all V2 languages), we can associate the satisfaction of the EPP to the [Spec, I] position. Now, just as in English, in these V2 languages the EPP has to be satisfied in the majority of cases, but it can be satisfied by subjects or non-subjects, as in Spanish. Examples from Yiddish are presented in (72).

(72) a. [$_{IP}$ Dos yingl vet   oyfn veg zen a   kats].
              the boy will on-the way see a   cat
              'The boy will see a cat on the way.'

       b. [$_{IP}$ Oyfn veg   vet   dos yingl zen a   kats].
              on-the way will the boy   see a   cat
              'On the way, the boy will see a cat.'

       c. *Oyfn veg [$_{IP}$ dos yingl vet zen a   kats].
              on-the way   the boy   will see a   cat   (Santorini 1992)

However, as discussed, these languages have a property absent in both English and Spanish: once [Spec, I] is occupied by either the subject or a topic, fronting of another constituent is not tolerated, as in (72c). I take this to be a prohibition against the kind of adjunction to IP observed in (65) and (69). Specifically, Yiddish is like English in that the EPP has to be satisfied, and it is like Spanish in that it can be satisfied by constituents other than the subject, but it is different from both Spanish and English in that it does not tolerate adjunction to IP once [Spec, I] is occupied. These properties are derived by the constraint hierarchy in (73). In this hierarchy, EPP is undominated (as in English), the whole of the Pole Hierarchy outranks SUBJCASE (as in Spanish), but crucially *ADJUNCTION outranks TOPICFIRST, thus preventing multiple topicalization by adjunction to IP.[44]

(73) EPP » *ADJUNCTION » TOPICFIRST » *Pole/Reason » . . . » *Pole/Agent » SUBJCASE

Future research should determine if a similar analysis can be developed of V2 languages where the verb instead moves from I to C. Finally, there is a prediction made by the present analysis that requires future corroboration. The ranking FULL-INTER » *Pole/*Reason* » . . . » *Pole/*Experiencer* » EPP » *Pole/*Agent* results in a language where only *agents* are displaced to [Spec, I] to satisfy the EPP. Since ergative languages tend to distinguish *agents* from all other semantic roles and grammatical relations, it seems to me that this prediction should ideally be tested in languages displaying syntactic ergativity.

3.6 CONCLUSIONS

In this chapter I have proposed that the unmarked word order observed in transitive, psych and unaccusative clauses in Spanish is dependent on structural markedness considerations. Poles with different semantic roles instantiate different degrees of markedness, and beyond a certain degree it is better to leave clauses without a Pole, in violation of the EPP. The scale of structural markedness responsible for these effects can be formalized by Harmonic Alignment of a scale of semantic roles with a structural prominence scale that incorporates the notion of the Pole. Embedding the EPP in the subhierarchy of markedness constraints that results from Harmonic Alignment then provides an analysis of the relevant word order facts. The resulting analysis also accounts straightforwardy for the unmarked word order observed in impersonal passives, *pro*-dropped constructions and in clauses with different kinds of psych verbs, and it can accommodate the basic word order facts observed in impersonal constructions.

The analysis developed in this chapter and the previous one constitutes the core of my proposal. However, the markedness constraints in the Pole Hierarchy are not only relevant for defining the unmarked word order in Spanish. As I discuss in the chapters that follow, the sensitivity of the Pole to the semantic role of the constituent that occupies it can also be observed in topicalization and *wh*-interrogatives. This provides further support for my approach, and allows us to develop an analysis where a number of left-peripheral word order phenomena in Spanish in general and in Mexican Spanish in particular are directly linked to the properties of the Pole.

Chapter Four
Word Order and Information Structure

In this chapter I discuss how information structure considerations (namely, focus and topicalization) modify the unmarked word order attested in Spanish in general and in Mexican Spanish in particular. The interaction between information structure and word order has been dealt with extensively in the OT literature, and so in this chapter I concentrate on two specific issues. The first one is to show how word order variation resulting from focus in Mexican Spanish can be readily accounted for under the proposal developed in the previous chapter, on the one hand, and on the other, that the resulting analysis is consistent with previous optimality theoretic work in this area. The second issue relates to how topicalization in Mexican Spanish provides further support for the notion of the Pole, and for an analysis that appeals to this notion to explain word order phenomena. Specifically, I show how my proposal explains why the relative order of multiple topics in the left periphery is dependent on their semantic role.

4.1 PERTURBATIONS OF THE UNMARKED WORD ORDER

Perturbations of the unmarked word order for different classes of predicates in declarative clauses in Spanish are widely attested, and this phenomenon has received considerable attention both in traditional grammars (see, for example, Gili y Gaya 1961) and in the theoretically-oriented literature (e.g. Bolinger 1954–55, Hatcher 1958, Meyer 1972, Contreras 1976, Silva-Corvalán 1983, Fant 1984, Vallduví 1992, Casielles-Suárez 1995, Zubizarreta 1998, *inter alia*). Some examples are presented below. The transitive clauses (1a-b) do not display the unmarked SVO word order, and the subjects of psych and unaccusative predicates in (1c) and (1d), respectively, appear in the preverbal position, contrary to what is observed in the unmarked case. The free translations of these examples are only meant to convey their approximate translation to English, and not their structural equivalence to the corresponding English forms (see §4.3 below).

(1) a. Ayer compró Juan el periódico.   Adv V S O
       yesterday bought Juan the newspaper
       'Yesterday Juan bought the newspaper.'

     b. El periódico lo compró Juan.   O V S
        the newspaper ACC-CL *bought Juan*
        'The newspaper, John bought it .'

     c. Los chocolates le gustan a Juan.   S V IO
        the chocolates DAT-CL *like.*3p *to Juan*
        ' Chocolate, Juan likes.'

     d. Tu hermano llegó.   S V
        your brother arrived
        'Your brother arrived.'

The standard diagnostic for determining that the word orders in (1) correspond to marked word orders is to test whether they can be felicitously uttered in an out-of-the-blue context or sentence focus context, as answers to questions like *'what's been happening?'* or *'what happened?.'* All the examples in (1) are infelicitous in such a context.

Since the earliest theoretical works on Spanish listed above, perturbations of unmarked word order like those in (1) have been linked to information structure (focus, topicalization, discourse prominence, etc.). It is not possible to review in any detail all the different analyses of these perturbations that have been proposed in the literature. Rather, my working assumption will be that what all these examples have in common is that the preverbal XP corresponds to a topic, which is followed by one or more focal elements (see Vallduvi 1992, Zubizarreta 1998, 1999).[1] Consequently, my analysis of the perturbations of the unmarked word order in (1) relies on the topic/focus articulation.

The relation between word order and information structure has been widely discussed in the OT literature (Legendre et. al. 1995; Samek-Lodovici 1996; Costa 1998, 2001; Grimshaw and Samek-Lodocivi 1998; Choi 1999, *inter alia*), particularly with respect to focus. These analyses highlight the fact that OT is an ideal framework for dealing with word order permutations induced by information structure considerations and their relation to "optionality."

In representational frameworks like GB word order permutations that do not result in truth-conditional differences are mostly unproblematic. To the extent that sentences like those in (1) meet a set of well-formedness conditions, they can simply be thought of as alternative options (subject to pragmatic considerations) for expressing the same truth-conditional content of the corresponding cases that display the canonical word order. With the development of notions like Economy of Movement and Economy of Structure, central notions for both Minimalism and OT syntax, optionality becomes a serious problem, though. If movement takes place exclusively to satisfy conditions on derivations or representations, then it can never be optional, strictly speaking. As such, either word order permutations like those in (1) are not optional or they directly falsify the hypothesis of Economy of Movement.

Most OT literature on this issue holds that word order permutations induced by information structure are not optional (Samek-Lodovici 1996; Costa 1998; Grimshaw & Samek-Lodovici 1998; Choi 1999), but rather result from the need to accommodate conflicts between the syntactic requirements that derive the unmarked word order and a number of discourse requirements codified as universal constraints. OT analyses capitalize on two properties of this framework to flesh out the idea that optionality is only apparent. On the one hand, in OT the constraints that regulate the syntax and those that relate to discourse considerations are not in different levels of representation/well-formedness evaluation. Rather, EVAL considers a set of candidates with respect to both sets of constraints simultaneously. As a result, the interaction between syntax and information structure can be captured directly. On the other hand, sentences that display the same truth-conditional properties but different word orders can be characterized in OT as optimal outputs for *different* inputs, under the assumption that features conditioned by discourse contexts (such as [topic], [focus]) are represented in the input. In other words, if SVO and OVS are both grammatical options in a language, then SVO is the optimal realization of an input x and OVS is the optimal realization of an input y, where the sets of discourse features of x and y are distinct. The ranking of constraints that are sensitive to the discourse features represented in the input determine which is the optimal candidate in each case.[2]

In what follows, I adopt the basic conclusions of the Optimality-theoretical analyses of word order and information structure cited above. However, I argue that the notion of the Pole is crucial for understanding the word order facts specific to Spanish. For the purpose of developing the analysis I first consider focus and its analysis in the section that follows. Topicalization is addressed in section §4.3. After presenting the basic analysis of topicalization, I address the interaction between topics and foci, and I conclude this chapter with the analysis of multiple topicalization.

4.2 FOCUS

The precise characterization of focus has been extensively debated in the literature, and many problematic issues remain to be solved. Here I simply assume the characterization of focus proposed in Halliday (1967), Rochemont (1986) and Kiss (1998). Terminological issues apart, these analyses propose that there are two fundamentally different kinds of focus, *contrastive focus* and *presentational focus*. Contrastive focus expresses a quantification-like operation that involves exhaustive identification on a set of entities.[3] As noted in Kiss (1998), in terms of its semantics the constituent that corresponds to the contrastive focus represents the value of the variable bound by an abstract operator expressing exhaustive identification. An example from Hungarian is presented in (2).[4]

(2)   HUNGARIAN
      Tegnap este   **MARINAK**   mutattam   be   Pétert
      last   night Mary.DAT   *introduced*-I PERF *Peter*.ACC
      'It was TO MARY that I introduced Peter last night.'   (Kiss 1998: 247)

Example (2) expresses the exhaustive identification characteristic of contrastive focus, since it means that out of set of individuals present in the domain of discourse, it was Mary and no one else that Peter was introduced to by the speaker. Halliday (1967) further proposes a definition of contrastive as "contrary to some predicted or stated alternative." This can be most clearly observed in so-called correction contexts, such as the one below (taken from Schwarzschild 1999). I assume that this is one of the pragmatic readings of contrastive focus that follows from its expression of exhaustive identification.

(3)   a.   John's mother voted for Bill.
      b.   No, she voted for **JOHN**.

On the other hand, presentational focus simply corresponds to information that is not part of the common ground (the common ground being roughly the information shared by the speaker and the hearer). Consider the Hungarian example in (4).

(4)   HUNGARIAN
      Tegnap este   be   mutattam   Pétert   MARINAK.
      last   night PERF *introduced*-I *Peter*.ACC *Mary*.DAT
      'Last night I introduced Peter TO MARY.'   (Kiss 1998: 247)

In contrast with (2), the presentational focus in (4) does not express exhaustive identification. Consequently, (4) does not imply that *Mary* was the only person that *Peter* was introduced to by the speaker. It merely presents *Mary* as "new" information that is not part of the common ground.[5] In relation to the correspondence between presentational focus and "new" information, Halliday (1967) suggests that presentational foci correspond to the constituent in the answer to a *wh*-question that corresponds to the *wh*-operator in the question, as in (5). This is a standardly accepted diagnostic for presentational foci in other analyses that postulate the existence of two kinds of focus (Kiss 1998, Zubizarreta 1998), and I will make use of it in what follows.

(5)   a. Who screamed?
      b. JOHN screamed.

Languages can distinguish these two types of foci in various ways (syntactically, morphologically and intonationally) but the syntactic contrast observed in Hungarian examples above is particularly illustrative. As discussed in Kiss (1998), contrastive foci in this language must appear in the immediate preverbal position, as in (2). However, presentational foci (*information focus* in Kiss' terminology) are not subject to this restriction and typically appear in the post-verbal field instead, as in (4). There are languages where the formal distinction between these two types of foci is not just distributional. Korean, for example, further encodes these two different kinds of foci morphologically (see Choi 1999: 88–90). Also, Zubizarreta (1998) claims that Spanish distinguishes contrastive and presentational foci intonationally (see also Silva-Corvalán 1983 and Fant 1984), although clearly more experimental research is required to settle this issue.

However, there do not appear to be absolute cross-linguistic correlations between the two kinds of foci and the way that they are formally marked. For instance, in Hungarian contrastive foci have a fixed position and presentational foci show a fairly free distribution, but the exact opposite situation is attested in Peninsular Spanish, as we will see shortly. Rather, it seems that the differences that hold cross-linguistically between these two kinds of foci are interpretive and pragmatic in nature. As noted in Kiss (1998), contrastive foci take scope, but presentational foci do not; presentational focus can project, but contrastive focus cannot. Also, as noted in Gundel (1999), every sentence has a presentational focus (see also Vallduví 1992 and Lambrecht 1994), but not every sentence has a contrastive focus. Accordingly, although I make use of word order diagnostics for distinguishing theses two types of focus in Spanish, no claim is made here as to whether these word order properties hold in other languages.

A final note on terminology is relevant here. When the focus corresponds to a single argument of the verb, as in (2–5), it is usually referred to as a *narrow focus,* a term I adopt in the analysis below. However, (descriptively, at least) the focus can correspond to a constituent larger than an argument, as in cases of VP, IP or sentence focus. In what follows I use the term *focus domain* (Lambrecht 1994) to refer to these cases.

4.2.1 Focus in Spanish

The analysis of focus that I develop concentrates on presentational focus and not on contrastive focus, for reasons to be outlined in what follows. For the purpose of defining the set of data that the analysis deals with, in this subsection I briefly describe the differences in word order between presentational and contrastive focus in Spanish.

In Spanish, subject focus often has very visible effects, since a constituent which occurs preverbally in the unmarked case, occurs instead in the post-verbal field when it is focussed. This phenomenon is termed (free) subject inversion (Bolinger 1954–55, Contreras 1976, Torrego 1984, Lambrecht 1994, Ordóñez 1998, Zubizarreta 1998) and it is observed across different varieties of Spanish. Some examples are presented in (6–7). Mexican Spanish, however, does not allow for VOS clauses with an empty preverbal position, in contrast with Peninsular and other varieties of this language. In all these cases the direct object can be alternatively dropped, in which case it is cross-referenced by the corresponding object clitic, yielding a VS sentence.[6]

(6)   PENINSULAR SPANISH/ MEXICAN SPANISH

Los discos   los   compró una   [$_{FOC}$ muchacha].[7]
the records   ACC-CL   *bought   a   girl*   OVS
'A GIRL bought the records.'

(7)   a.   PENINSULAR SPANISH (Zubizarreta 1998: 126)
Está buscando   una secretaria [$_{FOC}$ el jefe de la fábrica].   VOS
is   looking-for a   secretary   the factory's foreman
'The factory's FOREMAN is looking for a secretary.'

b.   MEXICAN SPANISH
??Compró el periódico Juan.   VOS
bought   the newspaper Juan

In both Mexican Spanish and in the varieties of Spanish analyzed in Zubizarreta (1998) (Peninsular and Rioplatense Spanish), inverted subjects can correspond to either presentational or contrastive foci.[8] This is shown in (8–9), which correspond to my own data. The inverted subject in (8b) corresponds to the *wh*-operator in the question in (8a), and it is also compatible with the "correction" context in (9).

(8) INVERTED PRESENTATIONAL SUBJECT FOCUS

    a. Quién compró los discos?
       'Who bought the records?'

    b. Los discos los   compró una MUCHACHA.
       the records ACC-CL *bought a   girl*   O V S
       'A GIRL bought the records.'

(9) INVERTED CONTRASTIVE SUBJECT FOCUS

    a. Me   dicen   que unos estudiante compraron los discos.
       to-me they-say that some students   bought   the records.
       'They tell me that some students bought the records.'

    b. No, los discos los   compró una MUCHACHA.
       no   the records ACC-CL *bought a   girl*   O V S
       'No, a GIRL bought the records.'

Zubizarreta (1998) further claims that in the varieties of Spanish she considers, presentational foci can only appear in the sentence final position. My own research indicates that this is also the case in Mexican Spanish. The distribution of contrastive focus in Spanish is considerably more complex, though. In Mexican Spanish, contrastive foci typically appear in sentence final position, just like presentational foci. However, when the subject in focus is highly definite and individuated (typically a proper name or a pronoun) it can also appear in its canonical preverbal position. This is shown in example (10), originally from Zubizarreta (1998).[9]

(10) MARÍA me   regaló la botella de vino.
     María to-me gave the bottle of wine
     'MARÍA gave me the bottle of wine.'

In other varieties of Spanish, the situation is even more complex. In the varieties of Spanish in Zubizarreta (1998) contrastive foci can also appear *in situ*[10] (see also Fant 1984), even when they do not correspond to the subject. This is shown in (11). Furthermore, as shown in (12) they can also be fronted to the left periphery (Hernanz & Brucart 1987, Casielles-Suárez 1995, Zubizarreta 1998; see Rizzi 1997 and Kiss 1998 for Italian).

(11) CONTRASTIVE FOCUS IN-SITU: Zubizarreta (1998).

>La camarera del hotel puso la VALIJA   sobre la cama (y   no   el maletín).
>*the hotel's attendant   put   the briefcase on   the bed and   not   the briefcase*
>'The hotel's chambermaid put the SUITCASE on the bed, not the briefcase.'

(12) PREPOSED CONTRASTIVE FOCUS: Zubizarreta (1998).

>Las ESPINACAS detesta Pedro (y   no   las papas).
>*the spinach   hates   Pedro and   not   the potatoes*
>'SPINACH Pedro hates, (not potatoes).

My data on fronted and in-situ contrastive focus in Mexican Spanish is too scant for me to draw any conclusions at this point. Speakers of Mexican Spanish, however, readily reject cases of preposed foci like (12), and to my ear, they are downright ungrammatical. In-situ foci do not appear to be fully ungrammatical, and they are in fact attested in some cases, but they mostly sound extremely unnatural and are clearly not as common as they are in Peninsular Spanish. Given these complications, in what follows I only provide an analysis of presentational focus, whose behavior is more systematic. Unless otherwise noted, from this point onwards I use the term "focus" to refer exclusively to presentational focus.

4.2.2 Subject Presentational Foci

I first address the most simple cases of subject focus, which correspond to those instances where the object of a transitive sentence is dropped. I will address the cases where the object is not dropped (examples (6–7)) once the basics of the analysis of topicalization are introduced in §4.3. Consider the felicity contrast in (13), which illustrates the requirement that foci be sentence final in Spanish.

(13) Quién compró los discos?
      'Who bought the records?'

>a. #[Una muchacha]_{FOC} los   compró.   **S V**
>   *a   girl*   ACC-CL   *bought*

b. Los   compró [una muchacha]_{FOC}.   V S
   ACC-CL *bought   a   girl*
   'A GIRL bought them.'

The felicitous answer where the subject is in focus, (13b), does not follow the word order observed in transitive clauses in the unmarked case. In §3
I argued that fronting of an *agent* subject was the result of the need to satisfy
the EPP, which in Spanish is prioritized over the marked structure that
results from having an *agent* as the Pole of the clause. But clearly the EPP is
not being satisfied in (13b), since the clause lacks a Pole altogether.[11]

Now, subject inversion in Spanish is often analyzed as an operation
that results in a compromise between focus and intonation requirements.
Under the assumption that foci need to be signaled with the nuclear accent
(the most prominent accent in the clause: Jackendoff 1972; Selkirk 1984,
1995, among many others), and under the assumption that this accent is
necessarily clause final in Spanish (e.g. Ladd 1996), a subject in focus must
appear in the clause final position to comply with the intonational prominence requirement on foci (Contreras 1976, Zubizarreta 1998, Büring &
Gutiérrez-Bravo 2001, Gutiérrez-Bravo 2002a). In what follows, I adopt this
general line of analysis.[12]

Following Samek-Lodovic (1996), Costa (1998) and Grimshaw &
Samek-Lodovici (1998), I assume that foci are specified as such in the
input by the feature [focus]. I further assume that the requirement that
foci be signaled with the nuclear accent corresponds to the FOCUSPROMI-
NENCE constraint of Büring & Gutiérrez-Bravo (2001).

(14) FOCUSPROMINENCE (FP)

Focus is most prominent.

I take FOCUSPROMINENCE to be a constraint that regulates the correspondence between a [focus] feature in the input and a constituent signaled with the nuclear accent in the output (i.e., it requires a focus to be
intonationally the most prominent constituent in a clause).[13] I further
assume the analyses in Büring (2001) and Büring & Gutiérrez-Bravo
(2001), which suggest that every focal element in the clause is subject to
it. When the subject is the only element specified as a focus, it is the only
constituent subject to this constraint. When both the verb and the subject (or some other argument or adjunct) are foci, both are subject to it,
and in cases of sentence focus every element in the clause is required to
satisfy it.

The FOCUSPROMINENCE constraint crucially interacts with the constraints that govern the formation of phonological phrases, as argued for in Truckenbrodt (1999), Büring & Gutiérrez-Bravo (2001) and Szendröi (2001). For full details related to phonological phrasing and intonational prominence in Spanish, I refer the reader to the analysis in Büring & Gutiérrez-Bravo (2001). In what follows, it will be enough to note that in the case of Spanish, where the nuclear accent is clause-final, FOCUSPROMINENCE is violated whenever there is a constituent in focus that does not occupy the clause-final position.

With these considerations in mind, consider again the VS order in (13a), where the *agent* subject is in focus. These examples show that Mexican Spanish, like other dialects of Spanish, prioritizes the requirement that presentational foci be intonationally prominent (and thus appear in the sentence final position where the nuclear accent falls) over the requirement to have the Pole position filled. To derive this result, it is only necessary to rank the FOCUSPROMINENCE constraint above EPP. The resulting analysis is shown in tableau (15) below, where (15b) emerges as the winner despite its violation of EPP. In (15) and the tableaux that follow, the constituent on which the nuclear accent falls is indicated in small caps.[14]

This analysis is similar in its essentials to previous OT analyses of focus-driven subject inversion (Samek-Lodovici 1996; Costa 1998, 2001; Grimshaw & Samek-Lodovici 1998) which propose that a language displays subject inversion when the constraint on foci outranks the structural requirement on subjects (either the SUBJECT or the SUBJCASE constraint). In this way, my proposal is compatible with the conclusion that these analyses arrive at. However, my analysis is different in two important respects.

First, in my OT analysis there is no direct link between word order and focus interpretation. As discussed originally in Gutiérrez-Bravo (2002a), the relevant effects are mediated by intonational considerations.[15] Secondly, my analysis does not resort to a subject condition, but rather to the interaction between the EPP and the markedness constraints in the Pole Hierarchy. This difference has no consequences in simple cases like (15), but its relevance

(15)   INPUT: <buy (x, y), x=a girl (Ag), x=[focus], y= *pro* [3rd.PL](Th)>

	FOCUS PROM	EPP	*Pole/ Agent
a. [IP [una muchacha]Foc LOS COMPRÓ [VP]] **SV**	*!		*
☞ b. [IP los compró [VP [UNA MUCHACHA]Foc]] **VS**		*	

emerges once we consider more complex cases, such as sentence focus, which I analyze in the next subsection.

4.2.3 Sentence Focus

It is a well-known fact about Spanish and other subject-inversion languages that the word order perturbations observed when the subject is in focus are not possible in cases of sentence focus, that is, when every constituent in the clause is a focus (see Contreras 1976, Fant, 1984, to cite just a few references). This is illustrated by the contrast in felicity between SVO and OVS in (16). Recall that OVS is the typical realization in Mexican Spanish of clauses with the subject in focus when both the subject and the object are realized as lexical XPs (see §4.2.1).

(16) Qué pasó?
 What happened?'

    a. Una muchacha compró los discos.   S V O
       a   *girl*   *bought* *he records*
      'A girl bought the records.'

    b. #Los discos los   compró una muchacha.   O V S
      the records ACC-CL *bought* *a*   *girl*

In Costa's (1998) analysis of sentence focus in Portuguese it is proposed that the unmarked SVO order emerges as the optimal output in these cases because the subject-inversion candidate (VOS in Portuguese) incurs a violation of the subject condition that is not necessary to satisfy the constraint on foci. Costa (1998) relies on the ALIGNFOCUS constraint of Grimshaw & Samek-Lodovici (1998) that requires foci to be rightmost, and which is vacuously satisfied in cases of sentence focus. He observes that as a result of this, any order of the predicate and its arguments equally satisfies ALIGNFOCUS and so this constraint does not play any role in defining the optimal output. Since the

(17) Sentence Focus in Portuguese (Costa 1998)

    INPUT: < V(x,y), Focus: V(x,y) >

	ALIGN FOCUS	SUBJ-CASE
☞ a. [IP S V [VP O]]		
b. [IP V [VP O [VP S]]]		*!

effects of ALIGNFOCUS are neutralized in this case, other constraints determine the outcome. Concretely, in Costa's analysis the SUBJECTCASE constraint decides the outcome of the competition. This is shown in the tableau in (17) above, which summarizes the analysis in Costa (1998).

Costa points out that in sentence focus contexts we see an instance of the *emergence of the unmarked word order*. In other words, even though Portuguese displays numerous word order permutations as the result of being a discourse-configurational language, the unmarked word order, regulated in its entirety by syntactic constraints, emerges as the optimal output when the constraints related to the discourse are neutralized.[16]

Costa's analysis embodies the important insight that in the case of sentence focus, focus-specific constraints play no crucial role in determining word order. Instead, the purely syntactic constraints are crucial. My analysis preserves this insight. However, in place of the syntactic-pragmatic constraint ALIGNFOCUS, my analysis appeals to FOCUSPROMINENCE, a constraint that regulates the correspondence between focus and pitch accent. Furthermore, the way in which my analysis explains why SVO is the felicitous order in sentence focus contexts is crucially different. This is most clearly observed in the contrast between SVO and OVS in (16). The competition between these two structures is shown in tableau (18) below, where I take the fronted object in OVS clauses to correspond to the Pole ([Spec, I] in this particular case; see §4.3.2 and §4.3.3 for further discussion).

Recall that the definition of FOCUSPROMINENCE is such that every focal element (whether it is an argument or a predicate) must be signaled with the nuclear accent. In cases of sentence focus the verb and both its arguments are all focal elements. Since the sentential accent can only signal one of these elements, cases of sentence focus will always bring with them violations of FOCUSPROMINENCE. In both (18a) and (18b), only the sentence-final constituent can satisfy FOCUSPROMINENCE, and so each candidate incurs two violations of this constraint, one corresponding to the verb, the other one to the argument in [Spec, I]. As in Costa's analysis, the word order effects driven by the condition on foci are neutralized in this case, since word order perturbations can no longer prevent violations of FOCUSPROMINENCE. As a result, the SVO candidate

(18) INPUT: <buy (x, y), buy=[focus], x=a girl (Ag), x=[focus], y=the records (Th), y=[focus]>

	FOC PRO	*Pole/ Theme	EPP	*Pole/ Agent
☞ a. [IP [una muchacha]Foc [compró]Foc [VP [LOS DISCOS]Foc]]	**			*
b. [IP[los discos]Foc [los compró]Foc [VP [UNA MUCHACHA]Foc]]	**	*!		

emerges as the winner because the OVS candidate incurs in a violation of *Pole/Theme that does not improve the structure in any way.

The analysis above highlights the relevance of structural markedness in my approach. As we have seen, in previous OT analyses based on Case (Costa 1998, 2001) or a subject condition (Samek-Lodovici 1996, Grimshaw & Samek-Lodovici 1998), the OVS candidate (18b) would be ruled out because it violates the Case/Subject condition, since the subject is not in [Spec, I]. Yet, as argued in the preceding chapter, it is problematic to derive the unmarked word order of the winning candidate (18a) through such a condition in Spanish, so in my analysis it plays no role in deciding the outcome of the competition.

Two further observations become relevant here. The first is that the EPP does not play a role in deciding the outcome either, since it is satisfied in both candidates, by the subject in (18a) and by the fronted object in (18b). And second, Economy of Structure and Economy of Movement do not play a role in deciding the outcome either. In both cases [Spec, I] is projected and both cases show the same number of movement operations; one of the arguments of the verb moves to [Spec, I] and the other one remains in its VP-internal position. Rather, what decides the outcome in (18) is structural markedness. The OVS candidate is more marked than the SVO candidate because it has a *theme* as its Pole. This results in the fatal violation of *Pole/Theme that crucially tilts the balance in favor of the SVO candidate which shows a lower degree of structural markedness. Unlike Costa (1998) and similar analyses, in my proposal the SVO candidate does not surface as the winner because it satisfies a well-formedness condition (say SUBJCASE) that the subject-inversion candidate fails to satisfy. Instead, its relative degree of structural markedness is what makes it optimal when compared with the OVS candidate.

In this way, my analysis is reminiscent of the analysis of word order in Spanish in Contreras (1976), who suggests that the contrast between (19a) and (19b) is also an issue of the relative markedness of the semantic role of the constituent that occupies the preverbal position. In Contreras' analysis, however, the relevant markedness distinction has to do with the Theme/Rheme dichotomy dating back to the Prague Circle tradition. In a nutshell, Contreras proposes a hierarchy where *agents* are more marked Rhemes (i.e. foci) than (semantic) *themes* or *patients*. Since Rhemes have to be aligned to the right edge of the clause in accordance with this hierarchy, the SVO word order corresponds to the one that is least marked with respect to the Rheme hierarchy, and so it is signaled as the unmarked order.

There are two ways in which my analysis is different from the one in Contreras (1976), though. First, in my proposal the relevant distinction is a distinction made purely in terms of structural markedness. This kind of markedness is defined in part with respect to the Pole, but is ultimately better understood as a property of the clause as a whole. For instance, in the discussion of unaccusative verbs I argued that a clause with a *theme* as the Pole is more marked than a clause without a Pole. But there is nothing inherent about *themes* functioning as Poles that entails that this should be so. It is the relative ranking of the EPP (a purely structural constraint), with respect to *Pole/Theme that defines the relative markedness of these two possible clauses and consequently defines the one that corresponds to the unmarked word order. Clearly enough, in a language that had the opposite ranking (i.e. EPP » *Pole/Theme) a clause with a *theme* as the Pole would be less marked than a clause without a Pole, and so it would correspond to the unmarked word order in this case.

The second way in which my proposal differs from Contreras' is that it rejects the hypothesis that discourse considerations such as Theme/Rheme play a role in defining unmarked word order (recall that in the analysis of unmarked word order that I developed in the preceding chapter constraints related to the discourse did not play any role). In departing from this hypothesis, I depart from its fundamental assumption, namely, that there is an inherent relation between certain semantic roles (i.e. *agents*) or grammatical relations (i.e. *subjects*) and certain pragmatic relations such as topic (or Theme, in Contreras 1976). This is an issue that has been much discussed in the literature on Spanish (and many other languages) with respect to the relation between subjects and topics, and so it is taken up in detail in the analysis of topicalization that I present in the following section.

Summarizing the discussion so far, the analysis of focus-driven subject inversion in Mexican Spanish developed in this section highlights two important properties of my approach. First, there is no incompatibility between the claim that clauses with focus-driven subject inversion lack a Pole (and therefore fail to satisfy the EPP) and the claim that the EPP is an active requirement in Mexican Spanish. In the OT proposal I have developed, this is the result of a ranking where FOCUSPROMINENCE outranks EPP. Secondly, the facts observed in sentence focus support my proposal that structural markedness plays a fundamental role in defining word order in Spanish. In my analysis the unmarked SVO order emerges in cases of sentence focus not because it satisfies a well-formedness condition that the subject inversion candidate OVS fails to meet. Rather, both orders satisfy the EPP, but SVO emerges as the output because it has a lower degree of structural markedness with respect to the Pole than the OVS candidate.

4.3 TOPICALIZATION

As in many other languages, topicalization results in perturbations of the basic word order of Spanish. We will see that these perturbations conflict with the scale of structural markedness (the Pole hierarchy) proposed in §3. Hence an adequate analysis of Spanish word order must include an account of topicalization. The account of the basic cases is fairly straightforward and provides further support for a definition of the EPP that appeals to the notion of the Pole. More complex are cases in which two constituents occur in the preverbal field. Here, the semantic role-sensitivity of the Pole, as embodied in the Pole Hierarchy, plays a crucial role in fixing their relative order.

Before addressing these issues, I will lay out my basic assumptions about topicalization. Topicalization remains one of the most obscure aspects of the syntax-pragmatics interface, and there is no agreement in the literature as to how to define sentence topics and how to characterize them formally.[17] Since it is not the purpose of this work to address the semantic and pragmatic properties of sentence topics, my characterization of topicalization in Spanish is fairly basic and relies mostly on syntactic criteria to identify topical XPs.[18]

By topicalization I mean the operation whereby a referential expression signaled as the sentence topic is displaced to a left-peripheral position. This is shown for a direct object in (19a) and for a temporal adverbial in (19b).[19]

(19) a. El periódico   lo   compró Juan.   O V S
       the newspaper ACC-CL *bought*   *Juan*
       'The newspaper, John bought it.'

     b. Ayer   compró Juan el   periódico.   Adv V S O
       yesterday *bought* *Juan* *the* *newspaper*
       'Yesterday Juan bought the newspaper.'

I assume that topicalization can fulfill either of two functions. In the first one, topicalization establishes a pragmatic relation of aboutness that holds between a referent and a proposition with respect to a particular context, such that a sentence topic is (broadly) the syntactic constituent that the proposition is about (Kuno 1972, Gundel 1974, Dik 1978, Reinhart 1982; see also Lambrecht 1994). The second function that sentence topics can have is to "limit the applicability of the main predication to a certain restricted domain . . . the topic sets a spatial, temporal or individual framework within which the main predication holds" (Chafe 1976:50).

In (19a) the left-peripheral XP 'the newspaper' is in an aboutness relation with the rest of the sentence, whereas in (19b) 'yesterday' anchors the rest of the sentence in a specific time frame. Despite their differences in function, these two kinds of topic are equally required to appear in a left-peripheral position. Furthermore, fronted topics of both kinds create islands for extraction (see Rochemont 1989; for Spanish, see Goodall 2001). This is shown in the examples below. The topic in (20a) corresponds to the direct object of the lower verb. In (20b) and (20c) it corresponds to a temporal and a locative expression, respectively. I adopt this syntactic test as the primary diagnostic for identifying sentence topics.[20]

(20) a. *A quién crees   [que el premio se   lo   dieron]?
           to whom you-think that the prize DAT-CL ACC-CL they-gave
           ('Who do you think that the prize they gave to?')   (Goodall 2001)

      b. ??Qué dices   [que ayer   compró Juan]?
          what you-say that yesterday bought Juan
          ('What are you saying that yesterday Juan bought?')

      c. *Cuántas personas decidieron   [que en Mérida van   a entrevistar]?
          how-many persons   you-PL-decided that in Mérida you-PL-go to interview
          ('How many people did you decide that in Mérida you are going to interview?)'

It is also important to note that even though the topic in (19a) is doubled by a clitic whereas the one in (19b) is not, this does not necessarily indicate that the fronted XPs in (19) are formally different *qua* topics.[21] Rather, this difference seems to be the result of the fact that Spanish has a fairly impoverished clitic inventory, as far as Romance languages go (in contrast, in other Romance languages locative, temporal and genitive/partitive XPs can be doubled by a clitic; see Vallduví (1992) for Catalan and Zubizarreta (1999) for Italian and French).

I also assume that sentence topics are crucially distinct from *discourse* topics. Discourse topics can be thought of as referential expressions that are both discourse-old and *active* in the sense of Chafe (1976, 1987) and Lambrecht (1994), where Chafe (1987:22ff) defines an active referent as one "that is currently lit up, a concept in a person's focus of consciousness at a particular moment." As noted in Lambrecht (1994), active referential expressions are typically realized as unstressed pronouns or as zero or null forms, and so I take this formal encoding as the *prima facie* diagnostic for discourse topics.[22]

A further difference between sentence topics and discourse topics is relevant here. It has often been pointed out that discourse-topicality is a property that can extend across a (potentially very large) number of sentences. In contrast, sentence topicality is a relational property that topic constituents have by virtue of being in a particular relation (aboutness, anchoring) with other elements of the clause, a relation that is usually signaled by word order (see especially Reinhart 1982, Vallduví 1992 and Lambrecht 1994).[23] In this respect, I assume that a fundamental difference between sentence and discourse topics is that a sentence topic cannot be realized by an unstressed or null form, and instead it must be realized as a full lexical XP (or as a stressed pronoun) in a left-peripheral position, in which I essentially follow the analysis of sentence topics in Vallduví (1992).[24]

After these considerations, the characterization of sentence topics that we arrive at is that a sentence topic is a full lexical XP that is part of the common ground and which is displaced to a left-peripheral position from the position it would occupy in the unmarked case. The diagnostic that I resort to for identifying sentence topics relies on the fact that topics create islands for extraction. With this characterization of sentence topics in mind, we can turn to the interaction of topicalization with the EPP and with the markedness constraints in the Pole hierarchy.

4.3.1 Topicalization and the Pole

Consider the examples first introduced in §4.1 as (1), and reproduced here as (21). Recall that I take all these cases to involve topicalization of the XP that appears in the preverbal position, with one or more focal elements following the topic.

(21) a. Ayer   compró Juan el periódico.   **Adv V S O**
        yesterday bought Juan the newspaper
        'Yesterday Juan bought the newspaper.'

   b. El periódico lo   compró Juan.   **O V S**
        the newspaper ACC-CL *bought Juan*
        'The newspaper, John bought it.'

   c. Los chocolates le   gustan a Juan.   **S V IO**
        the chocolates DAT-CL *like.3p to Juan*
        ' Chocolate, Juan likes.'

   d. Tu hermano   llegó.   **S V**
        your brother   arrived
        'Your brother arrived.'

Fant (1984) made the observation that in Spanish (all else being equal), all that is required for a *theme* argument to qualify as a topic and be fronted to the preverbal position is to have an instantiation in the previous discourse. Furthermore, under certain discourse conditions (whose precise characterization awaits future research) topicalization is obligatory in Spanish. Thus there is a robust contrast in felicity between (22a), where the unaccusative subject is fronted, and infelicitous (22b), which corresponds to the unmarked word order.[25]

(22) A: Estábamos esperando a que [llegara *tu hermano*] para ir a la fiesta pero no vamos a poder ir.

'We were waiting for [*your brother* to arrive] so that we could go to the party, but we're not going to be able to go.'

B: Por qué?
'Why?'

A: a) Porque [tu hermano llegó],   pero no trajo   el coche.   S V
because your brother arrived but   not brought the car
'Because your brother arrived, but he didn't bring the car with him.'

b) #Porque [llegó   tu hermano],   pero no   trajo   el coche.   V S
because   arrived your brother   but   not brought   the car

Based on this observation, I assume in what follows that being discourse-old is a sufficient condition for an argument or adjunct to appear as a sentence topic.[26] Following the discussion in the two preceding chapters, my proposed analysis for the examples in (21) is that in all cases the fronted topic corresponds to the Pole of the clause ([Spec, I] in this case). This raises two separate issues with respect to my analysis of unmarked word order in §3. The first one is that in my analysis *agents* constitute the least marked instance of a Pole, but in (21a-b) it is a different argument or adjunct that occupies the Pole position. The second issue is that I suggested that *themes* are prevented from occupying the Pole in the unmarked case because of the ranking *Pole/Theme » EPP, but clearly this state of affairs does not hold of (21b-d). In what follows I argue that both of these issues can be understood as the result of the interaction between the requirement that sentence topics appear in a left peripheral position, the EPP, and Economy of Structure considerations.

Recall from §3.5 that I take topics to undergo fronting because of the TOPICFIRST constraint.[27]

(23) TOPICFIRST   (Costa 2001:176)

Topics are sentence initial; nontopics cannot be topicalized.
Failed by topics that are not sentence initial, and by topicalized nontopics.

At this point, I propose two modifications of Costa's constraint. First, it seems to me that the clause of this constraint that states that non-topics cannot be topicalized can be independently captured by Economy of Structure and Economy of Movement considerations. In terms of my analysis, for example, unnecessary fronting of a non-topic results in a higher degree of structural markedness than the one of a candidate that does not display gratuitous topicalization (this is an issue that will become clearer in the discussion that follows). Accordingly, I will leave this second clause of the constraint out. Second, I propose defining TOPICFIRST as a gradient constraint. The purpose of this is to allow a topic to move as far to the left as possible, even when for some reason it cannot end up being the clause initial constituent. My proposed modification of TOPICFIRST is as follows.

(24) TOPICFIRST

A topic is the initial constituent of a [+verbal] Extended Projection.
If *XP* is a topic, then *XP* c-commands every head *Y* and every maximal projection *ZP* in the Extended Projection, where *Y* is a head not contained by *XP*, and *ZP* is a maximal projection that neither contains nor is contained by *XP*.
-*Violated once by every head Y or every ZP that c-commands a topic.*

The crucial aspect of my analysis of topicalization in Spanish is that in the examples in (21), the fronted topics automatically satisfy the EPP constraint by virtue of moving into the Pole position to satisfy TOPIC-FIRST. This is supported by the evidence from ellipsis discussed in §2, which indicates that topics and subjects occupy the same position in Spanish (Ordóñez & Treviño 1999). The relevant paradigm is repeated in (25).

(25) a. Luis reprobó a   Ernesto, pero [Juan no___].
        Luis failed   ACC *Ernesto* *but*   *Juan* *not*
        'Luis failed Ernesto, but Juan didn't.'

b. Invitó   a   Luis, pero [a   Juan no____].
   he-invited   ACC   *Luis but*   ACC   *Juan not*
   'He, invited Luis, but Juan, he, didn't (invite).'

c. En ese café   cobran   carísimo,   pero [en el otro no____].
   in that coffee.shop   they.charge   very.expensive   but   in the other not
   'In that coffee shop they charge a lot, but in the other one they don't.'

I first exemplify my analysis of topicalization with the case that corresponds to the topicalized subject of an unaccusative predicate, since it corresponds to the simplest instance of topicalization. We have seen that in this case a subject *theme* appears in the preverbal position, contrary to what is observed in the unmarked case. Since topicalization overrides the unmarked word order, TOPICFIRST must outrank *Pole/Theme in Spanish. The analysis of example (21d) is presented in tableau (26) below.

Candidate (26b), which corresponds to the unmarked word order, loses because of its violation of TOPICFIRST, since the verb in I c-commands the topic. Candidate (26a) wins despite its violation of *Pole/Theme, which would be fatal if the subject were not a topic. Notice that the winning candidate further satisfies the EPP by virtue of placing the subject in [Spec, I] in order to satisfy TOPICFIRST. This is irrelevant for the evaluation of this particular example (since TOPICFIRST is the constraint that decides the outcome of the competition) but the fact that fronted topics get to satisfy EPP as a side effect of complying with TOPICFIRST will be crucial when we consider more complex cases later in this chapter and in the following one.

In Spanish constituents with any semantic role can appear as fronted topics in the preverbal position. Examples (21a) and (21b) show a temporal expression and *theme* direct object functioning as a topic, respectively. Examples with locative XPs, and manner and reason adverbs are presented below.

(26) INPUT: <arrive (x), x=your brother (Th), x=[topic] >

	TOPIC FIRST	*Pole/ Theme	EPP
☞ a. [IP tu hermano llegó [VP]] **SV**		*	
b. [IP llegó [VP tu hermano]] **VS**	*!		*

(27) a. En este bar escribió Max su primera novela.
   in this bar wrote   Max his first   novel
   'In this bar, Max wrote his first novel.'   (Zubizarreta 1998:101)[28]

   b. De esta manera concluyeron las negociaciones entre   los dos   partidos.
   in this way   finished   the negotiations   between   the two   parties
   'In this way, the negotiations between the two parties came to an end.'

   c. Por eso no ha terminado Luis la carrera.
   for that not has finished   Luis the college.degree
   'Because of that, Luis hasn't finished his college degree.'

Under our assumption that all these topics occupy the same position, (27) indicates that TOPICFIRST outranks the whole of the Pole Hierarchy. This is because, all else being equal, an XP is not excluded from the Pole position when it corresponds to a topic, irrespective of how low its semantic role in the Thematic Hierarchy might be. The ranking of the relevant constraints so far is thus the one in (28).

(28) TOPICFIRST » *Pole/Reason » . . . » *Pole/Theme » EPP »*Pole/Experiencer »
   *Pole/Agent.

4.3.2 Vacuous Structure

The analysis in (26) assumes that if a topic gets fronted, it lands in the Pole specifier, and we have seen evidence from ellipsis that this is correct. However, it is clear that GEN can generate other structures where a topic is fronted to satisfy TOPICFIRST without making it the Pole of the clause. The relevant candidates are presented in (29).

(29) a. $[_{IP} \text{tu hermano}_i [_{IP} \underline{\quad} \text{llegó}_j [_{VP} t_i t_j]]]$.
        your brother   *arrived*

   b. $[_{XP} \text{tu hermano}_i [_X \emptyset] [_{IP} \underline{\quad} \text{llegó}_j [_{VP} t_i t_j]]]$.
        your brother   *arrived*

   c. $[_{XP} \text{tu hermano}_i [_X \text{llegó}_j] [_{IP} \underline{\quad} t_j [_{VP} t_i t_j]]]$.
        your brother   *arrived*

A candidate like (29a) adjoins the topic to IP, so TOPICFIRST is satisfied, but it leaves the specifier of IP empty, so there is no violation of

*Pole/Theme.[29] A candidate like (29b) also satisfies TOPICFIRST and avoids a violation of *Pole/Theme by projecting an extra XP with a null head above IP to host the topic in its specifier.[30] Candidate (29c) is just like (29b), the only difference is that in this case the verb in I^0 further moves to the head position of XP. Since these candidates only violate EPP, which is ranked below *Pole/Theme, one of them would emerge as the winner under our current set of constraints.

As surface strings the candidates in (29) are no different from the winning candidate (26a), but it is still necessary to distinguish them. As I show later in this chapter and in the following one, candidates where topics are adjoined to IP, as in (29a), or where an extra XP is projected above IP, as in (29b) (but not as in 29c) can in fact emerge as winners in more complex clauses. However, this is not the typical situation, as the evidence from ellipsis indicates. This makes it necessary to rule out the candidates in (29), where the topic does not occupy the same position that a preverbal transitive subject would occupy in the unmarked case. For this purpose I propose the constraints against vacuous structure below (see also Grimshaw 1997 and Legendre et.al. 1995), which I suggest belong to the family of constraints that regulate Economy of Structure.

(30)   NO VACUOUS STRUCTURE

Structure is only projected to satisfy the lexical and/or feature requirements of a head.

a.   *VACUOUS-XP
No vacuous projection; violated by projections of a head with no inherent lexical or featural content.

b.   *ADJUNCTION
No adjunction; violated by XP or head adjunction structures.

The definition of *ADJUNCTION is straightforward. The reason for proposing the *VACUOUS-XP constraint requires some discussion. Recall that in §2.1.2 I introduced the concept of *vacuous XP.* There I suggested that this is an XP that has no inherent features of its own, whether because the features of its head are exactly those of the phrase that is immediately subjacent to XP (i.e., IP recursion) or because its head lacks features altogether (other than the {F} value that it has simply for being part of the Extended Projection). *VACUOUS-XP is precisely the constraint that penalizes such a structure, and as such it is closely related to the MINIMAL PROJECTION constraint discussed in Grimshaw (1997), which requires that "a functional projection make a contribution to the functional representation of the extended projection that it is part of, thus ruling out empty projections" (Grimshaw 1997: 374, fn.1).[31]

My conception of *VACUOUS-XP differs from Grimshaw's MINIMAL PROJECTION in one important respect, though. Ultimately, *VACUOUS-XP is best conceived as a constraint that penalizes a DEPENDENCY violation (McCarthy & Prince 1995), and not just an Economy of Structure violation. This is because candidates that project an XP with a "dummy" head (either null or overt) are including a head in the output that does not have any corresponding element in the input. In other words, projecting *any* phrase (whether vacuous or contentful) will result in a number of violations of the constraints that regulate Economy of Structure (see Grimshaw 1997). But projecting a vacuous XP further carries with it a DEPENDENCY violation. It is this kind of violation that *VACUOUS-XP specifically targets. Given that projecting a vacuous XP brings with it a DEPENDENCY violation, but adjunction does not, I further assume as a working hypothesis that universally *VACUOUS-XP outranks *ADJUNCTION.

I also assume that *VACUOUS-XP is violated irrespective of whether the head of the vacuous XP remains null, as in (29b), or whether it is filled by movement of a contentful head, as in (29c). Candidates like (29b) and (29c) are different in that the former violates the OBLIGATORYHEAD (Ob-HD) constraint of Grimshaw (1997), whereas the latter does not. Yet they both violate *VACUOUS-XP because they introduce a head X^0 which has no correspondent in the input.[32] In other words, movement into the head position of a vacuous XP does not prevent a violation of *VACUOUS-XP.

Now, by ranking both *VACUOUS-XP and *ADJUNCTION over *Pole/Theme, we arrive at the right result, as shown in (31). Candidate (31b), which corresponds to (29a), loses to candidate (31a) because of its violation of *ADJUNCTION. Candidates (31c) and (31d), where a vacuous XP is projected to host the topic in its specifier in order to avoid a violation of *Pole/Theme, are ruled out because of their violation of *VACUOUS-XP,

(31) INPUT: <arrive (x), x=your brother (Th), x=|topic| >

	TOPIC FIRST	*VAC XP	*ADJ	*Pole/ Theme	EPP
☞ a. [IP [tu hermano]Top llegó [VP]]				*	
b. [IP [tu hermano]Top [IP __ llegó [VP]]]			*!		*
c. [XP [tu hermano]Top ∅ [IP __ llegó [VP]]]		*!			*
d. [XP [tu hermano]Top llegó [IP __ *t* [VP]]]		*!			*

independently of whether or not the verb moves to the head position of XP.

For the time being we have no evidence for the relative ranking of TopicFirst with respect to either *Adjunction or *Vacuous XP; any ranking of these three constraint will give the right result since the winning candidate satisfies them all. Later in this chapter I will argue for the relative ranking of TopicFirst and *Adjunction.

4.3.3 Topic and Focus

At this point, we can return to the OVS examples introduced in the section on focus. Recall that in Mexican Spanish OVS corresponds to the order observed in clauses where the subject is in focus, and where both the subject and the object are realized as lexical XPs.

(32)   Quién compró los discos?
       Who bought the records?'

    a. #[Una   muchacha]$_{FOC}$ compró los discos.   **S V O**
        a   girl   *bought   the records*

    b. Los discos los   compró [una muchacha]$_{FOC}$.   **O V S**
       the records ACC-CL *bought   a   girl*
       'A GIRL bought the records.'

I suggest that (32b) involves both focalization of the subject *and* topicalization of the direct object. Notice that the fronted object in (32b) has an instantiation in the previous discourse (i.e., in the *wh*-question) and so it meets the sufficient condition required of sentence topics.

In terms of my analysis, the object DP is fronted to the Pole position to satisfy TopicFirst. The subject DP in focus, on the other hand, remains in its VP-internal position. After V-to-I movement the subject ends up being to the sentence final constituent, so it receives the nuclear accent and Focus-Prominence is satisfied. This analysis is presented in (33). At present I have

(33)   OVS clauses; subject focus, object topic.
    INPUT: <buy (x, y), x=a girl (Ag), x=[focus], y=the records (Th), y=[topic]>

	FOCUS PROM	TOPIC FIRST	*Pole/ Theme	EPP
a. [$_{IP}$ [una muchacha]$_{Foc}$ compró [$_{VP}$ [LOS DISCOS]$_{Top}$]] **SVO**	*!	*!		
☞ b. [$_{IP}$ [los discos]$_{Top}$] los compró [$_{VP}$ [UNA MUCHACHA]$_{Foc}$] **OVS**			*	

no clear evidence for the relative ranking of FOCUSPROMINENCE with respect to TOPICFIRST and *Pole/Theme but this bears no consequences for the data under consideration, since the winning candidate does not violate either.[33]

I noted in §4.2.3 that OVS clauses are not felicitous instances of sentence focus in Spanish, for reasons of structural markedness. At this point, we can add a further observation to that analysis. A topical DP with a *theme* semantic role (whether a DO or an unaccusative subject) can occupy the Pole in order to satisfy TOPICFIRST. But in cases of sentence focus every element of the clause is a focus and so TOPICFIRST has no say in the matter. As discussed in §4.2.3, the competition between the SVO and OVS candidates is then decided by structural markedness considerations. The SVO candidate, which has an *agent* as the Pole, emerges as the winner by virtue of having a degree of structural markedness lower than that of the OVS candidate, which has a *theme* as the Pole.

We have seen how the requirements of TOPICFIRST can make an unaccusative subject or a direct object surface in the Pole, contrary to what is observed in the unmarked case. In this analysis, the EPP is satisfied as an indirect consequence of topicalization. One further observation is important at this point. In unaccusative clauses the *theme* subject is the only argument of the verb, and in OVS clauses with subject focus there is an independent condition that prevents the subject from surfacing as the Pole, namely, the requirement that it appear in the sentence-final position in order to satisfy FOCUSPROMINENCE. However, the analysis also accounts for cases where an *agent* subject could in principle surface as the Pole, but where in fact it does not, because another topical XP has already been fronted (thus satisfying the EPP), which makes movement of the *agent* subject to [Spec, I] unnecessary. This can be seen in Adv-VSO sentences like (21a), repeated here as (34).

(34) Ayer   compró Juan el periódico.   **Adv V S O**
     yesterday bought Juan the newspaper
     'Yesterday Juan bought the newspaper.'

The analysis I propose for this example is one where the fronted adverbial corresponds to the topic, and the rest of the clause corresponds to the focus. This is in accordance with the characterization in Zubizarreta (1998) of XP-VSO sentences in Spanish as *topic-comment* structures. The crucial question that we need to address is what prevents the subject from surfacing in its canonical preverbal position in *topic-comment* sentences like (34). Observe that satisfaction of FOCUSPROMINENCE is not an issue here. Given that the focus domain consists of subject, the verb, and the object, any order of these three constituents will still result in two violations of FOCUSPROMINENCE, since only one of them (the one in sentence final position) can be signaled with the sentential accent (see §4.2.3).

This is what makes (34) crucially different from the case of subject focus in (33). In (34) the *agent* subject could in principle surface in the preverbal position, providing the clause with the least marked instance of a Pole. But in my analysis, such a structure is ruled out by Economy of Structure considerations. In order to have both the *agent* subject in [Spec, I] and to satisfy the TOPICFIRST requirement on the topical temporal adverb, an extra layer of structure would have to be projected to host the topic. The resulting structure loses to the one where the only fronted element is the topic, which satisfies the EPP in [Spec, I] as a consequence of complying with TOPIC-FIRST. The desired result is achieved by ranking both *VACUOUS-XP and *ADJUNCTION above all the constraints in the Pole Hierarchy. The ranking of the relevant constraints so far is presented in (35).

(35)   TOPICFIRST, *VACUOUS XP » *ADJUNCTION » *Pole/Reason » . . . » *Pole/Theme »
         EPP » *Pole/Experiencer » *Pole/Agent.

The analysis of (34) under this ranking is shown in tableau (36). Candidate (36b) projects a vacuous XP to host the topical temporal adverb in its specifier; TOPICFIRST is satisfied, and a violation of *Pole/Temporal is avoided by having the topic outside the Pole position. Instead the EPP is satisfied by the subject *agent,* which, as mentioned, constitutes the least marked instance of a Pole. But the resulting violation of *VACUOUS XP proves fatal in my proposed constraint ranking of Spanish. The situation with candidate (36c) is in essence the same, with the exception that instead of projecting a vacuous XP, this candidate adjoins the topic to IP, and so it is ruled out because of its violation of *ADJUNCTION. In this way, candidate (36a) emerges as the optimal realization of the *topic-comment* input.[34]

(36) 'Yesterday Juan bought the newspaper'; Topic= *ayer* 'yesterday'

   INPUT: <buy (x, y; z), buy=[focus], x=Juan (Ag), x=[focus],

   y=the newspaper (Th), y=[focus]; z=yesterday (Temp), z=[topic] >

	TOPIC FIRST	*VAC XP	*ADJ	*Pole/ Temp	EPP
☞ a. [IP [ayer]Top compró [VP Juan el periódico]]. **Adv-VSO**				*	
b. [XP [ayer]Top Ø [IP Juan compró [VP el periódico]]]. **Adv-SVO**		*!			
c. [IP [ayer]Top [IP Juan compró [VP el periódico]]]. **Adv-SVO**			*!		

We are now in a position where we can address one of the central empirical observations of this work, the fact that VSO clauses with an empty preverbal position are not tolerated in Mexican Spanish. A relevant paradigm reflecting this state of affairs is presented in (37) below. Following the discussion of adverbial expressions and word order in §2.1.1, I assume that *ayer* 'yesterday' in (37a) and (37c) can be base-generated at the left edge of VP and V-to-I movement derives the order in which the verb precedes the adverb (Pollock 1989). For (37b) I assume that the adverb moves from its base position to [Spec, I].

(37) Mexican Spanish

    a. Juan compró ayer   el periódico.   **S V Adv O**
       Juan bought   yesterday the newspaper
       'John bought the newspaper yesterday.'

    b. Ayer   compró   Juan el   periódico.   **Adv VSO**
       yesterday bought Juan the newspaper
       'Yesterday John bought the newspaper.'

    c. *Compró ayer   Juan el   periódico.   **V Adv SO**
       bought   yesterday Juan the newspaper

In my analysis the unacceptability of (37c) is explained by the fact that it is never an optimal candidate under the ranking of constraints of Mexican Spanish. Consider first the SV-Adv-O example (37a). When there is no XP specified as a topic, the SV-Adv-O candidate, which has the least marked instance of a Pole, emerges as the winner as a result of the ranking *Pole/Temporal » EPP » *Pole/Agent. This analysis is presented in (38). In this tableau, candidate (38b), where the adverbial XP moves to the Pole position, loses because of its violation of *Pole/Temporal. Candidate (38c), which corresponds to (37c), does not violate any of the constraints in the Pole Hierarchy by leaving the Pole position empty, but loses to (38a) because of its violation of EPP.

(38) No topic (i.e. sentence focus); 'Juan bought the newspaper yesterday.'

INPUT: <buy (x, y; z), x=Juan (Ag), y=the newspaper (Th); z=yesterday (Temp)>

	*Pole/ Temp	EPP	*Pole/ Agent
☞ a. [IP Juan compró [VP ayer el periódico]]. **SV-Adv-O**			*
b. [IP ayer compró [VP Juan el periódico]]. **Adv-VSO**	*!		
c. [IP compró [VP ayer Juan el periódico]]. **V-Adv-SO**		*!	

(39) Topic = *ayer* 'yesterday': 'Yesterday Juan bought the newspaper.'

INPUT: <buy (x, y; z), x=Juan (Ag), y=the newspaper (Th);   z=yesterday (Temp),

z=[topic] >

	TOPIC FIRST	*Pole/ Temp	EPP	*Pole/ Agent
a. [$_{IP}$ Juan compró [$_{VP}$ [ayer]$_{Top}$ el periódico]]. **SV-Adv-O**	**!			*
☞ b. [$_{IP}$ [ayer]$_{Top}$ compró [$_{VP}$ Juan el periódico]]. **Adv-VSO**		*		
c. [$_{IP}$ compró [$_{VP}$ [ayer]$_{Top}$ Juan el periódico]]. **V-Adv-SO**	*!		*	

Consider now an input where the adverb is a topic, as in the analysis of (37b) in (36). As shown in tableau (39), the optimal candidate in this case is the one where the temporal adverb surfaces as the Pole in order to satisfy TOPICFIRST. The other two candidates, where the adverb is not the clause-initial element, lose because of their violations of TOPICFIRST.

Crucially, the V-Adv-SO candidate that leaves the Pole position empty does not emerge as a winner in either (38) or (39), and in this way (37c) is accounted for. In other words, given the ranking of constraints in Mexican Spanish there is no input that will have VSO as its optimal output. This, I claim, is what makes transitive clauses with an empty preverbal position ungrammatical (see the characterization of ungrammaticality in OT syntax in §1.2).[35]

It is worth highlighting the importance of this result by comparing a contrast in grammaticality like the one above with a contrast in felicity. Such a contrast is observed in the examples in (32), repeated here as (40).

(40) Quién compró los discos?
     Who bought the records?'

    a. #[Una muchacha]$_{FOC}$ compró los discos.   S V O
       a   girl   bought   the records

    b. Los discos los   compró [una muchacha]$_{FOC}$.   O V S
       the records ACC-CL *bought   a   girl*
     'A GIRL bought the records.'

The SVO clause in (40a) is obviously not an ungrammatical sentence, in contrast with (37c). It is in fact the felicitous word order in cases of sentence focus, as discussed in §4.2.3. In terms of my analysis, the difference between infelicity and ungrammaticality is that an infelicitous sentence *does* emerge as an optimal output for *some* input under the constraint ranking of the language. In a context where a sentence is judged as infelicitous, this is because it does not correspond to the candidate that the constraint ranking selects as the winner for the input defined by this context.

This analysis achieves two things. First, it dispels the potential criticism that comparing infelicitous and ungrammatical sentences as part of the same candidate set involves comparing two completely different sets of phenomena governed by different grammatical principles. Second, it is no longer necessary to claim (for theory-internal reasons) that all losing candidates correspond to ungrammatical sentences, which involved claiming that, for instance, the SVO sentence in (40a) *is* ungrammatical (not just infelicitous) in a subject focus context (cf. Grimshaw & Samek-Lodovici 1998).

4.3.4 Presentational clauses

The discussion so far raises the question of what the analysis should be of VSO clauses in those varieties of Spanish that do allow for them. Here I cannot provide a detailed analysis of these varieties, but some tentative observations can be made at this point. Niño (1993) suggests that VSO clauses in Spanish are presentational in nature.[36] An example is presented below (presumably from Venezuelan Spanish).

(41) Cazaron   los hombres un ciervo.   **VSO**
      hunt-3PL-PAST *the men*   *a deer*
      'The men hunted a deer.'   Niño (1993: 2)

Niño notes that (41) has a reading where the proposition is described as an activity, very much in character with a presentational function.[37] Niño further observes that many instances where VSO clauses are slightly deviant are improved when a topical temporal adverb appears in the preverbal position, a pattern reminiscent of Mexican Spanish. Following Diesing (1990), Niño takes this position to be the position also occupied by fronted subjects, namely [Spec, I]. The basis of Niño's analysis is to claim that there are discourse conditions that allow a VSO sentence to "stand on its own" without the need to project [Spec, I]. Niño proposes that these are the discourse conditions that require a presentational sentence. But those clauses that are not signaled as presentational require an element in [Spec, I], the subject in the unmarked case, or a temporal adverb functioning as a topic.

I suggest that the OT proposal I have developed is compatible with Niño's analysis under the following assumptions. Assume that the presentational nature of a proposition is expressed in the input by a feature [thetic], and that the correspondence between this feature in the input and the output representation is governed by the constraint in (42).

(42) THETIC CONDITION (THET-CON)

A [+verbal] extended projection is thetic iff its highest inflectional element c-commands all of the arguments of the lexical head of the extended projection.

As such, this is a purely descriptive constraint, and it should presumably be derived by more subtle semantic considerations. However, it will suffice for illustrating the point at hand. The variety of Spanish described in Niño (1993) can now be characterized as having the ranking THET-CON » EPP. In other words, when the input bears the feature [thetic], the optimal output corresponds to a VSO clause, which violates the EPP because it lacks a Pole altogether, but satisfies THET-CON because the verb in I^0 (asymmetrically) c-commands all of its arguments. However, when the input does not bear this feature, then the effects of THET-CON are neutralized, and the EPP once again plays a crucial role. The Pole must now be filled, either by the subject or by a fronted topic, and in this case the variety of Spanish in Niño (1993) behaves similarly to Mexican Spanish.

On the other hand, Mexican Spanish would be characterized by the opposite ranking, EPP » THET-CON. Given this ranking, the optimal candidate is one that has a fronted XP as a Pole, even if this means that the condition on presentational sentences is violated. This is illustrated for the simple transitive sentence (41) in the tableau in (43). In the input, [TH] stands for the abbreviation of the feature [thetic]. Notice that candidate (43a) violates THET-CON because the subject in [Spec, I] c-commands the verb in I^0.

In other words, by prioritizing the satisfaction of the EPP, transitive clauses in Mexican Spanish can in a sense be unfaithful to the semantic specification of an input as [thetic]. Ultimately, my sense is that this phenomenon is best conceived as an instance of neutralization, as understood in phonology (see also Legendre et. al. 1998, and McCarthy 2002). In the same way that a feature distinction present in underlying segments can be neutralized in the

(43) MEXICAN SPANISH: Thetic input of a transitive predicate.

INPUT: <[TH] hunt (x, y), x=the men (Ag), y=a deer (Th)>

	EPP	THET CON	*Pole/ Agent
☞ a. [IP los hombres cazaron [VP un ciervo]] **SVO**		*	*
b. [IP cazaron [VP los hombres un ciervo]] **VSO**	*!		

surface representation, the ranking of constraints in Mexican Spanish is such that it neutralizes two different inputs, $<V(x, y)>$ and $<[TH]\ V(x, y)>$, into the same surface representation, SVO.[38]

Notice that this result can be achieved because the EPP in an OT analysis is always an active requirement of the grammar, even if it can be overruled in some cases because of its ranking relative to other constraints. Once again, if we were to claim that Mexican Spanish has an active EPP requirement absent in VSO varieties of Spanish we would be at a loss in explaining why they behave similarly when a transitive clause does not have a presentational reading (i.e., in the SVO unmarked order and XP-VSO *topic-comment* sentences).

4.3.5 VOS clauses

At this point we can provide an analysis of the VOS clauses first introduced in §4.2.1. As already noted, VOS clauses can only have an interpretation where the subject is the only constituent in focus. Furthermore, such clauses are not tolerated in Mexican Spanish. In providing an account of these clauses, I follow the analysis in Ordóñez (1998). Ordóñez proposes that VOS clauses are derived by scrambling of the direct object, as in (44), originally from Torrego (1984). I also follow the analysis in Zubizarreta (1998), where this scrambling operation is driven by the need to make the subject in focus the clause-final constituent, in order for it to be signaled by the nuclear accent.

(44) $[_{IP}$ Contestó $[_{VP}$ la pregunta$_i$ $[_{VP}$ Juan t_i]]]   V O S
     answered   *the question*   *Juan*
     'JUAN answered the question.'

My suggestion is that VOS clauses in Peninsular and other varieties of Spanish are presentational clauses (as defined in the previous section) where the subject further bears the [focus] feature. The direct object scrambles to allow the subject to appear in the clause-final position, but it remains in a position where it can be c-commanded by the verb in I^0, in compliance with THET-CON.

Now, the current analysis accounts for the absence of VOS clauses in Mexican Spanish without the need of any extra machinery. We have seen in the previous section that THET-CON is a fairly low-ranked constraint in Mexican Spanish, and concretely, it is outranked by the EPP. Further notice that scrambling of the direct object in (44) results in adjunction, and that *ADJUNCTION outranks both the EPP and all of the constraints in the Pole Hierarchy. The relevant ranking is repeated in (45).

(45) TOPICFIRST, *VACUOUS XP » *ADJUNCTION » *Pole/Reason » . . . » *Pole/Theme » EPP » *Pole/Experiencer » *Pole/Agent.

(46)   MEXICAN SPANISH: Thetic input of a transitive predicate with subject in focus.

INPUT: <[TH] answer (x, y), x=Juan (Ag), x= [focus], y=the question (Th)>

	*ADJ	*Pole/ Theme	EPP	THET CON
a. [IP contestó [VP la pregunta [VP Juan]]] **VOS**	*!		*	
☞ b. [IP la pregunta la contestó [VP Juan]] **OVS**		*		*

Under this ranking, VOS does not emerge as the winning candidate for a thetic input with the subject in focus, as shown in tableau (46). Since the subject is in focus, the direct object has to move to move from its base position to allow the subject to be clause-final. The VOS candidate (46a) achieves this by scrambling the direct object, while the OVS candidate (46b) moves the direct object into the Pole instead. However, the violation of *ADJUNCTION that the VOS candidate incurs proves fatal when compared with the violation of *Pole/Theme of the OVS candidate. Consequently, even though the VOS candidate satisfies THET-CON and thus it is faithful to the [thetic] specification in the input, it loses to the OVS candidate, which violates THET-CON but avoids adjunction and further satisfies the EPP.[39] The structure and gloss of the winning candidate is presented in (47).

(47)   [IP La pregunta$_i$ la   contestó   [VP Juan t_i]]   O V S
          the question ACC-CL. *answered*   *Juan*
          'JUAN answered the question.'

Notice that this is a case where the direct object occupies the Pole position even though it is not specified as a topic in the input.[40] The result of this is that the analysis in (46) again corresponds to an instance of neutralization. Given the constraint ranking of Mexican Spanish, the thetic input <[TH] V(x, y), x=[focus]> and the non-thetic input <V(x, y), x=[focus], y=[topic]> (see §4.3.3) both have OVS as their output representation. In this way, the absence of VOS clauses in Mexican Spanish is accounted for.

4.3.6 Default Topics

I now consider an alternative to the analysis of unmarked word order developed in §3, which emerges from the discussion of topicalization. I have argued that different kinds of XPs can appear in the Pole and satisfy the EPP by virtue of being topics. Yet this raises the question of whether this could be the factor that derives unmarked word order in the first place. That is, we need to consider if subjects in the unmarked SVO order might surface in the preverbal position because they are "default" topics.

In fact, the analysis of subjects as default topics in Spanish has been fairly widespread in the literature, starting with Meyer (1972). This idea has gained even more appeal in recent years, as there is some evidence that pre-verbal subjects in Spanish behave like left-dislocated XPs in an A-Bar position (see Ordóñez & Treviño 1999). Yet, there are a number of empirical and conceptual reasons that make the *default topic* analysis problematic.

Empirically, we have seen in §3.4 and §4.3 that fronted topics create islands for extraction, but Goodall (2001), who also argues that preverbal subjects in Spanish move to satisfy the EPP, notes that fronted subjects do not lead to island effects. The relevant contrast is repeated in (48a-b). As mentioned in §4.3 (fn. 19), subjects clearly functioning as topics (such as fronted unaccusative subjects) do not lead to such strong island effects, but there is still a contrast between (48b) and (48c-d).[41]

(48) a. *A quién crees   [que el premio se   lo   dieron]?
          to whom you-think that the prize   DAT-CL ACC-CL they-gave
          (Lit. 'Who do you think that the prize they gave to?')

      b. A quién crees   [que Juan le   dio el premio]?
          to whom you-think that   Juan DAT-CL gave the prize
          'Who do you think that Juan gave the prize to?'   (Goodall 2001)

      c. ?Cuándo$_i$ dices [que tu   hermano llegó t_i]?
          when   you-say that your brother   arrived.
          'When did you say that your brother ARRIVED?'

      d. ??Cuándo$_i$ dices [que el calentador explotó t_i]?
          when   you-say that the heater   exploded.
          ('When did you say that the water heater exploded?')

Providing a formal characterization of the notion of default topic is equally (if not more) problematic. Claiming that a subject corresponds to the default topic amounts to assigning a specific pragmatic property to a specific grammatical relation. In both Minimalist and OT analyses this ultimately amounts to saying that the subject bears the feature [topic] by virtue of its grammatical relation. But if this is so, then we need some mechanism to remove this feature when the subject is clearly not functioning as a topic, as in the subject inversion cases we have discussed throughout this work. Furthermore, such a mechanism would face serious problems in accounting for cases of sentence focus. The standard assumption in these cases is that every element in the clause is focal, including the subject, so this would also be a case where the subject's default [topic] feature would have to be removed.

But, crucially, the subject still appears in the preverbal position in cases of sentence focus (see §4.2.3), which disconfirms the hypothesis that its movement to the preverbal position is dependent on having a feature [topic] in the default case.

Even assuming that such a feature removal mechanism could be developed and defined in some coherent way, the resulting analysis would still make the wrong predictions with respect to word order. Concretely, if subjects bear a default [topic] feature and if they appear in the preverbal position in transitive clauses as a result of bearing this feature, then it goes unexplained why in psych predicates it is the dative *experiencer* and not the subject that appears in the preverbal position in the unmarked case. Notice that even if we assign the default [topic] feature not to the subject, but to the argument of the verb that ranks highest in the thematic hierarchy, we still get the wrong result. This is because the *theme* argument of unaccusative clauses and impersonal passives would still be assigned this default feature (since there is no *agent* or *experiencer* argument in this case) and would be predicted to undergo fronting as the default topic in the unmarked case, contrary to fact. In my analysis, where the unmarked word order is derived in a way that is entirely independent of topicalization, all these complications are avoided.

4.3.7 Multiple Topics

To conclude this chapter, I show how the analysis of topicalization accounts for cases where there is more than one sentence topic. Spanish readily allows for clauses with multiple topics, as is well known.[42] Some examples are presented below.

(49) a. Esta carta el criado   la   trajo   para mí.
          this letter the servant ACC-CL *brought for me*
          'This letter the servant brought for me.'   (Contreras 1976)

      b. En este bar, Max escribió su primera novela.
          in this bar Max wrote   his first   novel
          'In this bar, Max wrote his first novel.'   (Zubizarreta 1998:102)

      c. Ayer   a   María la   vieron   con su   novio.
          yesterday ACC *María* ACC-CL *they-saw with her   boyfriend*
          'Yesterday they saw Mary with her boyfriend.'   (Hernanz & Brucart 1987:82)

In examples like (49a) and (49b) one of the fronted topics corresponds to the subject, but this is not a necessary requirement, as shown in (49c), where the fronted topics correspond to a temporal adverb and the direct object. Notice that in (49) we observe a situation different from the one in *topic-comment* sentences that have a single topic, namely, this is a case where extra structure *is* projected to accommodate the multiple topics. This means that Spanish prioritizes the requirement to have topics in a leftmost position over complying with Economy of Structure (as first suggested in §3.5). In terms of my analysis, this means that TOPICFIRST must outrank at least one of the NO VACUOUS STRUCTURE constraints in (30). So, in principle, there are two possible analyses of the examples in (49). In one analysis, one of the topics surfaces in the Pole and the leftmost topic is adjoined to IP (which violates *ADJUNCTION). In the other, one of the topics also surfaces in the Pole, but the leftmost topic is in the specifier of a vacuous XP projected to host the topic (which violates *VACUOUS-XP). These two alternatives are presented for (49c) in (50).[43]

(50) a. $[_{IP}$ Ayer $[_{IP}$ a   María   la   vieron $[_{VP}$ con   su   novio]]].
         yesterday   ACC *María* ACC-CL *they-saw*   *with*   *her boyfriend*
         'Yesterday they saw Mary with her boyfriend.'

     b. $[_{XP}$ Ayer   Ø $[_{IP}$ a   María   la   vieron $[_{VP}$ con   su   novio]]].
         yesterday   ACC *María* ACC-CL *they-saw*   *with*   *her boyfriend*
         Yesterday they saw Mary with her boyfriend.'

However, given our working hypothesis that *VACUOUS-XP outranks *ADJUNCTION (§4.3.1), the adjunction structure in (50a) will surface as the winner irrespective of whether TOPICFIRST outranks both *VACUOUS-XP and *ADJUNCTION or just *ADJUNCTION. This is shown in tableau (51), where it can be seen that the reverse ranking of *VACUOUS-XP and TOPICFIRST gives the same result.

(51) INPUT: <see(w, x; y, z), w=*pro* [3rd.Pl.], x=María, x=[topic]; y=yesterday, y=[topic], z=with her boyfriend >

	*VAC XP	TOPIC FIRST	*ADJ
☞ a. $[_{IP}$ [ayer]$_{Top}$ $[_{IP}$ [a Maria]$_{Top}$ la vieron $[_{VP}$ con su novio]]]		*	*
b. $[_{XP}$ [ayer]$_{Top}$ ο $[_{IP}$ [a Maria]$_{Top}$ la vieron $[_{VP}$ con su novio]]]	*!	*	
c. $[_{IP}$ [ayer]$_{Top}$ vieron $[_{VP}$ [a Maria]$_{Top}$ con su novio]]		**!	
d. $[_{IP}$ [a Maria]$_{Top}$ la vieron $[_{VP}$ [ayer]$_{Top}$ con su novio]]		**!	

Let us go through the candidates in (51) one by one. Observe that violations of TopicFirst are unavoidable when more than one topic is involved: even if both topics appear in a left-peripheral position, as in (51a) and (51b), the topic in the Pole is c-commanded by the leftmost topic, which results in one violation of TopicFirst (recall that TopicFirst is violated once for every XP or X^0 that c-commands a topic). However, the gradient definition of TopicFirst that I propose still makes each topic move as much as possible to the left periphery to avoid even more violations of this constraint. This is most clearly observed in candidates (51c) and (51d). These candidates have one topic in the Pole, but leave the other one in its VP-internal position. The result is that neither of these candidates violates *Vacuous XP nor *Adjunction.[44] However, by doing so they incur in an extra violation of TopicFirst. This is because in these two candidates (as opposed to 51a and 51b) both the topic in [Spec, I] *and* the verb in I^0 c-command the topic. The extra violation of TopicFirst proves fatal, and so candidates (51c) and (51d) are ruled out of the competition. Candidates (51a) and (51b) satisfy TopicFirst as much as possible by fronting both topics to a left peripheral position, which results in the projection of extra structure to host the second topic.[45] When comparing this pair, candidate (51b)'s violation of *Vacuous XP proves more costly than candidate (51a)'s violation of *Adjunction, and so (51b) loses to (51a). Incidentally, notice that in my analysis the gradient definition of TopicFirst captures the same effect that is achieved in Rizzi (1997) with multiple Topic Phrases, with the added advantage that it simplifies the structure of the left periphery considerably.[46]

Since the data under consideration does not allow us to determine the strict ranking between *Vacuous-XP and TopicFirst, I will leave these constraints unranked with respect to one another. The full ranking of the constraints relevant to topicalization thus corresponds to (52).

(52) *Vacuous XP, TopicFirst » *Adjunction » *Pole/Reason » *Pole/Manner-
      Temporal » *Pole/Locative » *Pole/Theme » EPP » *Pole/Experiencer »
      *Pole/Agent.

As such, (51) provides the basic analysis of multiple topicalization. There is, however, one more important property of multiple topic constructions that has not been observed in the literature (to the best of my knowledge), namely, that the relative order of the multiple topics is not entirely free. By and large, examples of multiple topicalization in the literature follow a pattern where the innermost topic (i.e., the one immediately to the left of the verb) is the one that ranks higher in the Thematic Hierarchy (§3.2.1). The examples in (49) all show this pattern. In (49a) and (49b) the two topics are a *theme* and *agent,* and a *locative* and an *agent,* respectively. In both cases the *agent* is the innermost topic. Notice again that this pattern is not dependent on the presence of a subject or an *agent.* In (49c) the two topics are a *temporal* adverbial and a *theme* direct object, and, again following the Thematic Hierarchy, the *theme* is the innermost topic.

In fact, when asked to judge examples with multiple topics without any preceding context, speakers systematically prefer this pattern. Some examples are presented below. The semantic role and relative order of each of the topics is presented to the right of each example.

(53) MULTIPLE TOPICS: NO PRECEDING CONTEXT

    a. Por eso Pedro visita a   sus padres todos los años.
       for that Pedro visits ACC *his parents all   the years*
       'Because of that, Pedro visits his parents every year.'   ***Reason > Agent***

    b. #Pedro por eso visita a   sus padres todos los años.
       Pedro for that visits ACC *his parents all   the years*   ***Agent > Reason***

(54) a. El periódico   Pedro lo   compró ayer.
       the newspaper Pedro ACC-CL *bought   yesterday*
       'The newspaper, Pedro bought it yesterday.'   ***Theme > Agent***

    b. ??Pedro el periódico lo   compró ayer.
       Pedro the newspaper ACC-CL *bought yesterday*   ***Agent > Theme***

(55) a. En Tijuana a Pedro le   molesta el ruido del   tráfico.[47]
       in Tijuana to Pedro DAT-CL *bothers the noise of-the traffic*
       'In Tijuana, the noise from traffic bothers Pedro.'   ***Locative > Exper***

    b. #A Pedro en Tijuana le   molesta el ruido del   tráfico.
       to Pedro in Tijuana DAT-CL *bothers he noise of-the traffic* ***Exper > Locative***

(56) a. De esta manera ayer   se redactó el texto final.
       of this   way   yesterday CL *wrote the text final*
       'In this way, the final text was written yesterday.'   ***Manner > Temporal***

    b. #Ayer   de esta manera se redactó el texto final.
       *yesterday of this   way   * CL *wrote   the text final*   ***Temporal > Manner***

Once again, It should be underlined that the (b) examples in (53–56) are simply infelicitous in the absence of any context, rather than ungrammatical. Although at this point I cannot characterize the pragmatic and discourse properties that license them, they can be readily found in spoken and written texts. As such, it appears that the pattern where the innermost topic ranks higher in the thematic hierarchy simply corresponds to the unmarked (or least marked) pattern of multiple topicalization. Impressionistically, it seems to me that the opposite pattern (where the innermost topic ranks lower in the thematic hierarchy) necessarily gives the innermost topic a contrastive reading (see Lambrecht 1994 for the notion of *contrastive topic*). In contrast, in the unmarked pattern the innermost topic can, but need not have a contrastive reading. Settling this issue goes beyond the scope of this work. What we need at this point is to define some diagnostic for the unmarked multiple topicalization pattern observed in the (a) examples in (53–56) that neutralizes the pragmatic conditions under which the opposite pattern is licensed. I suggest that contrastive verb or adverb focus provides such a diagnostic.

We have seen in (§4.2) that contrastive foci mostly appear in the sentence final position in Mexican Spanish, in which their behavior is akin to that of presentational foci. Consider now a case of contrastive verb or adverb focus, where the clause under consideration has two XPs that function as either arguments or adjuncts of the verb. FOCUS PROMINENCE requires that the verb or adverb in focus appear in the clause final position. If the two XP arguments or adjuncts have an instantiation in the previous discourse, they meet the sufficient requirement to function as sentence topics (see §4.3.1) and FOCUS PROMINENCE can be satisfied by fronting these XPs to the left periphery, after which the verb or adverb corresponds to the clause-final constituent. Crucially, it seems reasonable to assume that in this case neither of the two XPs moves to the left periphery as the result of its specification as a contrastive topic. Rather, given that they both meet the sufficient condition to function as sentence topics, they simply move out of the way to allow the verb or adverb to receive the nuclear accent in the clause-final position. In this context, we expect the (unmarked) pattern in (53–56) to emerge and this is indeed what is observed. Some examples are presented below.

(57) CONTRASTIVE VERB/ADVERB FOCUS
    A. Pedro escribió la carta.
        Pedro wrote   the letter
        'Pedro wrote the letter.'

a. B. No, la carta Pedro la   MANDÓ.   *Theme > Agent*
   no the letter Pedro ACC-CL sent
   'No, Pedro SENT the letter.'

b. B. ??No, Pedro la carta   la   MANDÓ.   *Agent > Theme*
   no, Pedro the letter ACC-CL sent

(58) A. Al   comité   le   molesta su actitud.
    to-the board-of-directors DAT-CL bothers his attitude
    'His attitude irritates the board of directors.'

a. B. Al contrario,   su actitud al   comité   le   ENCANTA.
   to-the contrary his attitude to-the board-of-directors DAT-CL charms
   'On the contrary, the board of directors LOVES his attitude.' *Theme > Exper*

b. B. #Al contrario, al   comité   su actitud le   ENCANTA.
   to-the contrary to-the board-of-directors his attitude DAT-CL charms
                                                        Exper > Theme

(59) A. Llueve mucho en Tijuana por eso.
    it-rains much   in Tijuana for that
    'That is why it rains a lot in Tijuana.'

a. B. Al contrario   por eso por eso   llueve POCO.   *Reason > Loc*
   to-the contrary for that in Tijuana it-rains few
   'On the contrary, that's why in Tijuana it rains so LITTLE.'

b. B. #Al contrario, en Tijuana por eso llueve POCO.   *Loc > Reason*
   to-the contrary in Tijuana for   that it-rains few

Now the crucial observation is that the unmarked multiple topicalization pattern is exactly what my proposal predicts it should be. In my analysis, topics are fronted to the Pole specifier and this is a specifier position that is sensitive to the semantic role of the constituent that occupies it. As such, XPs whose semantic role ranks low in the Thematic Hierarchy are more marked Poles than XPs whose semantic role ranks high in the hierarchy. When there is a single topic, the issue of relative markedness does not arise. But when there are two topics, the constraint ranking I have proposed so far predicts that the topic that ranks higher in the Thematic Hierarchy will be the one that surfaces as the Pole (i.e., the innermost topic), all else being equal. This is because the resulting construction shows a lower degree of structural markedness than

(60) INPUT: <rain (w; x, y, z), w=*pro* [3rd.SG], x=little, x=*focus*, y=in Tijuana, y=[topic],

z=for that reason, z=[topic]>

	*ADJ	*Pole/ Reason	*Pole/ Locative
☞ a. [IP por eso [IP en Tijuana llueve [VP poco]]]	*		*
b. [IP en Tijuana [IP por eso llueve [VP poco]]]	*	*!	

the alternative where the topic that ranks lower in the Thematic Hierarchy
surfaces as the Pole. In terms of the OT analysis developed so far, this alternative is ruled out because it violates a constraint that is ranked higher in the
Pole Hierarchy than the one violated by the attested output. This analysis is
presented for (59) in tableau (60).

Recall that both the *reason* and the *locative* adjuncts have to move to the
left periphery in order to allow the focussed adverb *poco* 'few, little' to appear in
the sentence final position. As in any multiple topic construction, a violation of
*ADJUNCTION is unavoidable if both XPs are to be hosted in the left periphery.
The final decision then rests on the markedness constraints of the Pole Hierarchy, and so candidate (60b), which places the *reason* adverbial in [Spec, I] loses
because of its violation of *Pole/Reason. The winning candidate instead adjoins
the *reason* adverbial to IP and makes the *locative* PP the Pole, which is the best
outcome given this state of affairs. The ranking in (52) equally accounts directly
for all the contrasts in (53–59), as I leave for the reader to verify.

The multiple topicalization data not only provide further support to
my analysis where the Pole is a position that can host fronted topics. These
same facts also disconfirm alternative analyses where all fronted topics land
in a position other than the Pole (i.e. the analysis in Goodall 2001; analyses
where every topic is adjoined to IP as in Contreras 1991; or analyses where
they land in the specifiers of multiple Topic Phrases, as in Rizzi 1997), since
in these analyses it would go unexplained why the relative order of multiple
topics is subject to thematic considerations.

Finally, the multiple topicalization facts also provide evidence against
an alternative analysis of the unmarked word order in Spanish based on
Alignment Constraints (McCarthy & Prince 1993).[49] In such an alternative
analysis, instead of having the markedness constraints in the Pole Hierarchy,
it would be possible to derive a hierarchy of alignment constraints sensitive
to semantic roles, as in (61).[50] Once we have these constraints, the unmarked
word order of transitive, psych and unaccusative clauses in Spanish discussed
in the previous chapter can be accounted by the ranking in (62), where STAY
immediately outranks ALIGN (THEME-L).

(61) ALIGN (AGENT-Left) » ALIGN (EXPERIENCER-Left) » ALIGN (THEME-Left) » . . .

(62) SPANISH
ALIGN (AGENT-Left) » ALIGN (EXPERIENCER-Left) » STAY » ALIGN (THEME-Left) » . . .

The logic behind this kind of analysis is that every constituent with the specified semantic role has to be aligned with the left-edge of the clause, but STAY, the constraint that penalizes syntactic displacement, can signal the cut-off point at which it is better to leave a constituent in its base position than to move it to the left edge to satisfy the corresponding alignment constraint. As can be seen in tableau (63) below, in the unmarked case VSO and OVS transitive sentences are ruled out because the *agent* subject is not left-aligned with IP.[51]

In the case of unaccusative sentences, the violation of STAY that results from aligning the *theme* subject with the left edge of the IP proves fatal, and the winning candidate is the one where the subject stays in its VP-internal position, as I leave for the reader to verify.

My proposal and the alternative Alignment proposal I have sketched out are not equivalent, though. The Alignment analysis makes a clear prediction: all else being equal, the *agent* will appear at the leftmost position in the clause. My proposal makes a different prediction: all else being equal, the *agent* will appear in the Pole specifier, which will sometimes, but not always, correspond to the leftmost position in the clause. The prediction made by the Alignment analysis is not borne out by the multiple topicalization data, where the leftmost topic is the one whose semantic role ranks lower in the thematic hierarchy. In contrast, by appealing to the notion of the Pole as a position that is sensitive to thematic information, but which is not defined with respect to the left edge of the clause, my analysis derives the correct result.

(63) TRANSITIVE CLAUSES: UNMARKED WORD ORDER.

'A girl bought the records' = (16) in §4.2.3.

INPUT: <buy (x, y), x=a girl (Ag), y=the records (Th)>

	ALIGN AGENT-L	STAY	ALIGN THEME-L
☞ a. [IP una muchacha₁ compró [VP t₁ los discos]] **SVO**		*	*
b. [IP compró [VP una muchacha los discos]] **VSO**	*!		*
c. [IP los discos₁ los compró [VP una muchacha t₁]] **OVS**	*!	*	

4.4 CONCLUSIONS

In this chapter I have shown how the proposal developed in §2 and §3 can be extended to account for perturbations of the unmarked word order that result from information structure considerations. We have seen that focus-driven subject inversion in Spanish can be accounted for with the ranking FOCUSPROMINENCE » EPP, and that the resulting analysis still predicts correctly that SVO will be attested output in cases of sentence focus, which is consistent with previous OT analyses of focalization and word order. With respect to topicalization, the central claim has been that the relevant facts can be explained by an analysis where sentence topics are fronted to the Pole specifier in order to satisfy TOPICFIRST. Alternatives where topics are fronted to a position other than the Pole are ruled out because of Economy of Structure considerations, all else being equal. In this analysis, fronted topics simultaneously satisfy the EPP by virtue of moving to the Pole specifier, and this explains why it is not necessary for the subject to move to [Spec, I] when some other argument or adjunct functions as a topic, as in XP-VSO *topic-comment* sentences. The proposed ranking of constraints for Mexican Spanish further explains why VSO and VOS clauses with an empty preverbal position are ungrammatical in this variety of Spanish. Lastly, we have seen that data from multiple topicalization provide further support for this proposal, since this data cannot be accounted for straightforwardly in analyses where topics land in a position other than the Pole, or in analyses where the unmarked word order is derived by alignment constraints.

Chapter Five.

Wh-Interrogatives and Word Order

In the previous chapter, I have discussed the word order effects that result from the interaction between the constraints that derive the unmarked word order in Spanish and those related to information structure. In this final chapter I discuss the effects on word order that result from the interaction of these two sets of constraints with the constraints that govern the behavior of *wh*-interrogatives. My central claim about the word order of *wh*-interrogatives is that fronted *wh*-operators in Spanish have the Pole as their landing site, all else being equal. Accordingly, they satisfy the EPP and make fronting of an *agent* subject or a dative *experiencer* unnecessary. However, a conflict arises when there is both a topic and a *wh*-operator in the representation, since the Pole is also the landing site of topics, as discussed in §4. I argue that the relative word order of topics and *wh*-operators that is observed in this case can be understood as the result of the interaction between the TopicFirst constraint, the constraints that penalize vacuous structure, and the constraint that derives *wh*-movement in the first place.

5.1 *WH*-INTERROGATIVES IN SPANISH[1]

In this section, I introduce the two issues that will be the subject of analysis in this final chapter, both of which are related to *wh*-movement in interrogative clauses. The first one concerns the relative word order of fronted *wh*-operators with respect to subjects that would occupy the preverbal position in the unmarked case. The second issue concerns the relative word order of fronted *wh*-operators with respect to fronted topics. The discussion of these issues in this section is essentially descriptive. I delay theoretical considerations until sections §5.2 and §5.3.

One of the most notable and amply studied characteristics of Spanish is that, in a number of dialects in this language, the preverbal position cannot be occupied by the subject when a *wh*-operator is fronted in interrogative clauses (Meyer 1972, Torrego 1984, Groos & Bok-Bennema 1986, *inter alia*). This is shown by the examples in (1–3) from Mexican Spanish.[2]

(1) a. Qué compró Juan?
   what bought Juan
   'What did Juan buy?'

  b. *Qué Juan compró?
   what Juan bought

(2) a. Cuándo compró Pedro el periódico?
   when bought Pedro the newspaper
   'When did Pedro buy the newspaper?'

  b. *Cuándo Pedro compró el periódico?
   when Pedro bought the newspaper

(3) a. Por qué compró Pedro el periódico?
   why bought Pedro the newspaper
   'Why did Pedro buy the newspaper?'

  b. ??Por qué Pedro compró el periódico?
   why Pedro bought the newspaper

However, it is also well known that not every variety of Spanish behaves in this way. Torrego (1984) noted for Peninsular Spanish that preverbal subjects are not allowed when the *wh*-operator corresponds to an argument, as shown in (4), but they are permitted otherwise, as shown in (5). It is also well known that the Caribbean varieties of Spanish allow preverbal subjects with any kind of *wh*-operator, as shown in (6).

(4) PENINSULAR SPANISH: Torrego (1984)[3]

  a. Qué querían esos dos?
   what wanted those two
   'What did those two want?'

  b. *Qué esos dos querían?
   what those two wanted

(5) a. Cuándo Juan consiguió por fin abrir la puerta ayer?
   when Juan got at end open the door yesterday
   'When did John finally get to open the door yesterday?'

   b. Por qué Juan quiere salir antes que los demás?
   why Juan wants to leave before that the others
   'Why does Juan want to leave before the others?'

(6) CARIBBEAN SPANISH (Puerto Rico): Suñer (1994)[4]

   a. Qué Ivan dijo de eso?
   what Ivan said of that
   'What did Ivan say about that?'

   b. Cuándo un implante dental es exitoso?
   when an implant dental is successful
   'When is a dental implant successful?'

In his cross-dialectal OT analysis of *wh*-questions in Spanish, Bakovic (1998) discovered that there is an intricate implicational relationship among the types of *wh*-phrases that can co-occur with preverbal subjects in any given variety of this language.[5] Given the scale in (7) (see §3.2), if preverbal subjects are allowed with a *wh*-operator with a semantic role X, then they are also allowed with *wh*-operators with every semantic role less prominent than X.

(7) Bakovic (1998: 37)
   ARGUMENT > LOCATION > MANNER > REASON

In other words, if a variety of Spanish allows a direct object operator to co-occur with a preverbal subject, then it allows every kind of *wh*-operator to do so. This corresponds to the Caribbean variety illustrated in (6). Similarly, if a variety allows for preverbal subjects to co-occur with a *manner wh*-operator, then it also allows for preverbal subjects to co-occur with *reason* operators. Crucially, there is no variety that, say, allows preverbal subjects to co-occur with *manner wh*-operators but not with *reason* operators.

Bakovic further discovered that some varieties display matrix-subordinate asymmetries in this respect. Descriptively, some varieties allow for preverbal subjects to co-occur with *wh*-operators in embedded interrogatives where this would not be allowed in matrix interrogatives. The cases where preverbal subjects co-occur with *wh*-operators in embedded interrogatives follow the same implicational relation discussed above, but there is a further implicational relationship at play here. If preverbal subjects are not allowed with *wh*-operators of type X in embedded interrogatives, then this pattern is also disallowed in matrix questions, but not vice versa. As noted by Bakovic, this means that there are varieties of Spanish where preverbal subjects in embedded interrogatives are allowed to co-occur with more kinds of *wh*-operators than in matrix interrogatives, but there is no variety in his survey where preverbal subjects in matrix interrogatives are allowed to co-occur with more kinds of *wh*-operators than in embedded interrogatives.

The variety of Mexican Spanish under consideration here is in fact a variety that displays such a matrix-subordinate asymmetry. In contrast with (3b), preverbal subjects are allowed to co-occur with a *reason* operator in embedded interrogatives, as shown in (8a).[6] However, when the *wh*-operator is a *manner* operator, there is no asymmetry. Co-occurrence of a preverbal subject and a *manner wh*-operator is disallowed altogether, as shown in (9) and (10).

(8) a. Yo quiero saber [por qué   Pedro   compró   el periódico].
         I want   know   why   Pedro   bought   the newspaper
         'I want to know why Pedro bought the newspaper.'

     b. Yo quiero saber [por qué   compró   Pedro   el periódico].
         I want   know   why   bought   Pedro   the newspaper
         'I want to know why Pedro bought the newspaper.'

(9) a. Cómo   arregló   Pedro   la tele?
         how   fixed   Pedro   the T.V.
         'How did Pedro fix the T.V.?'

     b. *Cómo Pedro arregló la tele?
         how   Pedro fixed   the T.V.

(10) a. Yo quiero   saber   [cómo   arregló   Pedro   la tele].
         I   want   to.know how   fixed   Pedro   the T.V.
         'I want to know how Pedro fixed the T.V.'

     b. *Yo quiero saber   [cómo   Pedro   arregló   la tele].
         I   want   to.know how   Pedro   fixed   the T.V.

The relevance of the contrasts in (8–10) for our analysis is straightforward. In an analysis where fronted *wh*-operators occupy the Pole (see §2.3.1) the pattern observed in Mexican Spanish in (1–3), (9) and (10) is unsurprising. Since the *wh*-operator occupies the Pole position, it also satisfies the EPP and fronting of the subject becomes unnecessary. However, the presence of both a preverbal subject and a *reason wh*-operator in (8a) now requires an explanation.

The second issue that I address in this chapter concerns the relative word order of fronted topics and *wh*-operators. In Spanish, topics typically precede *wh*-operators, as is well known (see Meyer 1972, Fontana 1994, Zubizarreta 1998, *inter alia*). This is the case both when the topic corresponds to a subject and to a non-subject, as shown in (11).[7] The reverse order is not possible, as shown in (12) for a DO topic.

(11) a. Juan cuándo llegó?   **Top -** *Wh*
          Juan when   arrived
          'When did Juan arrive?'

      b. Los discos quién los   compró?
          the records who ACC-CL *bought*
          'Who bought the records?'

(12) *Quién   los discos   los   compró?   *Wh* **- Top**
         who   the records ACC-CL *bought*

Within an analysis of the left periphery along the lines of Rizzi (1997), this fact would follow if in Spanish all Topic Phrases dominate the phrase whose specifer hosts the *wh*-operator (a Focus Phrase in Rizzi 1997). This would be in contrast with what is observed in Italian, where there are Topic Phrases both above and below the Focus Phrase.

(13) a. ITALIAN   [. . . . [$_{TopP*}$ [$_{FocP}$ [$_{TopP*}$ [. . . .   ]]]]]   (Rizzi 1997)

      b. SPANISH: [. . . . [$_{TopP*}$ [$_{FocP}$ [. . . .]]]]

However, the Mexican Spanish pattern cannot be reduced to (13b), since when the *reason* operator in embedded interrogatives is involved, we find exactly the order [$_{FocP}$ [$_{TopP}$ [. . .]]], which is not permitted under (13b). This is shown in the examples in (14). Notice that this is the reverse order from the one observed in (11).

(14) a. Yo quiero saber   [por qué ayer   llegó   tarde Juan].   *Wh* **- Top**
          I want to know   why   yesterday arrived late Juan
          'I want to know why Juan arrived late yesterday.'

      b. Yo quiero saber [por qué al   presidente le   toman   esa clase de fotos.]
          I want to know why   to-the president DAT-CL *they.take that kind of photos*
          'I want to know why they take that kind of pictures of the president.'

This characteristic is not specific to Mexican Spanish. As noted in Suñer (1994), in Caribbean Spanish, where preverbal subjects can co-occur with all kinds of *wh*-operators, the position that corresponds to the subject can be alternatively occupied by a topic. This is shown in (15) (glosses are my own).

(15) PUERTO RICAN SPANISH (Suñer 1994)

    a. A qué   ahora/estos días   se   dedica?
       to what now/these   days   CL devote
       'To what does she devote herself now/these days?'

    b. Qué al   Rafo le   han   hecho?
       what to-the Rafo DAT-CL *they.have done*
       'What have they done to Rafo?'

Furthermore, when the *reason wh*-operator is involved in Mexican Spanish embedded interrogatives, the order [$_{\text{TopP}}$ [$_{\text{FocP}}$ [. . . .]]] is disallowed, again contrary to (13b). This shown in (16), to be compared with (14).

(16) a. ??Yo quiero saber   [ayer   por qué llegó   tarde Juan].   **Top - *Wh***
       I want to.know yesterday why   arrived late Juan

    b. *Yo quiero saber   [al   presidente por qué le   toman
       I want to.know to-the president why   DAT-CL they.take
       esa   clase de fotos].
       that kind of photos

In an exploded CP analysis like (13), the data in (14) and (16) cannot be accounted for straightforwardly. Such an analysis would need to stipulate a template of C-related projections ([$_{\text{FocP}}$ [$_{\text{TopP}}$ [. . . .]]]) for embedded interrogatives with reason operators, and a different template altogether ([$_{\text{TopP}}$ [$_{\text{FocP}}$ [. . . .]]]) for all other cases. Furthermore, even if this were a possibility such an analysis would still need to provide an explanation of why this asymmetry exists in the first place.[8]

    My analysis of topicalization (§4.3) does not involve Topic Phrases, and so it avoids these problems altogether. However, the data in (11–12), (14) and (15) still requires an explanation. Clearly, simply stipulating that TOPICFIRST is undominated in Mexican Spanish, as assumed in §4.3, will not suffice. This is because the wrong result would be derived for (14) where the *wh*-operator precedes the topic.

    In the remainder of this chapter, I provide an analysis of the facts from Mexican Spanish. I argue that the sensitivity of [Spec, I] to the semantic role of the constituent that occupies it is crucial for understanding the matrix-subordinate asymmetry discussed above, which in turn provides further evidence for the notion of the Pole. Before developing the analysis, it is necessary to determine what exactly triggers the fronting of interrogative *wh*-operators in Spanish.

5.2 DERIVING *WH*-MOVEMENT

For the purpose of analyzing the facts just discussed, I essentially adopt the analyses of *wh*-movement in interrogatives of Cheng (1991) and Ackema & Neeleman (1998a, 1998b). Cheng (1991) proposes that *wh*-fronting in interrogatives in languages like English takes place to type (i.e. to mark) the clause as a *wh*-interogative. Other languages, like Chinese and Japanese, use *wh*-particles for this same purpose. This is expressed in the Clausal Typing Hypothesis in (17).

(17) Clausal Typing Hypothesis   (Cheng 1991: 30)
      Every clause needs to be typed. In the case of typing a *wh*-question, either a *wh*-particle in C^0 is used or else fronting of a *wh*-word to the Spec of C^0 is used, thereby typing the clause through Spec-head agreement.

Cheng thus develops a transformational analysis where the scope and absorption properties of *wh*-operators are universally satisfied at LF. The difference between languages that show overt *wh*-movement *vs.* those that do not ultimately corresponds to a difference between languages that do not have true interrogative complementizers (and which accordingly resort to *wh*-movement to signal the clause as an interrogative) and those that do.[9]

  Cheng's analysis explains why in clauses with multiple *wh*-phrases like (18), one of the *wh*-phrases stays in-situ. In order to satisfy the typing requirement, it is only necessary to move one of them to Spec-CP. Any other movements are ruled out by Economy of Movement.[10]

(18) $[_{CP}$ Who$_i$ $[_{IP}$ t$_i$ bought what]]?   (Cheng 1991: 30)

  Ackema & Neeleman (1998a, 1998b) develop an OT analysis of *wh*-interrogatives closely related to Cheng's. They propose that in languages like English, interrogative operators are fronted to satisfy the Q-MARKING constraint in (19). This implies that in these languages Q-MARKING outranks STAY.

(19) Q-MARKING: Ackema & Neeleman (1998b: 16; 1998a:447)
A question must be overtly Q-Marked.
In a question, assign a [+Q] feature to the constituent corresponding to the proposition.

In interrogative clauses, Q-MARKING requires that the proposition that is immediately subjacent to CP (VP in Ackema & Neeleman 1998a) be assigned the feature [Q] by C through head-complement agreement. There are two ways in which this can occur. The first one is when C inherently bears the [Q] feature (*whether, if*), as in (20). In this respect Ackema & Neeleman's analysis departs from Cheng's.

(20) John wonders [if   [$_{VP}$ you have seen the soccer match]].
                       [Q] ⇨ [Q]

The second way is when the [Q] feature is provided by a *wh*-phrase. In this case, the head of the phrase above VP first acquires the [Q] feature through Spec-head agreement with the *wh*-phrase. After this, the VP acquires the [Q] feature through head-complement agreement, as illustrated in (21).

(21) [What   have   [$_{VP}$ you seen]]?
         [Q] ⇨ [Q] ⇨ [Q]

This proposal explains why adjunction of the *wh*-operator to IP (or VP in Ackema & Neeleman's terms) in English, as in (22), is not an option, since the appropriate Spec-head configuration is not established.

(22) *[$_{VP}$What   [$_{VP}$ you have seen]]?

As in Cheng (1991), a central characteristic of this proposal is that the movement of *wh*-operators (in some languages) is independent from scope considerations. However, in contrast with Cheng's proposal, in Ackema & Neeleman's analysis there are languages where overt *wh*-fronting is related to scope, namely, the Slavic languages that show multiple *wh*-fronting. They propose that besides Q-MARKING there is a constraint Q-SCOPE that requires *wh*-operators to c-command the constituent corresponding to the proposition. In languages like English, STAY outranks Q-SCOPE. As a result, once one *wh*-operator has been fronted to satisfy Q-MARKING in cases of multiple-*wh,* any other *wh*-operators remain in-situ. In contrast, the Slavic languages that show multiple *wh*-movement are characterized by a ranking where Q-Scope outranks Stay. With this ranking, the optimal pattern is the one where all *wh*-operators move to a scope position in the left periphery in the surface representation.[11] [12]

There are two minor technical issues that are somewhat problematic for the Q-Marking analysis, though. The first concerns subject *wh*-operators. Following standard OT assumptions, in this case the subject does not move beyond the position where it is assigned Case ([Spec, V]) in Ackema & Neeleman's proposal), as in (23). But now the VP that corresponds to the proposition is not assigned the [Q] feature in a head-complement configuration.

(23) [$_{VP}$ Who ate the bagels]?

To solve this problem Ackema & Neeleman (1998a) propose that feature percolation is an alternative way of Q-marking. The subject *wh*-operator in (23) provides the verb with the [Q] feature, which then percolates to the VP, satisfying Q-Marking. Although this is not a serious problem, ideally the effects in (20), (21) and (23) should all be derived by the same mechanism.[13]

The second problem is somewhat more delicate. Ackema & Neeleman (1998a) note that their analysis predicts that (24) should be a possible output in English (with a non-echo reading), contrary to fact. This is because the interrogative complementizer is all that is needed to Q-mark the VP, so the *wh*-operator does not need to be fronted.

(24) *Mary wonders [if John loves who].

To solve this problem, Ackema & Neeleman (1998a) propose the redefinition of Q-Marking in (25). This redefinition implies that every *wh*-operator in a clause must "discharge" (i.e. transfer) its own [Q] feature on the VP. For this to happen, every *wh*-operator must be in the appropriate Spec-Head configuration in the output. This condition is not met in (24), where *who* stays in-situ. Its [Q] feature is not "discharged" on the VP and so Q-Marking is violated.

(25) Q-Marking
      Mark the constituent corresponding to the proposition for every [Q] feature that it has present.

The new definition still rules out multiple *wh*-fronting in English. This is because only one *wh*-operator can be in the appropriate Spec-Head configuration to transfer its [Q] feature to the head that will ultimately Q-mark the VP.[14] Fronting of more than one *wh*-operator thus results in extra violations of STAY that cannot improve the structure with respect to Q-MARKING.[15] However, it seems to me that this new definition dilutes too much the distinction between *wh*-movement driven by clause typing and *wh*-movement driven by scope considerations. In both cases, every *wh*-operator must be fronted, but in languages where *wh*-movement is driven by clause typing, multiple *wh*-fronting happens to be ruled by the fact that only one *wh*-operator can be in the appropriate Spec-Head configuration that will allow it to transfer its [Q] feature to the VP.

To tackle these issues I propose that the effects of Q-MARKING can be reduced to a condition that requires the head of the highest phrase in the Extended Projection to bear the feature [Q] (without the need to Q-Mark VP or any other maximal projection). This is closer in spirit to Cheng's original proposal and avoids the two complications of the Q-MARKING analysis. I formalize this condition as in (26).

(26)   INTERROGATIVE CLAUSE CONDITION (ICC)
     A clausal Extended Projection is interrogative iff the head of the highest phrase
     in the Extended Projection bears the feature [Q].

I follow Ackema & Neeleman in assuming that this constraint can be satisfied in two different ways. The first is when the head of the highest phrase in the extended projection inherently bears the [Q] feature (i.e. by *whether* or *if* in English).[16] The second is by Spec-head agreement between a *wh*-operator and the highest head in the extended projection.[17] However, like Cheng (1991) and Rizzi (1996), and *contra* Ackema & Neeleman (1998a), I assume that the head involved can be either overt or null.[18] Specifically, I follow Cheng (1991) in assuming that in English subordinate interrogatives the appropriate Spec-head configuration is established between the fronted *wh*-operator and a null functional head, as in (27).

(27) I don't know [what   Ø   [$_{IP}$ you should wear to the party]].
                    [Q] ⇨ [Q]

The analysis of *wh*-interrogatives that results from the ICC captures Grimshaw's (1997, 2000) observations about Economy of Projection and is compatible with the analysis of *wh*-movement in English in Grimshaw (1997). Following Grimshaw (1997), when the *wh*-operator needs to land in

Spec-IP for independent considerations (i.e. Case for a subject *wh*-operator), it does not need to move any further (see (28a) below). In terms of my proposal this is because the ICC can be met without the need to project another phrase above IP. I^0 acquires the [Q] feature through Spec-head agreement with the *wh*-operator in Spec-IP and the ICC is satisfied. When Spec-IP is already occupied, CP is projected to host the *wh*-operator in its specifier, as in (28b). I-to-C movement in English follows from the high ranking of OBLIGATORY-HEAD (Ob-HD). The necessary Spec-head configuration is now established between the *wh*-operator and the inflectional head in C^0. In this way, (28a) and (28b) are both signaled as interrogatives by the same property (the [Q] feature in the highest head of the extended projection), in contrast with the Q-MARKING analysis.

(28) a. [$_{IP}$ Who ate the bagels]?

   b. [$_{CP}$ What did [$_{IP}$ John eat *t*]]?

Notice that another consequence of this analysis is that selection is no longer a problem (*cf.* Grimshaw 1997). A verb like *wonder* simply selects a [Q] sentential complement, as defined by the ICC. As long as the head of the highest phrase in the extended projection bears the feature [Q], it does not matter if the sentential complement is CP or IP. In both cases the result is head-to-head selection, as illustrated in (29).

(29) a. I wonder [$_{CP}$ which coat [$_{C}$ Ø] [$_{IP}$ you should wear]].
                              [Q]

   b. I wonder [$_{CP}$ if [$_{IP}$ he saw her]].
                        [Q]

   c. I wonder [$_{IP}$ who can bring the bagels]].
                        [Q]

Now, to address the problem presented by (24) (**Mary wonders if John loves who*), we need to consider how the ICC relates to the input. I assume that the interrogative value of a clause is specified in the input by an abstract morpheme [Q] (Baker 1970). The input of a *wh*-question like (30a) thus corresponds to (30b).

(30) a. What did you buy?

   b. < [Q] buy (x, y), x=[2nd.Sing], y= [+wh] >

It is important not to confuse the abstract morpheme [Q] with the operator *Q* of Legendre *et. al.* (1998), who also build on Baker's (1970) analysis. In my proposal [Q] is just an abstract morpheme that specifies an interrogative value, as in Baker's original analysis (it can be thought of as the shorthand notation of [+interrogative]). It does not represent a given scope, and I have only included it as the leftmost element of the input for illustration.[19] Under these assumptions, the ICC is a well-formedness condition on expressing the [Q] specification of the input in the syntactic representation.

Consider now the following. In an OT analysis, it is possible to assume that complementizers are never part of the input, as in Grimshaw (1997). This is a reasonable assumption, since the input is nothing more than a predicate-argument structure plus tense/aspect specifications, plus scope specifications for certain kinds of elements.[20] Accordingly, I assume that the presence of a complementizer in the output representation violates FULL-INTERPRETATION. Now we can analyze English (and Spanish) as languages characterized by the ranking ICC » FULL-INTERPRETATION » STAY. As shown in the tableau in (32) below, this ranking explains why (24) (repeated here as (31)) is ungrammatical. For the sake of exposition, I only include in the tableau the part of the input that corresponds to the embedded clause.

(31)   *Mary wonders [if John loves who].

With the ranking FULL-INTERPRETATION » STAY, the optimal candidate is the one that moves the *wh*-phrase to Spec-CP (candidate 32a), since this is less costly than to insert a complementizer in the representation. Candidate (32b), which does insert a complementizer, is ruled out by its fatal violation of FULL-INTERPRETATION. Trivially, candidate (32c) loses because of its violation of ICC, since in this case there is neither a *wh*-phrase nor a [Q] complementizer to signal the clause as an interrogative.

However, a crucial characteristic of my proposal is that in the absence of a *wh*-phrase, the ranking ICC » FULL-INTERPRETATION does force the

(32)   INPUT: < [Q](love (x, y)), x=John, y= [wh] >

	ICC	FULL-INTER	STAY
☞a. Mary wonders [who$_i$ John loves t_i].			*
b. Mary wonders [if John loves who].		*!	
c. Mary wonders [John loves who].	*!		

(33)   INPUT: < [Q](love (x, y)), x=John, y= Catherine >

	ICC	FULL-INTER
☞ a. Mary wonders [if John loves Catherine].		*
b. Mary wonders [John loves Catherine].	*!	

insertion of an interrogative C^0, because otherwise the ICC would be violated.[21] This is shown in tableau (33).

Having characterized my assumptions about the conditions responsible for the fronting of *wh*-operators in languages like English and Spanish, I now proceed to provide an account of the word order facts observed in *wh*-interrogatives in Mexican Spanish.

5.3 MATRIX INTERROGATIVES IN MEXICAN SPANISH

5.3.1 Basics of the analysis

Consider again matrix *wh*-interrogatives in Mexican Spanish. As discussed in §5.1, preverbal subjects cannot co-occur with *wh*-operators of any kind in this environment. The relevant examples are repeated in (34).

(34) a. Por qué compró   Pedro el   periódico?
          why   bought   Pedro the newspaper
          'Why did Pedro buy the newspaper?'

      b. ??Por qué Pedro   compró el   periódico?
          why   Pedro   bought   the newspaper

Following the analysis developed in chapters §2–4 and the characterization of *wh*-interrogatives in §5.2, my proposal is that all kinds of *wh*-operators in Spanish move into the Pole to satisfy the ICC. The structure of (34a) under this analysis is presented in (35) below. Here the fronted *wh*-operator is in the appropriate Spec-Head configuration. Accordingly, the verb in I^0 acquires the [Q] feature and the ICC is satisfied, since the highest head in the extended projection is specified for the feature [Q].

We have already seen in §2.3.1 that evidence from ellipsis supports an analysis where *wh*-operators occupy the Pole position, since they have the same distribution as preverbal subjects and fronted topics in elliptical constructions. The relevant paradigm is illustrated in (36).

(35)

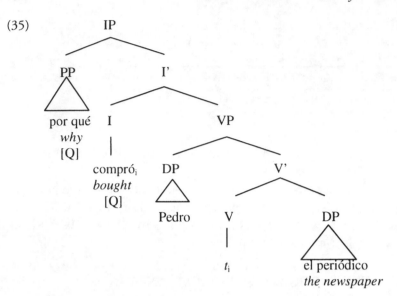

(36) a. Luis reprobó a   Ernesto, pero [Juan no___].
       Luis failed   ACC *Ernesto   but   Juan not*
       'Luis failed Ernesto, but Juan didn't.'

   b. En ese café   cobran   carísimo,   pero [en el otro no___].
      in that coffee.shop they.charge very.expensive but   in the other not
      'In that coffee shop they charge a lot, but in the other one they don't.'

   c. En ese café   cobran   carísimo,   pero [en dónde no ___]?
      in that coffee.shop they-charge very.expensive but   in where not
      'In that coffee shop they charge a lot, but where don't they?'
      (=That coffee shop is very expensive, but (then again) which one isn't?)

A further argument can be found in EPP effects. If a fronted *wh*-operator
occupies the Pole, it automatically satisfies the EPP. Accordingly, *wh*-move-
ment should be able to "rescue" constructions that would otherwise be ruled
out because of a violation of the EPP. This is indeed what is observed. I
argued in §3 that VSO clauses in Mexican Spanish are not tolerated because
of their violation of the EPP. However, *Wh*-VSO is clearly an acceptable
word order, as shown by the contrast in (37).

(37) MEXICAN SPANISH
     a. ??Compró Juan el periódico.   V S O
        bought   Juan the newspaper
        'Juan bought the newspaper.'

b. Por qué compró Pedro el periódico?   *Wh-*V S O
   why   bought   Pedro the newspaper
   'Why did Pedro buy the newspaper?'

5.3.2 Against inversion analyses

At this point it is worth comparing the analysis in (35) with alternative analyses that derive the corresponding surface word order by means of a movement operation akin to Subject-Aux inversion in English, a proposal first developed in Torrego (1984). Translating Torrego's proposal into contemporary terms,[22] in example (34a) the subject does occupy the preverbal "subject" position, but movement of the verb from I to C derives the observed surface order, as illustrated in (38).

(38) [$_{CP}$ Por qué compró$_j$ [$_{IP}$ Juan$_i$ t$_j$ [$_{VP}$ t$_i$ t$_j$ el periódico]]]?
         why   bought   Juan   the newspaper

From this perspective, (34b) and similar examples (examples (1b) and (1c) in §5.1) are ungrammatical because the verb has failed to move from I to C. This analysis is adopted in its essentials in the OT analysis of Spanish *wh*-interrogatives in Bakovic (1998), which I now discuss in more detail, since it is directly relevant to our analysis. Recall Bakovic's observation that the possibility of having a preverbal subject co-occur with a *wh*-operator obeys an implicational relationship along the scale in (7), repeated here as (39):

(39) ARGUMENT > LOCATION > MANNER > REASON

As discussed in §5.1, if a variety of Spanish allows a direct object operator to co-occur with a preverbal subject, then it allows every kind of *wh*-operator to do so. If a variety allows for preverbal subjects to co-occur with a *manner wh*-operator, then it also allows for preverbal subjects to co-occur with *reason* operators. But there is no variety that, say, allows for preverbal subjects to co-occur with *manner wh*-operators but not with *reason* operators.

    Consider now matrix interrogatives in one of the dialects in Bakovic's survey, Dialect-F. In this dialect, *location wh*-operators can co-occur with a preverbal subject, but argument *wh*-operators cannot. This is shown in (40).

(40) SPANISH DIALECT-F (Bakovic 1998)
      a. Dónde Miguel se fue?
         where   Miguel went.3s
         'Where did Miguel go?'

b. *Qué Miguel se comió?
   what Miguel ate.3s

c. Qué se comió Miguel?
   what ate.3s   Miguel
   'What did Miguel eat?'

In Bakovic's Extended Projection analysis (see §2.1.1), as in Torrego's original analysis, the subject in the examples (40) is found in the position where it is
base generated, namely [Spec, V].[23] In the inversion case (40c), a second VP is
projected to host the operator in its specifier. Since Bakovic assumes (*contra*
Grimshaw 1997) that GEN does not generate projections with a null head, the
verb obligatorily moves into the head position of the second VP. The resulting
structure is illustrated in (41a). In contrast, Bakovic suggests that when there is
no inversion, as in (40a), the fronted *wh*-operator is adjoined to the VP that
immediately dominates the subject, as in (41b). Although Bakovic's analysis is
different from Torrego's on this point, what is common to both analyses is that
the verb occupies a different position in *wh*-interrogatives with inversion than it
does in declaratives, just like the highest inflectional head does in English.

(41) a. $[_{VP2}$ qué$_i$ se comió$_k$ $[_{VP1}$ Miguel $t_k t_i$]].
          what   ate.3s   Miguel

      b. $[_{VP1}$ dónde$_i$ $[_{VP1}$ Miguel se fue t_i]].
          where   Miguel went.3s

To account for the contrast in (40), Bakovic proposes that the OP-SPEC constraint of Grimshaw (1997), which requires operators to occupy a specifier
position, be decomposed into the markedness hierarchy in (43). In this hierarchy each operator type has a separate OP-SPEC constraint referring to it.
Each of these constraints states that the corresponding operator must be in a
specifier position:

(42) OPERATOR IN SPECIFICER (OP-SPEC)
      Syntactic Operators must be in specifier position.   (Grimshaw 1997)

(43) ArgumentOP-SPEC » LocationOP-SPEC » MannerOP-SPEC » ReasonOP-SPEC.

The hierachical relation in (43) states that even though all kinds of operators must be in a specifier position, it is more important for operators that
correspond to arguments to occupy such a position than for all other kinds

of operators. Descending in the hierarchy, it is more important for *location* operators to be in a specifier position than for *manner* and *reason* operators to do so, and so on.

Given Bakovic's assumptions about sentential structure in Spanish (i.e., that an SVO clause, for instance, corresponds to the VP in which every argument is generated) the presence of a *wh*-phrase requires that a second VP be projected in order to satisfy the constraints in (43), all else being equal. However, because of Bakovic's assumption that GEN does not generate projections with a null head, a conflict now emerges between the constraints in (43) and STAY. This is because after projecting a second VP (VP2 in (41a)) the verb must move into the head position of VP2. This results in a violation of STAY that is not incurred when there is only one VP (as in (41b)). Under these assumptions, embedding STAY along the hierarchy in (43) will determine when and whether inversion is observed.

Bakovic's analysis of Dialect-F in (40) then runs as follows. This is a dialect that displays the ranking ArgumentOp-SPEC » STAY » LocativeOp-SPEC. When the *wh*-operator is an argument as in (41a), the high-ranking ArgumentOp-SPEC forces the projection of a second VP to host the operator in its specifier. The verb moves into the head position of the second VP and the inversion candidate (44a) in the tableau below wins. Candidate (44b), which instead adjoins the operator to VP, loses because of its violation of ArgumentOp-SPEC.

But when a *locative* operator is involved (as in (41b)), then the adjunction candidate wins, since the extra violation of STAY that would result from projecting a second VP and having the verb move into its head position proves fatal, as shown in tableau (45).

(44) 'What did Miguel eat?'

	ARGUMENT-OP-SPEC	STAY	LOCATION-OP-SPEC
☞a. [$_{VP}$ qué$_i$ se comió$_k$ [$_{VP}$ Miguel t_k t_i]].		**	
b. [$_{VP}$ qué$_i$ [$_{VP}$ Miguel se comió t_i]].	*!	*	

(45) 'Where did Miguel go?'

	ARGUMENT-SPEC	STAY	LOCATION-SPEC
a. [$_{VP}$ dónde$_i$ se fue$_k$ [$_{VP}$ Miguel t_k t_i]].		**!	
☞ b. [$_{VP}$ dónde$_i$ [$_{VP}$ Miguel se fue t_i]].		*	*

In dialects of Spanish that show obligatory inversion in matrix clauses for all kinds of operators, like Mexican Spanish, STAY is ranked below all of the hierarchy in (43).[24] In this way, a notable characteristic of Bakovic's analysis when compared with previous analyses of these facts is that it does not need to stipulate for each different dialect of Spanish when preverbal subjects are allowed to co-occur with a fronted *wh*-operator.[25]

However, a considerable number of works, most notably Goodall (1991a, 1991b), Suñer (1994) and Ordóñez (1997), have argued that the inversion analysis of Spanish *wh*-interrogatives is not adequate. These analyses have provided extensive evidence that the verb is in the same position in both declaratives and *wh*-interrogatives, and that this position corresponds to I^0. For the sake of exposition, here I reproduce only some of the arguments provided in these works.

Goodall (1991a) and Suñer (1994) note that Spanish has a class of adverbs like *apenas* 'barely,' *regularmente* 'usually,' etc. (highlighted in boldface below), which behave exactly like their English counterparts in that they can precede the highest inflected element when there is no *wh*-movement, as in (46). The crucial assumption necessary here is that these adverbs are adjoined to the I' level.

(46) a. [$_{IP}$ John [$_{I'}$ **barely** [$_{I'}$ could see the screen from that seat]]].

   b. [$_{IP}$ Juan [$_{I'}$ **apenas** [$_{I'}$ veía la pantalla desde ese asiento]]].
      Juan   barely   saw the screen   from that seat
      'Juan could barely see the screen from that seat.'   (Goodall 1991a)

These works note that in English, where I-to-C movement is attested, *wh*-fronting modifies the relative order of the adverb with respect to the highest inflected element. This can be seen in (47), where the adverb now appears after both the subject and the modal. But as noted by these works, in Spanish *wh*-fronting does not modify the relative order of the adverbial with respect to the inflected verb, as shown in (48). This shows that the verb is in the same position in declaratives and interrogatives.[26]

(47) a. From which seat could John **barely** see the screen?

   b. *From which seat **barely** could John see the screen?

(48) Desde cuál   asiento **apenas** veía   Juan la pantalla?
     from   which seat   barely   saw   Juan the screen
     'From which seat could Juan barely see the screen?'   (Goodall 1991a)

Suñer (1994) further notes that it is unlikely that this is the result of adverbs like *apenas* 'barely,' being head-adjoined to the verb, since the same pattern is observed in sequences with more than one adverb and/or with the sentential negation *no*. This is shown in (49), from Suñer (1994: 346).

(49) A quién ya casi no le escribes tú cartas?
    to whom already almost not DAT-CL *write you letters*
    'To whom do you write letters hardly at all anymore?'

    Suñer further points out that, contrary to what inversion analyses assume, the post-verbal position of subjects in *wh*-interrogatives in Spanish does not provide evidence that the verb has moved beyond the position it occupies in declaratives. This is most clearly seen in the fact that in the varieties that allow *wh*-operators and preverbal subjects to co-occur, the position occupied by the subject can alternatively be occupied by a topic (see §5.1). As shown in (50), in this case the subject indeed occupies a post-verbal position. However, it is clear that the verb has not moved into the head position of the phrase that hosts the *wh*-operator in its specifier, (C^0), because the verb is to the immediate right of the topic and not to the immediate right of the *wh*-operator.

(50) Suñer (1994: 351)[27]
    Por qué a Paco ya no lo aguanta nadie?
    why ACC *Paco already not* ACC-CL *can.stand no-one*
    'Why can't anybody stand Paco anymore?'

    Lastly, my own data from ellipsis (example (36c), repeated here as (51)) presents a further argument against the inversion analysis. Concretely, the fact that the presence of a polarity head to the right of the fronted *wh*-operator is required, and, more importantly, that the presence of the verb is not tolerated in Spanish elliptical constructions (see §2.1.3) is hard to reconcile with the inversion analysis, where the central claim is that the verb moves into the head position of the phrase that hosts the *wh*-operator in its specifier.[28]

(51) En ese café cobran carísimo, pero [en dónde no ___]?
    in that coffee.shop they-charge very.expensive but in where not
    'In that coffee shop they charge a lot, but where don't they?'
    (=That coffee shop is very expensive, but (then again) which one isn't?)

    Summing up, the evidence presented above points to the conclusion that the verb occupies the same position in Spanish *wh*-interrogatives that it

does in declaratives, which disconfirms an inversion analysis of *wh*-inter-
rogatives. My analysis in (35) is consistent with this conclusion, since the
verb is located in I^0 and the *wh*-operator in [Spec, I] (i.e. the Pole). Crucially, since the Pole is the landing site of *wh*-operators and since the Pole
is sensitive to the semantic role of the constituent that occupies it, the
facts discovered by Bakovic can now be accounted for by the markedness
constraints in the Pole hierarchy instead. This is a welcome result, since
the constraints in the Pole hierarchy also account for unmarked word
order and multiple topicalization. Analyzing the word order facts in
wh-interrogatives with these constraints thus provides a unified account
of these three phenomena.[29]

5.3.3   *Interrogative* wh-*operators in the Pole*

Consider now how the interaction between the Interrogative Clause
Condition (ICC) and the constraints developed in Chapters Three and
Four accounts for the word order facts observed in matrix *wh*-interrogatives
in Mexican Spanish. Recall that in this variety, pre-verbal subjects are not
tolerated in this context with any kind of *wh*-operators.

(52) a. Por qué compró Pedro   el   periódico?
        why   *bought*   *Pedro*   *the*   *newspaper*
        'Why did Pedro buy the newspaper?'

   b. ??Por qué   Pedro   compró   el periódico?
        why   *Pedro*   *bought*   *the newspaper*

Since a *reason* operator in Mexican Spanish can move into the Pole to satisfy
the ICC (see (35)), this indicates that ICC outranks *Pole/Reason. As shown
in tableau (53), the candidate that avoids a violation of *Pole/Reason by leaving the *wh*-phrase in-situ loses because of its violation of the ICC, since the
clause's interrogative specification in the input is not signaled in the output
representation.

(53) 'Why did Pedro buy the newspaper?'

Input: <[Q] buy (x, y; z), x=Pedro (Ag), y=the newspaper (Th); z= [wh] (Reason)>

	ICC	*Pole/ Reason
☞ a. [IP por qué compró Pedro el periódico].		*
b. [IP Pedro compró el periódico por qué].	*!	

(54) 'Why did Pedro buy the newspaper?'

INPUT: <[Q] buy (x, y; z), x=Pedro (Ag), y=the newspaper (Th); z= [wh] (Reason)>

	ICC	*VAC XP	*ADJ	*Pole/ Reason
☞ a. [IP por qué compró [VP Pedro el periódico]].				*
b. [IP por qué [IP Pedro compró [VP el periódico]]].	*!		*	
c. [XP por qué [ø][IP Pedro compró [VP el periódico]]].		*!		

In turn, the contrast between (52a) and (52b) is explained by Economy of Structure. Moving the subject into the Pole *and* also fronting the *wh*-operator requires projecting extra structure. In order to arrive at (52b), where the subject occupies the Pole position, there are two different possibilities. In one, the *wh*-operator is left-adjoined to IP; this violates *ADJUNCTION and also the ICC, because the *wh*-operator is not in a Spec-Head configuration with the highest head of the extended projection. In the other, an extra (vacuous) XP is projected in order to host the operator in its specifier. This satisfies the ICC but violates *VACUOUS-XP. Both alternatives are suboptimal when compared with the candidate where the *wh*-operator in the Pole simultaneously satisfies the ICC and the EPP without projecting any extra structure. The analysis is presented in tableau (54) above. Recall that the evidence from topicalization in §4.3 already determined that *VACUOUS-XP and *ADJUNCTION outrank *Pole/Reason. We cannot yet determine the ranking of ICC with respect to the constraints that penalize vacuous structure, since any ranking of these three constraints will give the right result in this case. Accordingly, for the sake of exposition, ICC is kept separate from these constraints in the tableau.

The analysis gives the same result for *wh*-operators with other semantic roles, since *Pole/Reason is the highest ranked of the constraints in the Pole Hierarchy. In all these cases the most harmonious candidate is the one where the *wh*-operator occupies the Pole, satisfying the ICC (and the EPP) and avoiding any violations of *VACUOUS-XP and *ADJUNCTION.

Consider now the relative word order of *wh*-operators and fronted topics. As discussed in §5.1, topics invariably precede *wh*-operators in Mexican Spanish matrix clauses. Examples are presented in (55).

(55) a. Pedro por qué se fue?
   Pedro why   CL *leave*
   'Why did Pedro leave?'

b. ??Por qué   Pedro   se   fue?
   why   *Pedro*   CL   *leave*

c. Los discos quién los   compró?
   the records who   ACC-CL   *bought*
   'Who bought the records?'

d. *Quién   los discos los   compró?
   who   *the records* ACC-CL   *bought*

The analysis developed so far, where fronting of topics is triggered by TOPIC-FIRST and fronting of *wh*-operators is triggered by the ICC, derives these word order effects without the need for any extra machinery. This is shown for (55c-d) in tableau (56) below: recall from §4.3 that we had already determined that TOPICFIRST outranks *ADJUNCTION.

The optimal candidate (56a) satisfies ICC by placing the *wh*-operator in the Pole position, and it satisfies TOPICFIRST by adjoining the topic to IP. All other candidates are less harmonious. Candidate (56b) satisfies TOPIC-FIRST by placing the topic in the Pole, and leaves the *wh*-XP in-situ, thus avoiding any violations of *VACUOUS-XP and *ADJUNCTION. However, the clause is not marked as an interrogative in this case, in discrepancy with the input, and so ICC is fatally violated.[30] Candidate (56c) instead satisfies ICC by having the *wh*-operator in the Pole and avoids any violations of *VACU-OUS-XP and *ADJUNCTION by leaving the topic in its base position, but now the violation of TOPICFIRST is fatal. Consider candidates (56d) and (56e), where the *wh*-operator precedes the topic. Candidate (56d) achieves this by placing the topic in the Pole and adjoining the *wh*-phrase to IP. This violates both ICC, since the highest head of the extended projection is not in a

(56) 'Who bought the [records]$_{TOP}$?'

INPUT: <[Q] buy (x, y), x=[wh] (Ag), y=the records (Th), y= *topic* >

	ICC	*VAC XP	TOPIC FIRST	*ADJ
☞ a. [$_{IP}$ Los discos [$_{IP}$ quién los compró [$_{VP}$]]].				*
b. [$_{IP}$ Los discos los compró [$_{VP}$ quién]].	*!			
c. [$_{IP}$ quién compró [$_{VP}$ los discos]].			*!*	
d. [$_{IP}$ quién [$_{IP}$ los discos los compró [$_{VP}$]]].	*!		*	*
e. [$_{XP}$ quién [ø][$_{IP}$ los discos los compró [$_{VP}$]]].		*!	*	
f. [$_{XP}$ Los discos [ø] [$_{IP}$ quién los compró [$_{VP}$]]].	*!	*		

Spec-Head configuration with the *wh*-phrase, and also TOPICFIRST, since the *wh*-phrase c-commands the topic. Candidate (56e) is similar, but it satisfies ICC by projecting a vacuous XP and placing the *wh*-phrase in its specifier. However, TOPICFIRST is still violated and a violation of *VACUOUS-XP is also incurred. Lastly, candidate (56f) shows the attested word order, but in contrast to the winning candidate (56a) it does so by projecting a vacuous XP to host the topic in its specifier. The resulting representation violates *VACUOUS-XP, but also ICC, since the highest head of the extended projection (X^0) is not in a Spec-Head configuration with the *wh*-phrase, and so this candidate loses to (56a).

Notice that the relevant word order effects are derived without resorting to a constraint that specifies the position of fronted *wh*-operators in terms of linear order or Left-Alignment. Instead, the conditions under which ICC is satisfied play a crucial role in determining the surface word order. This will be crucial in the analysis of subordinate interrogatives. Further observe that (56) also provides a ranking argument for ICC » *ADJUNCTION. Under the reverse ranking candidate (56b) would emerge as the winner, since it would be better not to signal the clause as an interrogative than to have a structure that resorts to adjunction, such as (56d). However, (56) still does not allow us to determine the relative ranking of ICC, *VACUOUS-XP, and TOPICFIRST because the winning candidate does not violate any of these constraints. The evidence that will allow us to determine the relevant ranking is found in the word order observed in subordinate interrogatives, which I address in the following section.

5.4 Embedded interrogatives

Recall from §5.1 that in subordinate interrogatives in Mexican Spanish a preverbal subject is allowed when the *wh*-operator is a *reason* operator, but not with other operators. The relevant contrast is repeated in (57).

(57) a. Yo quiero saber   [por qué Pedro compró el periódico].
        I want   to.know why   Pedro bought the newspaper
        'I want to know why Pedro bought the newspaper.'

     b. *Yo quiero saber   [cómo Pedro arregló la tele].
        I   want   to.know how   Pedro fixed   the T.V.

We have also seen in §5.1 why these facts are problematic for an analysis of the left-periphery in Spanish based on an exploded CP. Following the analysis developed so far, in which left-peripheral phenomena in Spanish are associated with the inflectional layer instead, I suggest an account of these facts that relies instead on the Pole and its relation to structural markedness.

In order to address this problem I assume first of all that, in accordance with the Extended Projection analysis, embedded interrogatives are IPs and not CPs, all else being equal (this means that CPs correspond exclusively to subordinate clauses headed by an overt C^0; see Doherty 1993, Grimshaw 1997, and our discussion in §5.2). Now, there are two observations that are crucial for understanding the contrast between (57a) and (57b). The first one is that the word order in (57a) is not the only option for embedded interrogatives with *reason* operators. The subject can alternatively appear in the post-verbal field, as in (58). Notice that the alternation between (57a) and (58) is reminiscent of the XP-VSO / XP-SVO alternation discussed in §4.3, where the subject is a topic in XP-SVO.

(58) Yo quiero saber   [por qué compró Pedro el periódico].
      I want to.know why   bought Pedro the newspaper
      'I want to know why Pedro bought the newspaper.'

The second relevant observation is that, as mentioned in §5.1, the position occupied by the subject in (57a) can alternatively be occupied by a fronted topic.

(59) a. Yo quiero saber   [por qué ayer   llegó   tarde Juan].
          I want to.know why   yesterday arrived late Juan
          'I want to know why Juan arrived late yesterday.'

      b. Yo quiero saber [por qué al   presidente le   toman esa clase de fotos.]
          I want to.know why   to-the president DAT-CL they.take that kind of photos
          'I want to know why they take that kind of pictures of the president.'

All this points to the conclusion that (57a) corresponds to a case where the subject is a topic, which therefore must be fronted to a left-peripheral position to comply with TOPICFIRST.[31] When the subject is not specified as a topic (i.e., example (58)), it surfaces in the post-verbal field, just like in the Topic-VSO sentences analyzed in §4.3, and in the *Wh*-VSO matrix interrogatives from the previous section.

Recall now from the previous sub-section that when there is both topicalization and *wh*-fronting in interrogatives, the *wh*-operator is fronted to the Pole position and the topic is adjoined to IP. This same pattern is observed in embedded interrogatives, although in many cases speakers find it degraded to some degree (in contrast with (57a) and (59)).[32] Examples are presented in (60). However, with one exception all speakers consulted reject this possibility when the *wh*-operator is a *reason* operator, as shown in (61) (cf. the examples in (59)).

(60) a. ?Yo quiero saber [al   presidente, cómo le   van   a   hacer
      I   want   know to-the president   how   DAT-CL they.go to make

      llegar esa carta].
      arrive that letter

      'I want to know how they are going to get that letter to the president.'

   b. ?Yo quiero saber   [ayer,   cómo llegó   Pedro].
      I   want   to.know yesterday   how   arrived Pedro
      'I what to know how Pedro got here yesterday.'

(61) a. *Yo quiero saber   [Pedro por qué compró el periódico].
      I   want   to.know   Pedro why   bought the newspaper

   b. *Yo quiero saber   [al   presidente por qué le   toman
      I   want   to.know to-the president   why   DAT-CL they.take

      esa   clase de fotos].
      that kind of photos

We can now begin to understand the pattern observed in (57–61) as follows. The structures in (60) and (61), where the topic is adjoined to the IP complement of the matrix verb, violate the prohibition against adjunction to complements (Chomsky 1986, McCloskey 1992, Grimshaw 1997). In this sense, these structures are more marked than the corresponding matrix interrogatives where a topic is adjoined to IP.[33] Consider now the examples in (61). These structures further have a *reason* operator as the Pole, and expressions with a *reason* semantic role constitute the most marked instance of a Pole, in accordance with the Pole hierarchy. Taking these considerations into account, my suggestion is that the embedded interrogatives in (61) correspond to the "worst of the worse" in terms of structural markedness: they resort to adjunction and they have the most marked instance of a Pole.

My proposal is that the degree of structural markedness of this case of the "worst of the worse" is such that an extra XP is projected above IP in order to avoid it. Once this extra XP is projected, there is no need to resort to adjunction. Instead there are now two different specifiers in the representation to host the two fronted constituents. I illustrate this analysis in (62),

(62)

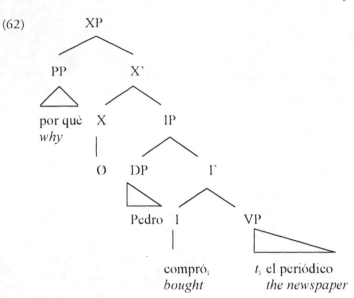

which corresponds to (57a). Notice that this is one of the structures ruled out in (56) for matrix clauses.[34]

In Chapter Two I proposed as a working hypothesis that in structures with vacuous XPs like (62), it is the specifier of IP that corresponds to the Pole, not specifier of XP.[35] Consequently, a property of (62) is that the *wh*-operator is not in the Pole. Embedded interrogatives like (63), where a negative XP occupies the immediate preverbal position, corroborate this hypothesis, since the Negative Pole Condition (§2.3.2) targets the Pole position and not the highest specifier of the Extended Projection.

(63) Yo quiero saber [$_{XP}$ por qué ∅ [$_{IP}$ nadie dijo nada].
      I want   to.know why   nobody said nothing
      'I want to know why nobody said anything.'

The examples in (62) and (63) further highlight the importance of the distinction between the Pole and the highest specifier of the extended projection. As we have seen in the analysis so far, the two coincide in many cases, but crucially not in the ones here. This is most clearly observed in the way in which (62) and (63) comply with the ICC. Previously we had seen cases where a fronted *wh*-operator satisfies the ICC by landing in the Pole, which also happened to be the highest specifier in the extended projection. In the structures in (62) and (63), the *wh*-operator is also in the highest specifier of the extended projection, and the ICC is satisfied because the *wh*-operator is in a Spec-Head configuration with the highest head of the extended Projection. But crucially, this specifier no longer corresponds to the Pole.

Consider now how we can account for the facts above with the analysis developed so far. We have seen that the constructions in (61) violate *Pole/Reason. They also violate the prohibition against adjunction to complements. This prohibition is defined in Grimshaw (1997) as the PURE-EP constraint in (64).

(64) PURITY OF EXTENDED PROJECTURE (PURE-EP)

No adjunction takes place to the highest node in a subordinate extended projection; and no movement takes place into the highest head of a subordinate extended projection.   (Grimshaw 1997:374)

I depart slightly from Grimshaw's definition by assuming that PURE-EP only penalizes adjunction to subordinate extended projections and not head movement. In this respect, the definition of PURE-EP that I assume is closer to the proposals of Chomsky (1986) and McCloskey (1992).[36]

At this point we need to formalize the fact that the degree of structural markedness in (61) corresponds to the worst of the worse. Following Aissen (1999a), I suggest that this can be achieved through Local Conjunction (Smolensky 1995) of the Pole Hierarchy with PURE-EP. Local Conjunction is the operation that conjoins constraints as in the definition in (65).

(65) The local conjunction of C_1 and C_2 in domain D, C_1 & C_2, is violated when there is some domain D in which both C_1 and C_2 are violated.

(Smolensky 1995)

The logic behind Local conjunction is that "two constraint violations are worse when they occur in the same location" (Smolensky 1995). Smolensky formalizes this by suggesting that there is a universally fixed ranking of C_1 & C_2 with respect to each of its conjuncts, as in (66).

(66) Universally, C_1 & C_2 dominates C_1, C_2.

Aissen (1999a) further proposes that the conjunction of a constraint C_1 with a subhierarchy of constraints (call it S_1) yields a subhierarchy of conjoined constraints (call it S_2) such that the hierarchical relations of S_1 are held constant in S_2. This is formalized as in (67).

(67) The local conjunction of C_1 with the subhierarchy $[C_2 \gg C_3 \gg \ldots \gg C_n]$ yields the subhierarchy $[C_1 \& C_2 \gg C_1 \& C_3 \gg \ldots \gg C_1 \& C_n]$

(Aissen 1999a)

Following these definitions, the local conjunction of PURE-EP with the Pole Hierarchy yields the markedness subhierarchy in (68). I assume that the domain relevant for evaluation corresponds to the clause.

(68) PURE-EP & *Pole/Reason » PURE-EP & *Manner » . . . » PURE-EP & *Pole/Agent

Introducing the constraints in (68) into the analysis has no effect on the account of word order in matrix interrogatives, because PURE-EP only targets subordinate clauses. Consider now how we can account for the facts in (57–61) with these constraints. I have suggested that when a *reason wh*-operator and a topic co-occur, an extra functional XP is projected above IP. This result is achieved by ranking [PURE-EP&*Pole/Reason] over *VACUOUS-XP. This is shown in tableau (69) below, which corresponds to example (57a). For simplicity, in the tableaux that follow only the part of the input that corresponds to the embedded interrogative is represented.

Candidate (69b) loses because it violates both components of the conjoined constraint. PURE-EP is violated because the topic is adjoined to IP and *Pole/Reason is violated because the *reason wh*-operator corresponds to [Spec, I]. Candidate (69a), which corresponds to the structure in (62), emerges as the winner.

This ranking still does not explain by itself why the relative order of the topic and the *wh*-operator is the reverse of the one observed in other kinds of interrogatives. This is because a candidate where the topic is in the specifier of XP also avoids a violation of [PURE-EP&*Pole/Reason], (even if the *reason*

(69) 'I want to know [why Pedro bought the newspaper].'

INPUT: < [Q](buy (x, y; z)), x=Pedro (Ag), x=*topic*, y=the newspaper (Th); z= [wh] (Reason) >

	PURE-EP & *Pole/Reason	*VAC XP
☞ a. [XP por qué [ø][IP Pedro compró [VP el periódico]]].		*
b. [IP Pedro [IP por qué compró [VP el periódico]]].	*!	

(70) 'I want to know [why Pedro bought the newspaper].'

INPUT: < [Q] (buy (x, y; z)), x=Pedro (Ag), x=*topic*, y=the newspaper (Th); z=[wh]
(Reason) >

	PURE-EP & *Pole/Reason	*VAC XP
a. [$_{XP}$ por qué [ø][$_{IP}$ Pedro compró [$_{VP}$ el periódico]]].		*
b. [$_{XP}$ Pedro [ø][$_{IP}$ por qué compró [$_{VP}$ el periódico]]].		*

(71) 'I want to know [why Pedro bought the newspaper].'
INPUT: <[Q] buy (x, y; z), x=Pedro (Ag), x=*topic*, y=the newspaper (Th);
z=[wh] (Reason) >

	ICC	PURE-EP & *Pole/Reason	TOPIC FIRST
☞ a. [$_{XP}$ por qué [ø][$_{IP}$ Pedro compró [$_{VP}$ el periódico]]].			*
b. [$_{XP}$ Pedro [ø][$_{IP}$ por qué compró [$_{VP}$ el periódico]]].	*!		
c. [$_{IP}$ Pedro [$_{IP}$ por qué compró [$_{VP}$ el periódico]]].		*!	

operator is the Pole in this case) since there is no adjunction and so PURE-EP is satisfied, as shown in (70).

With these elements in mind we can already determine that ICC outranks TOPIC-FIRST in Spanish. Otherwise the candidate where the topic precedes the *wh*-operator, candidate (70b) would surface as the winner.[37] The analysis is presented in tableau (71) above. Further notice these facts indicate that [Pure-EP&*Pole/Reason] also outranks TOPIC-FIRST. Otherwise the adjunction structure where the topic is the first constituent in the subordinate clause, candidate (71c), would emerge as the winner.[38]

Consider now embedded interrogatives with topics and other kinds of *wh*-operators, such as *manner wh*-operators. As discussed in §5.1 neither topics nor subjects can occupy the immediate preverbal position in these cases. The examples in (72) illustrate this for a non-subject topic.

(72) a. ?Yo quiero saber   [ayer,   cómo llegó   Pedro].
       I   want to.know yesterday how   arrived Pedro
       'I want to know how Pedro arrived yesterday.'

   b. *Yo quiero saber   [cómo ayer   llegó   Pedro].
       I   want to.know   how   yesterday arrived Pedro

The embedded interrogative in (72a) shows the same word order as the corresponding matrix interrogative. In terms of our analysis, this means that the

(73) 'As for yesterday, I want to know how Pedro arrived (then).'

INPUT: <[Q](arrive (x; y, z)), x=Pedro (Th); y=yesterday (Temp), y=*topic*, z=[wh] (Manner)>

	ICC	*VAC-XP	TOPIC FIRST	PURE-EP & *Pole/Manner
a. [_XP_ cómo [ø][_IP_ [ayer]_TOP_ llegó [_VP_ Pedro]]].		*!	*	
b. [_XP_ [ayer]_TOP_ [ø] [_IP_ cómo llegó [_VP_ Pedro]]].	*!	*		
☞c. [_IP_ [ayer]_TOP_ [_IP_ cómo llegó [_VP_ Pedro]]].				*

(74) Final Ranking of constraints for Mexican Spanish.

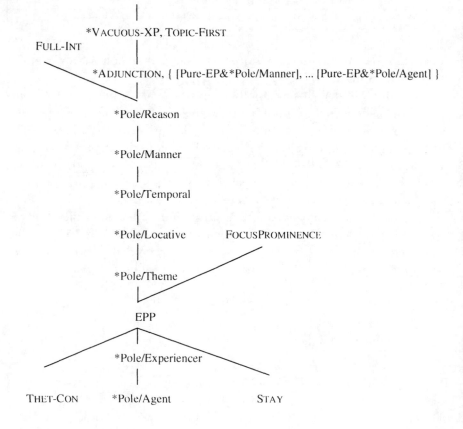

degree of structural markedness of a subordinate structure displaying adjunction plus a *manner wh*-operator functioning as the Pole is not high enough to warrant the projection of a vacuous XP above IP. This can be accounted for with a ranking where *VACUOUS-XP outranks the conjoined constraint [Pure-EP&*Pole/Manner] and the rest of the conjoined constraints in the subhierarchy in (68). The analysis is presented in tableau (73) in the preceding page.

In this case, the candidate that projects an XP above IP, candidate (73a), loses to the candidate displaying adjunction, candidate (73c), because the former's violation of *VACUOUS-XP proves fatal.[39] The optimal candidate violates the conjoined constraint [PURE-EP&*Pole/Manner], but given the constraint ranking of Mexican Spanish, this is better than projecting a vacuous XP above IP. Trivially, candidate (73b), which projects a vacuous XP and displays the attested word order by placing the topic in [Spec, X], violates both ICC and *VACUOUS-XP.

With this I conclude the analysis of the word order facts observed in *wh*-interrogatives in Mexican Spanish. As a summary of the analysis developed in this and in the preceding two chapters, the known rankings of the constraints involved are presented in the Hasse diagram in (74). In this diagram the notation {[PURE-EP&*Pole/Manner]. . . . [PURE-EP&*Pole/Agent]} encapsulates all the markedness constraints that result from the conjunction of PURE-EP with the constraints in the Pole Hierarchy below *Pole/Reason.

5.5 CONCLUSION

In this chapter I have extended the analysis developed in Chapters Two–Four to account for the word order facts observed in *wh*-interrogatives in Mexican Spanish. This analysis follows the analyses where *wh*-movement in languages like English and Spanish is derived by the need to signal the clause as an interrogative, and defines such a requirement as the ICC constraint. In this analysis, the optimal way to comply with the ICC and with Economy of Structure consists of placing a fronted *wh*-operator in the Pole, which in turn satisfies the EPP. This explains the cases where *wh*-operators are not allowed to co-occur with preverbal subjects. The relative word order of fronted topics and *wh*-operators in matrix interrogatives is derived by this analysis without the need for any extra machinery. In subordinate interrogatives, the sensitivity of the Pole to the semantic role of the constituent that occupies it is appealed to for explaining the matrix/subordinate asymmetry in word order observed in Mexican Spanish. The analysis makes use of Local Conjunction in order to explain why beyond a certain degree of structural markedness, the optimal structure is one that projects a vacuous XP above IP to host the *wh*-operator in [Spec, X] instead of in the Pole. The resulting analysis, which links *wh*-fronting to the inflectional layer in Spanish, avoids the problems that result in an exploded CP analysis of the relevant facts.

Notes

NOTES TO CHAPTER ONE

1. No free translations of these examples are provided in the original.
2. See also Contreras (1991) and Ordóñez & Treviño (1999).
3. This criticism holds not only of Alexiadou & Anagnostopoulou's analysis, but also of many other analyses that directly or indirectly deal with word order facts. Some exceptions are Contreras (1976) and Fant (1984) for Spanish, and Belletti & Rizzi (1988) for Italian.
4. Fant (1984) reports the same word order facts in (5) for Peninsular Spanish, but Zubizarreta (1998) reports a SV order for unaccusatives in an out-of-the-blue (sentence focus) context. The varieties of Spanish described in Contreras (1976) and Arnaiz (1998), show the same pattern as Mexican Spanish.
5. From here onwards, specific semantic roles are signaled in italics.
6. All these analyses are discussed in detail in Chapter Three.
7. Other varieties of Spanish do not necessarily behave in this way. For example, constructions like (6a), and (6b) have been reported to be fine in the varieties discussed in Gross & Bok-Bennema (1986), Contreras (1991) and Zubizarreta (1998), amongst others. I will not attempt to account for these cross-dialectal differences here, since this would require data that is unavailable to me at this point. In Chapter Four, however, I will briefly comment on a potential analysis to accommodate them.
8. The speakers of Mexican Spanish consulted judge VSO sentences as either strongly deviant or ungrammatical. My own judgments are that they are strongly deviant in most cases, but they become clearly ungrammatical if other elements such as adverbs also appear in the post-verbal field. The absence of the SVO/VSO alternation is not unique to Mexican Spanish. The deviant nature of VSO constructions with an empty preverbal position has also been reported in the varieties of Spanish described in Suñer (1994)

and Zagona (2002), and for matrix (though not subordinate) clauses in the variety of Spanish described in Contreras (1991). Even for some varieties that allow VSO with an empty preverbal position, Niño (1993) and Zubizarreta (1998:100–102) report that the typical pattern is one where a topic occupies the preverbal position.

9.   One should note from the start, though, that not all of the examples in (7) are discourse-equivalent. Examples (7a) and (7b) are felicitous in an out-of-the blue context, while (7c) is not, as noted originally in Fant (1984). Example (7c), has a reading where either the subject is a topic, or where the experiencer IO is in focus (or both). Similarly, not all of the constructions in (8) are discourse-equivalent. I return to this issue in Chapter Four.

10. Although more research is needed, there is some evidence that this property is not unique to Mexican Spanish. In her study of different kinds of VS constructions, based on data from numerous varieties of Spanish, Hatcher (1956) had already noticed the unusually high frequency with which the verb in these constructions is preceded by an adverbial XP. Luis Casillas (p.c.) further reports similar judgements for Caribbean Spanish (except for *wh*-interrogatives, which are addressed in Chapter Five).

11. Example (10) can also have a reading where the post-verbal subject DP is in focus (i.e. *a GIRL bought the records*). Again, I return to this issue in Chapter Four.

12. In Rizzi's proposal, Focus and Topic phrases are only projected when there are topics or foci that need to be fronted. Notice that once this possibility is allowed, the resulting analysis begins to look more and more like a simple restatement of the facts.

13. For example, a strict requirement on subjects to appear in [Spec, I] would rule out (18a) as a possible topicalization structure when the topic is not the subject. Notice that even in this case there would still presumably be at least two ways of satisfying the well-formedness requirements of TOPIC-FIRST, one for subjects and one for non-subjects.

14. Despite differences across theories, the majority of syntactic analyses in OT agree that the input does not contain any form of phrase-structural representation.

15. I will lay out my specific assumptions about the nature of the input and the candidates in the candidate set in the section that follows.

16. Strictly speaking, OT requires a strict ranking for every constraint in the grammar. It is very often the case, however, that the relative ranking between two or more constraints cannot be determined solely on the basis of the data that one is analyzing. It is in these cases that a dotted line is used. It has also been suggested extensively in the OT literature that constraints may be "tied" in some cases. Tied constraints will not be crucial for the analysis to be developed in what follows, and so I will not go into details about their formalization.

17. There are different ways in which candidate evaluation can be formally understood. One is the method of *Mark Cancellation* (Prince & Smolensky 2004). In this method, which can only be applied when a tableau compares two candidates, those violations that the two candidates share can be cancelled, after which the winning candidate is the one that satisfies the highest ranked constraint on which the two candidates conflict. See also McCarthy (2002) for a proposal in which EVAL is defined in terms of function composition.

18. As noted in Legendre et. al. (1998), arguments and adjuncts in the input are probably best viewed as nothing more than a lexical head plus a bundle of features, but providing such a representation will not be crucial for the discussion that follows.

19. The semantic role labels to be used in what follows are just labels that encapsulate finer semantic distinctions, such as those in Dowty (1991). Except for the discussion in §3.4, these finer distinctions will not be crucial for the analysis, and so I use the standard semantic role labels for convenience.

20. I refer the reader to McCarthy (2002) for further details on these issues, including discussion of computational models of OT that do not face the problems of efficiency of computation that have given rise to this debate.

21. Of course, GEN can also generate an S-structure like (28) without a trace as part of the candidate set. Such a candidate, however, would violate θ-MARK because there would be no link between the subject DP and the lexical projection of the verb that assigns it its semantic role. Since I assume that θ-MARK is undominated in Spanish, I do not consider such candidates here.

22. Although there is considerable murkiness about this issue in the literature, it is worth pointing out that these interpretations of STAY are not necessarily equivalent. Consider the case of Clitic Left-dislocation (CLLD) in Romance languages, which according to Cinque (1990) corresponds to an instance of base-generation (*ec* stands for *empty category*).

    (i) $[XP_i [_{VP} \ ec_i \ ]]$

    In a derivational model, (i) never violates STAY, since there is no movement involved. In a representational model, however the evaluation of (i) depends on how we define a chain. For example, if we define a chain as a syntactic object that has any null category (whether a trace, *pro*, or PRO) as its foot, then (i) would indeed violate STAY. This is the definition of chains that I will assume throughout this work, and consequently, I take all instances of CLLD to violate STAY. This assumption is not crucial to the analysis in any way.

23. This is also the characterization of ungrammaticality in McCarthy (2002).

NOTES TO CHAPTER TWO

1. The same applies to the nominal system, which I will not describe here, since I do not address nominal expressions in this work. See Grimshaw (2000) for details.

2. Grimshaw's definition does not distinguish between lexical nodes that are distinct from the head of the extended projection in the definition in (2) and those that are not. However, I believe that this distinction is necessary. Otherwise V could not be the extended head of IP because there is a lexical node (i.e. an {F0} node) that intervenes between IP and V, namely VP.

3. See Grimshaw (2000: 117) for an alternative formulation where the {F} value of YP can instead be higher or equal to that of X.

4. The purpose of the discussion that follows is to provide some independent support for the assumptions that; a) clauses with a tense specification always have an inflectional functional layer, and; b) that the inflectional layer is fundamentally distinct from the "complementizer layer" or C-layer. These are standard assumptions in transformational frameworks, but not in OT syntax, hence the need to address them in more detail.

5. Perhaps a specifier position in a VP shell (Larson 1988), but I will not go into details here.

6. See Haegeman (1995), though, for convincing evidence against such an analysis.

7. See also Zwart (1997).

8. Rizzi (1997: 284–285).

9. For example, my proposal does not contemplate the existence of either Topic or Focus phrases, and will consider topicalization and *wh*-movement as movement into the I-system, as in Zubizarreta (1998).

10. In fact there are analyses like Contreras (1991) and Ordóñez & Treviño (1999) where it is claimed that the subject does not move to [Spec, I] at all. I discuss these analyses in Chapter Four and in §2.2.1, respectively.

11. Some analyses, like Zubizarreta (1998) involve a combination of these two hypotheses.

12. The same is true of psych and unaccusative sentences, although, to the best of my knowledge, their word-order interaction with negation has not been as thoroughly discussed in the literature. Contreras (1976) does report, however, that predicates that show an unmarked VS order switch to an unmarked SV order in the presence of sentential negation. My judgments do not correspond to this, but it does seem that [S Neg V] unaccusative sentences have a freer distribution than, say, [S V] sentences where the subject is topicalized. It seems to me that in these cases there is an entirely different factor at play, namely, having the subject outside the scope of sentential negation. This is an important issue, since it would show that the interpretive properties of scope-taking elements also play a role in determining word order in Spanish, but one that cannot be addressed here.

13. Laka (1990) labels this Polarity Phrase 'Σ-Phrase.'
14. Analyses where nominative Case is assigned in [Spec, I] still face the separate problem of how to account for nominative DPs that do not appear in the preverbal position. I address this issue in detail in the following chapter.
15. See Brucart (1999) for a list and description of the polarity elements that can appear in these constructions, and their relation to the polarity of the antecedent clause.
16. An account of this difference between Spanish and English is developed in López (1999), to which I refer the reader for details.
17. Strictly speaking, TP ellipsis in Laka's analysis.
18. Phrasal ellipsis in Spanish and English is different in other respects besides the category of the elided XP. See López (1999) for discussion.
19. Here I have concentrated on the evidence provided by ellipsis, since it will also be relevant for supporting some of the other claims developed in this chapter. Further evidence against the adjunction analysis of negation, however, can be found when Spanish is compared to other Romance languages. Zanuttini (1997a, 1997b), for example, notes that in some Romance languages and dialects the preverbal negation is indeed adjoined to the verb. However, Zanuttini notes that whether the preverbal negation is an independent head (as in Spanish and Italian) or whether it is adjoined to the verb, crucially correlates with different sets of properties. For instance, preverbal independent negative heads can negate the clause by themselves, whereas adjoined preverbal negative heads require an extra negative element to fulfill this function (this is the case of *ne* in literary French). I refer the reader to Zanuttini (1997b) for further details on these issues.
20. This kind of analysis was originally proposed for Yiddish by Diesing (1990).
21. As pointed out to me by Judith Aissen (p.c.), the constructions in (26) and (27) below must be distinguished from one where the relevant XP follows the negation, as in (i.b):

> (i) a. Invitó   a   Luis, pero [a   Juan no ___]
>   *he-invited* ACC *Luis* *but*   ACC *Juan not*
>   'He invited Luis, but Juan, he didn't (invite).'
>
>   b. Invitó   a   Luis, (pero) [no   a   Juan].
>   *he-invited* ACC *Luis* *but*   *not* ACC *Juan*
>   'He invited Luis, (but) not Juan.'

Constructions like (i.b) are better analyzed as instances of stripping, since they differ from those cases involving true phrasal ellipsis in that they cannot appear in embedded contexts, a well-known characteristic of stripping also attested in English (Jackendoff 1972; the English examples are from López & Winkler 2000: 648).

(ii) *Invitó a Luis, pero creo que [no a Juan].
he-invited ACC *Luis but I-think that not* ACC *Juan*

(iii) a. Sam read many books but not novels.
b. *Sam read many books but I think that [not novels].

In contrast, as noted in López & Winkler (2000), the fact that constructions like (i.a) can appear in embedded contexts, as in (iv), argues against their analysis as instances of stripping and in favor of their analysis as true instances of phrasal ellipsis.

(iv) Invitó a Luis, pero creo que [a Juan no ___].
he-invited ACC *Luis but I-think that* ACC *Juan not*
'He invited Luis but I think that Juan, he didn't (invite).'

Furthermore, with an overt affirmative polarity head, the construction where the XP precedes the head is perfect, but the one where it follows it is not.

(v) a. No invitó a Luis, pero [a Juan sí ___].
not he-invited ACC *Luis but* ACC *Juan yes*
'He didn't invite Luis but Juan, he did (invite).'

b. ??No invitó a Luis, pero [sí a Juan].
not he-invited ACC *Luis but yes* ACC *Juan*

22. All the examples below are from Mexican Spanish. See Sánchez-López (1999) for other examples.

23. Throughout this work, I adopt the (first) definition of c-command in Reinhart (1981: 612):

(i) Node A c(onstituent)-commands node B iff the branching node most immediately dominating A also dominates B.

See also Barker & Pullum (1990) for a more precise definition of this command relation.

24. As will be argued in the following chapter, my proposal crucially departs in this respect from related considerations developed in Grimshaw (1997).

25. This contemporary conception of the EPP is of course very different from Chomsky's (1981,1982) original definition of this principle, which made

crucial reference to the subject of the clause. See McCloskey (1997, 2001) for discussion.

26. By inherent features I mean the features that are specified as part of the lexical entry of a head. The functional specification of each head (discussed in relation to (1)), i.e. its {F} value, will indeed be different for I and the head of YP in (32b), but {F} is not an inherent feature. Rather, as discussed in §2.1.1, its value is defined relationally, depending on the position that each head occupies in the Extended Projection.

27. Here I will not attempt to give a comprehensive definition of 'subject,' since there are considerable differences across theoretical frameworks with respect to how to characterize subjecthood (see McCloskey 1997 for discussion). Instead I will rely on the standard diagnostics for identifying subjects in languages like English and Spanish, such as verb agreement and nominative Case.

28. The distinction between subject and Pole also accommodates languages that have no EPP effects, but where subjects still need to be licensed in a specific position outside VP, such as Irish (McCloskey 1996, 2001; see also Alexiadou & Anagnostopoulou 1998 and the comments on their analysis in §1.1). Irish is a strict VSO language, whose basic word order is argued by McCloskey to result from the following two considerations: (i) V raises to T (and no further) in finite clauses, and (ii) the EPP is inactive in this language, so the specifier of the highest inflectional phrase (TP in McCloskey's analysis) is always empty. However, McCloskey identifies a position in the inflectional layer below TP where subjects move to have their nominative Case licensed, as is evidenced by stranded quantifiers, word order of the subject DP with respect to the main verb in periphrastic aspects, and other facts. McCloskey argues convincingly that the evidence from Irish indicates that two properties previously associated with the grammatical subject (nominative Case and satisfaction of the EPP) must be kept distinct. In terms of my proposal, Irish is a language where clauses do not have a Pole. However, I follow McCloskey's analysis in that this does not entail that there will not be other positions in the inflectional layer that license properties typically associated with subjects, such as nominative Case. See §3.4.

29. The notion of the Pole, however, is not incompatible with frameworks where the subject grammatical relation is a primitive of the theory. Rather, in my view satisfaction of the EPP would need to be kept separate from the characteristics that define subjecthood in such frameworks.

30. Clearly enough, the Pole and the logical subject can still overlap in many cases. Example (33) is arguably a case where the three relevant notions, grammatical subject, logical subject, and Pole, all overlap. The precise characterization of the relation between the Pole and the logical subject in these cases is an issue that I leave open for future research.

31. I assume that both topics and *wh*-operators are in a dependency relation with a null category in the VP (see §1.2.2 and §1.3.1). For the cases of ellipsis that follow, this means that *remnant* is to be understood as any displaced XP that is either an argument or an adjunct of the predicate elided along with the IP.

32. Some speakers of Mexican Spanish do find (38c) to be acceptable. In analyzing these examples, however, care should be taken not to confuse a small clause with two potential remnants; in the former case the resulting construction is fine because the small clause is the single constituent and so again we have a single remnant:

     (i)   Juan tiene [$_{SC}$ amigos en Barcelona], pero [$_{SC}$ amigos en
           Madrid] no.

           Juan has   friends in Barcelona but   friends in
           Madrid not

           'Juan has friends in Barcelona, but friends in Madrid he doesn't.'

     Accordingly, it may be possible that the speakers who accept (38c) might be giving the two XPs preceding *no* a small clause interpretation.

33. My own judgments are that both examples are ungrammatical, but (39b) is almost unparsable.

34. This is an issue that I address in detail in Chapter Four.

35. Observe that the fact that languages like English do allow for multiple remnants points to the conclusion that their absence in Portuguese and some varieties of Spanish is probably not due to pragmatic considerations.

36. There is considerable debate in the literature as to whether negative XPs in Romance languages are negative quantifiers or rather negative polarity items (see Haegeman 1995 for a brief overview of this debate). Settling this matter will not be crucial for our purposes, and so I will use the label *negative XP* throughout.

37. Zubizarreta (1998) reports that fronted negative XPs in these cases must be intonationally prominent. This does not correspond to my judgements and is not reported in other works dealing with these facts either (Fontana 1994, Suñer 1995, Sánchez-López 1999).

38. Despite their similarities there are important differences between the syntactic realization of negation in Spanish and Italian that space considerations prevent me from accounting for here (see Haegeman 1995, chap. 4 for an overview). At this point, I am unaware if similar differences exist between these two languages, on the one hand, and Portuguese, on the other. Furthermore, my own research points to the conclusion that considerable differences also exist between Mexican and Peninsular Spanish. To the best of my knowledge, however, the data presented in (43–47) is consistent in these two varieties of Spanish.

39. In terms of the definitions in (48) and (49), this means that every feature [NEG] that is semantically potent translates into a negative operator in the semantic representation. Not every negative concord language behaves in this way, though, as is well-known. For instance, Catalan (as described in Ladusaw 1992; glosses are my own), differs from Spanish in this respect. Both conditions are operational in this language, as can be seen in (i.a-b), but when a negative XP in the Pole co-occurs with the sentential negation, the result is not a double negation reading. This is shown in (i.c), which has the same meaning as (i.b).

    (i) a. No m'ha   telefonat ningú.
           not me-has telephoned nobody
           'Nobody has called me.'

        b. Ningú   ha   vist en Joan.
          nobody has seen John
          'Nobody has seen John.'

        c. Ningú no ha vist en Joan.
          nobody not has seen John
          'Nobody has seen John.'

Descriptively, we can say that Catalan is a language where the NEGATIVE HEAD CONDITION and the NEGATIVE POLE CONDITION cannot both be operational at the same time. Ultimately, in providing a full account of languages like Catalan, it would be necessary to determine which of the two negative conditions is neutralized in (i.c) and why, but dealing with this issue goes beyond the scope of this work. Notice, though, that from an OT perspective the fact that one condition can be made inactive under certain circumstances is far from being a surprising state of affairs.

40. See Haegeman (1995) for an analysis of West Flemish, a negative concord language that also allows for DN constructions in some cases. The cases where West Flemish shows DN readings are, however, very different from those in which the DN reading is observed in Spanish. This is an issue that should be the subject of future research.

41. This is one of the central observations behind my assumption that there is a fundamental difference between II-Projections (the projections in the inflectional layer) and K-Projections (the C-system).

42. Suñer (1995) provides an analysis of negation Spanish based on the Negative Criterion. However, in her analysis NegP is sandwiched in the middle of the inflectional layer, an analysis which we have seen runs into problems when ellipsis is considered. Consequently I have modified her analysis in accordance with the conclusions about sentential structure in Spanish that we have arrived at so far.

43.   Ultimately this condition would have to be expanded to include those cases where there is licensing of negative XPs across clause boundaries, but this is an issue I will not deal with here.

44.   Not every Romance language displaying negative concord behaves like this. Italian, for example, does allow for constructions like (62b) (see Haegeman 1995). This is a problem that cannot be addressed here, but one possibility is that Italian, in contrast with Spanish, does allow for multiple specifiers (cf §1.2.2). This would provide I^0 with two specifiers and so with two preverbal positions where the feature [NEG] would be semantically potent.

45.   Glosses are partially my own.

NOTES TO CHAPTER THREE

1.   As far as I have been able to determine from the literature, this is the unmarked word order that transitive sentences show in most varieties of Spanish. Costa (1998, 2001), however, reports a variety of Peninsular Spanish where VSO can also function as the unmarked word order. I refer the reader to Gutiérrez-Bravo (2002a) for a possible analysis of such varieties.

2.   Based on a different set of data, Goodall (2001) also arrives at the conclusion that the EPP is operative in Mexican Spanish, and, accordingly, that Alexiadou & Anagnostopoulou's proposal cannot be entirely correct. I refer the reader to Goodall's work for specific details.

3.   The analysis in Grimshaw (1997) is actually more complex than this. I will return to this analysis shortly. None of the OT analyses considered here provide a characterization of the notion of "subject," though. For the purposes of our discussion, unless otherwise noted, "subject" in what follows is to be understood pre-theoretically as the lexical XP that agrees with the verb (see §2.2.2).

4.   Psych verbs sometimes require a more elaborate discourse context as a diagnostic than the *'what's been happening?'* question-answer pair, presumably for pragmatic considerations. Fant (1984:109–114) carried out an experiment to test for their unmarked word order using a number of different contexts. In his results, psych predicates where the *experiencer* is a post-verbal dative XP and where the subject *theme* is realized overtly in the preverbal position, (i.e. the inverse order of (7)) are found to be felicitous only between 16.7 and 11.1% of the time.

5.   The glosses and free translations of (7a-b) are my own.

6.   For ease of exposition, in this tableau and the tableaux that follow I do not represent the violations of STAY that result from V-to-I movement, since they are irrelevant for the evaluation of the candidates. Further notice that the claim here is not that (8b) is an ungrammatical sentence in Spanish, but rather that it does not correspond to the unmarked word order (i.e. it is infelicitous in a sentence-focus context). Perturbations of this unmarked word order are addressed in the following chapter.

7. One could presumably develop an analysis where the subject of transitive clauses moves to [Spec, I] because of Case considerations, and the *experiencer* of psych clauses moves to this same position for other reasons. The proposal I will develop later in this chapter will provide a unified analysis of these two cases, though. Accordingly, it captures a generalization that is lost in an alternative where these two cases are analyzed separately.

8. Once we have seen this second formulation of SUBJECT, the reader may wonder if the formulation of the EPP that I propose is actually any different from it. They are in fact different, and they make different predictions in a number of cases. Space considerations do not allow me to discuss every difference between the two constraints, but the following two cases are illustrative. In cases of IP recursion, for example, Grimshaw's SUBJECT is defined in such a way that the subject/EPP condition has to be satisfied in the highest recursion of IP. As discussed in the previous chapter, in my proposal it is actually the specifier of the lower IP that counts as the Pole, so my proposal predicts that the EPP still has to be satisfied even when something occupies the specifier of the highest recursion of IP. This seems to be the case in negative inversion in English (which, as far as I can tell, involves IP recursion in Grimshaw's (1997) analysis). To the extent that expletives are attested in these constructions, this indicates that the preposed negative XP does not satisfy the EPP:

   (i) a. Seldom would it bother him that the mail arrived late.

        b. Under no circumstances will there be any exceptions made.

   A second difference between the two proposals has to do with the domain in which the EPP applies. In Grimshaw's definition, this domain includes VP, whereas in my proposal it does not. Accordingly, Grimshaw's constraint predicts that in contexts where there is no inflectional layer (or in languages where there might not be an inflectional layer at all) there should still be EPP effects, whereas my proposal predicts that there shouldn't. Settling this matter is an important empirical issue, but one that cannot be fully undertaken here. For the purposes of the discussion that follows it is enough to note that my definition of the EPP, and Grimshaw's second formulation of SUBJECT are not equivalent.

9. Glosses and free translations are my own. Observe that similar word order facts are also attested for unaccusative verbs in Italian (see Pinto 1994, Zubizarreta 1998, and Arnaiz 1998). Before the unaccusative hypothesis, Spanish verbs that show an unmarked VS order were characterized as presentational verbs (Hatcher 1956, Contreras 1976), but unaccusative verbs without a presentational function also show this pattern, as in (13c) and (13d).

10. Costa (1998: 348–352) notes that this is also a problem for unaccusative clauses in Portuguese, which allow both VS and SV orders in the unmarked

case. I refer the reader to Costa's work for a tentative solution to this problem. See also Gutiérrez-Bravo (2005a) for an alternative analysis of VS/SV alternations observed in the unmarked case.

11. In a way more or less analogous to the way in which Procrastinate, a general prohibition against movement, can only be overridden to make a derivation converge (Chomsky 1993).

12. Although clearly this can indeed be the case when only binary contrast are involved.

13. In Masullo (1993), however, these preverbal subjects are taken to be a kind of quirky subject. See Gutiérrez-Bravo (2005b) for evidence against such an analysis.

14. As in the previous chapters, throughout I assume V-to-I movement and movement of the constituent in [Spec, I] from its base position inside the VP. Following Suñer (1988) and Parodi (2003), I further assume that clitics in Spanish are instances of morphological agreement, and I represent them as such in the phrase markers that follow.

15. It is worth pointing out, however, that to the extent that one accepts the proposal that *wh*-extraction from certain contexts is only possible for constituents which bear roles from the higher end of the Thematic Hierarchy (Rizzi 1990, Cinque 1990), it is problematic for proposals where the *theme* ranks low in the hierarchy to explain why direct objects, for example, can typically undergo extraction from such contexts, whereas other more adjunct-like *wh*-operators do not. This same pattern is arguably also observed cross-linguistically in relative clause formation, as in work on the Accessibility Hierarchy (Keenan & Comrie 1977). Lastly, Torrego (1984), Suñer (1994) and Bakovic (1988) provide extensive evidence from *wh*-movement in Spanish that *themes* are thematically more salient than oblique arguments and adjuncts. I address this last issue in detail in Chapter Five.

16. To the best of my knowledge, the observation that a scale like (19) defines the possibility of a constituent occupying a peripheral position in Spanish was first made in Contreras (1976) with respect to the right periphery. I address Contreras' analysis in the following chapter.

17. Other authors, most notably Bakovic (1998), have developed markedness subhierarchies without making use of Harmonic Alignment. I discuss Bakovic's proposal in detail in Chapter Five.

18. See also Asudeh (2001) and Sharma (2001) for other implementations of Aissen's proposal.

19. Expressions with a *reason* semantic role display an irregular behavior in this respect though. For instance, when the *reason* expression is an adverbial clause it is typically the sentence-final constituent. This is consistent with the Harmony scale in (27b), in that the adverbial clause can be taken to be the most deeply embedded constituent in a VP shell (Larson 1988). However, other *reason* expressions (such as *for some reason*) typically appear in the left

periphery instead. It may be the case that some independent factor (such as scope) is responsible for the displacement of the *reason* adverb in these cases. This is an issue I leave open for future investigation.

20. It is worth pointing out that there is some evidence that in languages other than Spanish the Non-Pole constraints may well play a fairly important role in determining clause structure. English, for example, does not allow existential-*there* constructions with *agents,* and this can be the result of *Non-Pole/Agent ranking very high in this language. Other Germanic languages do allow for *agents* in existential constructions, as in Icelandic Transitive Expletive Constructions. However, Jonas & Bobaljik (1996) argue that in these cases the *agent* subject is in a VP-external position so again this might be the result of a high-ranking *Non-Pole/Agent constraint.

    The reader may also wonder if postulating the existence of the Non-Pole constraints does not inevitably lead to some bizarre typological predictions. For example, ranking all of the Non-Pole constraints above STAY derives a language where it is better to move every argument and adjunct out of the VP than to have them surface in their base position. Yet the analyses of polysynthetic languages in Jelinek (1984) and Baker (1995), where argument XPs are always adjoined to more peripheral positions, do not appear to be very different from this situation. Testing the full typological predictions that are derived from my proposal is of course an important issue, but one that lies beyond the scope of this work.

21. It must also be the case that EPP outranks STAY. Otherwise movement into the Pole position would be disallowed altogether. Since STAY does not play a crucial role in the evaluation of the candidates in what follows, for ease of exposition I will leave out of the tableaux this constraint and the traces it penalizes.

22. The same is true of some of the losing candidates in tableaux (32) and (33). Concretely, (32a) and (33a) are just infelicitous in a sentence-focus context. The distinction between infelicity and ungrammaticality in my analysis is dealt with in the following chapter. See also §1.2.2.

23. There are two other possible alternatives to the analysis of word order I have developed, one based on the notion of *default topic* and the other one based on Alignment constraints. Since the data that more strongly corroborate the adequacy of my analysis *versus* these alternatives comes from topicalization, I delay their discussion until the next chapter.

24. An issue that I leave open for future research is the word order of clauses with morphologically derived predicates, such as periphrastic passives, exemplified in (i).

    (i) Los delincuentes fueron capturados (por las autoridades).
        the criminals   were   captured   by the authorities
        'The criminals were captured by the authorities.'

In (i), the *theme* subject surfaces as the Pole, and the oblique *agent* appears in the post-verbal field, contrary to what would be expected in my analysis. Furthermore, the reverse order is not possible at all. One possible solution for this problem relies on information structure considerations. It has long been observed in the functional literature that the passive in English is chosen over the active when the *patient* is more discourse-prominent than the *agent* (Tomlin 1985, Thompson 1987). Discourse prominence is conditioned by several factors (empathy, topicality, discourse coherence) that are grouped together in Aissen (1999a) under the label *Thematic Prominence* (not to be confused with prominence along the Thematic role Hierarchy). Now it is also a well-known fact that the preverbal position in Spanish is typically a topic position, as I discuss in detail in the following chapter, and so it may be possible that it is also a position for discourse-prominent arguments. Consequently, if as argued in Aissen (1999a) active and passive sentences are members of the same candidate set, then a passive sentence like (i), where the *patient* surfaces in the prominent Pole position, emerges as the winner when the *patient* is more discourse-prominent than the *agent*.

25. The precise analysis of *pro*-dropped constructions depends largely on the assumptions that we start out with. In an OT analysis where there are no null subjects at all (Samek-Lodovici 1996), the EPP is violated in (37b), but this is still better than violating *Pole/Theme. In OT analyses that do allow for null subjects (Costa 1998), it is necessary to determine first if null elements can satisfy constraints like the EPP, CASE, etc., and then determine if there is any evidence that a *pro* is functioning as a Pole in *pro*-dropped constructions. Settling this issue goes beyond the scope of this work, but my proposal is compatible with either analysis.

26. Belletti & Rizzi (1988) in fact note that some verbs of the *preoccupare* class can have an interpretation where one of the arguments functions as an *agent*.

27. In this respect, it is relevant that Spanish *intimidar* in (41b) is not exactly equivalent to English 'to intimidate,' since the former necessarily implies that purposeful actions are taken to bring about the intimidation. Accordingly, (41b) cannot mean that the activists are intimidated simply because of the presence or the amount of power of the government.

28. My analysis thus resembles the analysis in Pesetsky (1995) (vs. the analysis in Grimshaw 1990) in suggesting that the subjects of psych verbs can display more thematic distinctions than what is standardly assumed (for example, in Belletti & Rizzi 1988). Ultimately, though, Linking analyses like Pesetsky (1995) and Grimshaw (1990), account for which argument of a predicate is mapped as the subject and/or the external argument. Word order, however, is a separate phenomenon. For instance, Grimshaw (1990) and Pesetsky (1995) both agree that a *cause* semantic role is usually enough for an argument of a psych predicate to be mapped as the subject (with the

observation that in Grimshaw's analysis the subject of a psych verb does not always correspond to the external argument). The Spanish data in (40–41) corroborate this hypothesis. However, this still does not account for the word order facts, as can be observed in these same data, because the subject occupies a different position in each case. It is precisely here that the finer semantic distinctions in Dowty (1991) become crucial.

29. The *dative/accusative* alternation is also reported for certain Italian verbs in Belletti & Rizzi (1988: 335, fn. 28). I am unaware if the alternation in Italian is also dependent on semantic entailments, or if it also results in a word order alternation, as it does in Spanish.

30. In some dialects of Spanish, human direct objects can be doubled by the clitic *le* (the so-called *leísta* dialects). Mexican Spanish is not one of these dialects, so it is certain that the *experiencer* in (42b) is a dative indirect object, and not a clitic left-dislocated direct object.

31. Ultimately, it seems feasible to develop a more refined analysis in which the Pole would be sensitive not to the broad semantic role labels I have been using so far, but rather to finer semantic distinctions such as those expressed in Dowty's Proto-Agent and Proto-Patient entailments. However, for the purposes of the chapters that follow, which concentrate on the properties of the Pole in relation to word order perturbations that result from topicalization and *wh*-movement, the broader semantic role labels will suffice.

32. Examples (45) and (46a) are taken from Fernández-Soriano (1999).

33. See Gutiérrez-Bravo (2005b) for further details.

34. The glosses are my own.

35. This is not an idiosyncratic characteristic of Spanish, of course. For example, French can express some possessive relations by realizing the possessed entity as a nominative DP and the possessor as a dative, as is well known. See also Aissen's (1999b) analysis of external possession in Tz'utujil (Mayan).

36. See the discussion on sentence topics in §4.3.

37. Definiteness and specificity are variables that are not controlled for in Fernández-Soriano's investigation. In most of her example sentences, the preverbal locatives are either deictic locative pronouns like 'here' or proper names corresponding to locations, whereas the post-verbal subjects are almost always indefinite or bare NPs. Given the nature of Spanish as a discourse-configurational language, it is fundamental to control for these variables.

38. Taken from Alexiadou & Anagnostopoulou (1999: 104): no free translation of this example is provided in the original. Although Alexiadou & Anagnostopoulou are not clear about this point, from this example it seems that the gist of the proposal in Huybregts (1996) is to analyze Arabic *inna,* traditionally taken to be a matrix complementizer, as an expletive element instead (many thanks to Anders Holmberg for clarification on this point).

39. The same kinds of languages result from having an undominated EPP and embedding FULL-INTER by itself in the Pole Hierarchy.

40. In this respect, however, it is important to note that the current analysis formally predicts a number of patterns that we do not expect to observe for independent reasons. For instance, a language with the ranking EPP » *Pole/Reason » FULL-INTER corresponds to a language that only inserts an expletive to prevent *Reason* adverbials from landing in [Spec, I]. Although only thorough empirical research of all languages displaying expletives can determine whether such a language exists or not, there is a reason why we do not expect this pattern to surface in the first place. Predicates do not typically have a *Reason* adverbial as their unique argument, so a clause with a reason adverbial will also include a number of other arguments with semantic roles more prominent in the Thematic Hierarchy than *Reason* (*Agent, Experiencer, Theme,* etc.). Although under the ranking under discussion it is true that a candidate that inserts an expletive will be more harmonious than a candidate that satisfies the EPP by moving the reason adverbial into [Spec, I], the expletive candidate will still be beaten by any candidate that instead moves an *Agent, Experiencer, Theme,* etc., into [Spec, T] for this purpose, and so the expected pattern does not surface

41. Henriquez-Ureña (1939:222), however, reports that expletive insertion was also observed in some Peninsular Spanish texts in the period going from the 16th to the 19th century.

42. The precise formulation of both TOPICFIRST and *ADJUNCTION is discussed in detail in the following chapter.

43. A detailed analysis of topicalization and multiple topicalization in Spanish is provided in the following chapter. The discussion addresses the focus reading that the post-verbal subject typically has in such cases.

44. The fact that numerous V2 languages permit leftward adjunction below IP in the form of scrambling is not problematic for this analysis. This is because the *ADJUNCTION constraint is not a total ban against adjunction structures. Rather, the ranking *ADJUNCTION » TOPICFIRST simply implies that adjunction to IP is not resorted to when topicalization at play. Scrambling is derived in any ranking where the interpretive and/or information structure constraints that trigger scrambling in turn dominate *ADJUNCTION. Alternatively, it maybe possible to derive the V2 pattern by means of an alignment constraint requiring the verb to be aligned with the left edge of the clause (say, ALIGN-V, L). Such a constraint requires the verb to be leftmost, but when it is dominated by EPP it yields to the requirement that the clause have a Pole. However, if ALIGN-V, L in turn dominates TOPICFIRST then we derive the V2 pattern, since at most one XP (the one that satisfies the EPP) will be allowed to intervene between the verb and the left edge of the clause. Space considerations, however, prevent me from developing this analysis in detail.

NOTES TO CHAPTER FOUR

1. These are not the only possible cases, of course. At the very least Spanish also shows cases where non-focal material (i.e. material that is already part of the common ground) does not undergo fronting to the left periphery, but rather stays in the post-verbal field (the *tail* in Vallduví 1992) and cases of multiple topicalization. I will have very little to say about the former case, which I leave open for future investigation. Multiple topicalization I will analyze in detail in the final subsection of this chapter.

2. This non-optionality approach to word order, however, has been challenged in work by Gereon Müller (see for example Müller 1999), based on data from German which, one should acknowledge, is considerably more complex than the data analyzed by the proponents of non-optionality. In the analysis that follows I will not take a strong stance on this debate. I will adopt the non-optionality approach as a working hypothesis, but I remain neutral with respect to the issue of whether or not word order variation can be truly optional in some cases.

3. Kiss (1998: 245) (who uses the term *identificational focus* instead of *contrastive focus*) defines it as follows: "(a contrastive) focus represents a subset of the set of contextually or situationally given elements for which the predicate phrase can potentially hold; it is defined as the exhaustive subset of this set for which the predicate phrase actually holds."

4. I represent presentational foci in small caps and contrastive foci in small caps in boldface. As in Kiss (1998), these various diacritics indicate neither pitch accent nor differences in pitch accent.

5. The label "new information" is somewhat misleading (hence the scare quotes). As noted in Vallduví (1992) and Lambrecht (1994), what is new (in terms of information structure) about *Mary* in cases like (4) is its relation with the rest of the proposition, not the referent of *Mary* itself. I refer the reader to these works for details.

6. Mexican Spanish does allow for VOS sentences if the preverbal position is occupied by another constituent, as in (i).

> (i) Ayer   compró el periódico   [$_{FOC}$ Juan].   **Adv V O S**
>   *yesterday   bought   the newspaper   Juan*
>   Yesterday JUAN bought the newspaper.'

My sense is that in these cases the direct object corresponds to the *tail* (see fn. 1), i.e., it is material that is part of the common ground and that must appear in the postverbal field (see Vallduví 1992). Analyzing these cases requires a detailed account of the behavior of *tails* in Spanish that cannot be undertaken here, so I leave the analysis of XP-VOS sentences for future investigation.

7. Alternatively, OVS sentences can be also compatible with an interpretation where both the subject and the verb are in focus (see Fant 1984, Zubizarreta 1998, Gutiérrez-Bravo 2002a).

8. Interestingly, Zubizarreta claims that in these cases the contrastive reading is available even when the focus does not bear the kind of pitch accent characteristic of contrastive foci. My impression is that this is also the case in Mexican Spanish, but experimental research is needed to support the validity of this claim.

9. Some speakers of Mexican Spanish (myself not included) further accept example (10) as an instance of presentational focus, i.e., as a reply to the *wh*-question "*Who gave you the bottle of wine?*." These speakers, however, still reject subject preverbal presentational foci when the subject is not a proper name. It seems to me that this is the result of pragmatic accommodation (see Lambrecht 1994). If the hearer assumes that the speaker is already presupposing the answer to the relevant question, he may use a contrastive focus as in (10) to disconfirm the speaker's presupposition. More research is needed to understand all the variables in play these cases. For the time being, however, I do not consider proper names in the discussion of presentational foci to follow.

10. By contrastive focus in-situ I mean the situation where a constituent can be contrastively focussed in its canonical position even when this position does not correspond to the clause final position.

11. Again, throughout I follow Suñer (1988) in analyzing accusative and dative clitics in Spanish like *los* in (13) as instances of morphological agreement and not as XPs or independent heads. This rules out the possibility that the EPP is satisfied by the clitic. In this kind of analysis, though, the clitic is coreferential with a *pro* that satisfies the verb's selection and theta requirements (Jaeggli 1982) and this raises the question of whether *pro* could satisfy the EPP in this kind of subject inversion sentence. Up to this point I have not found any evidence confirming or disconfirming such a possibility, but it should be noted that subject inversion in general is not dependent on some other argument of the verb (null or overt) satisfying the EPP. This is most clearly observed in VOS sentences from Peninsular Spanish, where both the arguments of the transitive verb are realized overtly in the post-verbal field.

12. In contrast, there are a number of OT analyses that derive the position of inverted subjects through a structural constraint on foci (usually an Alignment constraint) as in Samek-Lodovici (1996) and Grimshaw & Samek-Lodovici (1998), or through a combination of structural and intonational requirements (Costa 1998). I refer the reader to Gutiérrez-Bravo (2002a) for a critique of these analyses.

13. Technically, this is a simplified version of FocusProminence. In cases where there is more than one constituent in focus in languages like German, this constraint is responsible for ensuring that all of the focal constituents receive some

degree of intonational prominence through a pitch accent (all else being equal) even if only one of them can be signaled with the nuclear accent.

14. What prevents a preverbal focussed subject (such as the subject in 15a) from satisfying FOCUSPROMINENCE by receiving the nuclear accent *in-situ* are higher-ranked prosodic constraints that ensure that the nuclear accent is sentence-final in Spanish. See Büring & Gutiérrez-Bravo (2001) for details.

15. This difference is not immediately relevant for our purposes, so I refer the reader to Gutiérrez-Bravo (2002a) for discussion.

16. See Gutiérrez-Bravo (2002a) for an OT analysis of Peninsular Spanish along these lines.

17. For different analyses of sentence topics, see Kuno (1972), Chafe (1976), E. Prince (1981, 1984), Reinhart (1982), Vallduví (1992), Lambrecht (1994), and Choi (1999).

18. I am greatly indebted to Donka Farkas for helpful discussion of the relevant issues in the paragraphs that follow.

19. In what follows I do not consider hanging topics, which are topical expressions that are introduced by a locution such as *'with respect to . . .', 'as for . . .'*, etc., as in the English example in (i), and which behave differently from sentence topics in Spanish and other languages (see Zubizarreta 1999 for discussion and diagnostics):

> (i) With respect to John, he has agreed to take responsibility over the project.

20. This diagnostic is not as reliable when the topic corresponds to the subject, as in complement clauses with preverbal unaccusative subjects. In such cases extraction is still degraded but clearly better than in the examples in (20). At present I have no explanation for this fact.

21. This is in contrast with English which does have two formally different ways of expressing sentence topics, as is well known: topicalization and left-dislocation. Each is illustrated in the examples in (i), from E. Prince (1984).

> (i) a. Math courses I was never good at.
> b. This one book, I read it when I was a kid.

As is also well known, these two kinds of constructions have a number of different syntactic, intonational and pragmatic properties (see E. Prince 1981, 1984; Lasnik & Saito 1992, *inter alia*). For instance, left-dislocation involves a resumptive pronoun coreferential with the topic, but topicalization does not. Also, in topicalization the sentence topic necessarily shows some degree of intonational prominence (although it does not bear the most prominent accent in the clause. i.e., the nuclear accent), but this is a condition left-dislocated topics are not subject to. English further has preposed focus constructions, which are syntactically identical to topicalization, but which are different from topicalization differ in their intonational and pragmatic properties (E. Prince 1981). I refer the reader to Prince's work for details.

In this respect, there is no Spanish construction like (i.a) lacking a resumptive clitic that would be equivalent to English topicalization: clitic left-dislocation is the only possibility in such cases. The absence of the clitic in (19a), and in all other constructions involving fronted topical definite direct objects and indirect objects, would result in ungrammaticality, as is well known (see for example Suñer 1988, Zubizarreta 1999).

The reader should also be aware that by using the term *topicalization* I am not claiming that this phenomenon in Spanish is equivalent in its pragmatic properties to English topicalization (vs. English left-dislocation). At present, I do not know if Spanish topicalization fulfills the different functions of both English topicalization and left-dislocation, or if it corresponds to just one of them. See Casielles-Suárez (1995) for discussion of this issue in Catalan.

22. In my view, discourse topics are the kind of topic that is targeted by the DROP-TOPIC constraint of Grimshaw & Samek-Lodovici (1998), which requires expressions signaled as topics in the input to be left unrealized in the output. My analysis of topicalization addresses sentence topics and not discourse topics, so I do not discuss the DROPTOPIC constraint in what follows.

23. There are languages like English (Jackendoff 1972, E. Prince 1981, 1984) where sentence topics can also be signaled by purely intonational means, without displacement to a left-peripheral position. It seems to me that this option is not available in Spanish, but clearly extensive research is needed to clarify this issue.

24. Sentence topics are termed *Links* in Vallduví (1992).

25. Example (22) is my own. See Fant (1984) for similar contrasts in transitive constructions and psych predicates.

26. Having an instantiation in the previous discourse is a sufficient but not a necessary condition for topicalization. As discussed in the previous section, what characterizes the referent of a topic is that it is part of the common ground, and temporal expressions usually can be part of the common ground and function as topics even when they are not discourse-old. This is presumably because the speaker and the hearer share the assumption that an event necessarily involves a specific time at which it occurs.

27. A different approach to topicalization in OT can be found in Legendre et.al. (1995) and Legendre et. al. (1998). In these analyses topics are taken to be operators whose scope is specified in the input. Fronting of a topic is then derived by a faithfulness constraint that requires that the scope of the topic in the input be mapped into the surface representation. As noted in Costa (1998), however, numerous works have argued that topics do not behave like true operators (Cinque 1990, Lasnik & Stowell 1991, Müller &

Sternefeld 1993), and so deriving their behavior through scope considerations does not seem entirely adequate. Ultimately though, the contrast between long and embedded topicalization indicates that TOPICFIRST is not the only constraint at play in topic fronting. This is an issue that certainly deserves more attention, but for the purpose of analyzing the relation between topicalization, structural markedness, and the EPP, we can rely solely on the TOPICFIRST constraint.

28. Gloss and free translation are my own.

29. Contreras (1991) proposes that topicalization involves precisely this structure in Spanish.

30. Recall from the definition in §2.2.2 that the specifier of such a phrase (whether a recursion of IP or a fully vacuous XP) does not correspond to the Pole.

31. Grimshaw (1997) ultimately abandons the MINIMALPROJECTION constraint, claiming that its effects with respect to Economy of Structure can be captured independently by the STAY and Ob-HD constraints. Although this is true in a great many cases, independent violations of the STAY and Ob-HD constraints are not enough to rule out a candidate that does not abide by Economy of Structure when such a candidate satisfies a markedness constraint that outranks both STAY and Ob-HD. This is arguably the case in Spanish, where the relevant markedness constraint can be taken to be *Pole/Theme. We know that *Pole/Theme outranks STAY because *Pole/Theme outranks EPP and EPP in turn outranks STAY (§3.3.1). Evidence from *wh*-interrogatives, to be presented in the following chapter (§5.4., fn 34) further indicates that Ob-HD is fairly low-ranked in this language, possibly even outranked by STAY. As a result, a candidate that projects a vacuous XP to prevent a *theme* from landing in the Pole position indeed violates either Ob-HD (example 29b) or incurs an extra violation of STAY because of verb movement from I^0 to X^0 (example 29c), yet it will still win, because in either case it avoids a violation of the higher ranked *Pole/Theme. In other words, this is a case where the projection of extra structure is not entirely gratuitous, and so it cannot be ruled out independently by STAY and Ob-HD. This is where a constraint like MINIMALPROJECTION or *VACUOUS-XP becomes necessary.

32. The fact that (29b) violates Ob-HD but (29c) does not have any effect in the analysis that follows, since Ob-HD is a fairly low-ranked constraint in Spanish (see preceding note).

33. Recall that the evidence from subject inversion when the direct object is dropped only allows us to conclude that FOCUSPROMINENCE outranks EPP in Spanish.

34. Spanish does allow for Adv-SVO sentences like the losing candidates (36b,c), of course, but my claim is that in these cases the subject is also a topic. In contrast to what is observed in Adv-VSO sentences, if both the subject and the adverb are topics, they both have to be fronted to the left periphery to satisfy TOPICFIRST. This issue is discussed in detail in §4.3.5.

35. A further argument in favor of this characterization of ungrammaticality in OT, in this case related to the interaction between topicalization and negation, can be found in Gutiérrez-Bravo (2000).

36. This is consistent with the proposal in Alexiadou & Anagnostopoulou (1998) that VSO sentences in Spanish and Greek are closely related to Transitive Expletive Constructions in some Germanic languages.

37. It has also been noted in the literature that in VSO clauses the subject can sometimes be in focus. Niño (1993), however, argues convincingly that focussing of the subject is not the primary function of this kind of clause, a conclusion also arrived at in Zubizarreta (1998). Putting the analyses of these two authors together, it seems to me that these cases are instances of presentational sentences where the subject is a contrastive focus accented *in-situ* in its VP-internal position (see §4.2.1).

38. The current analysis thus avoids the problem of ineffability, in a way similar to the one proposed in Legendre et. al. (1998). It is not the case that a presentational input with a transitive predicate in Mexican Spanish has no output. Rather, given the ranking of constraints of Mexican Spanish, the output of such an input is not distinct from the output of a simple transitive input.

39. This indicates that THET-CON outranks *ADJUNCTION in Peninsular Spanish. Otherwise the VOS candidate in this variety would lose in the same way that it does in Mexican Spanish.

40. This indicates that topicalization is not the only factor that makes a constituent surface as the Pole that would not do so in the unmarked work order. This is an issue that should be addressed in future research.

41. The glosses of (48a-b) are partially my own. Here I will not attempt to provide an analysis of the contrast in (48), since such an analysis would require a detailed OT characterization of island effects. It needs to be pointed out that in Goodall (2001) the contrast between (48a) and (48b) is presented as evidence that subjects and topics occupy different structural positions in Spanish. However, independently of what the analysis of topic islands ultimately is, Goodall's claim is difficult to reconcile with the data from ellipsis and the distribution of non-subject negative XPs discussed in §2.

42. See also Vallduví (1992) for Catalan and Rizzi (1997) for Italian. Recall that in §3.5 I argued that this is one of the two fundamental differences between Spanish and V2 languages.

43. Recall that I assume that Spanish does not allow for multiple specifiers (§1.2.2). Consequently, I do not consider such an option for the cases at hand.

44. More generally, they comply better with Economy of Structure than the attested output.

45. As opposed to what we see in the *topic-comment* sentences with a single topic discussed in §4.3.3, the projection of extra structure is not gratuitous when multiple topics are involved. Rather, it is necessary in order to violate TOPICFIRST as little as possible.

46. Ultimately, this issue is not just a question of simplicity of the resulting structure. Analyses that postulate the existence of Topic Phrases usually run into problems when it needs to be determined what the status of such phrases is with respect to locality, adjacency, etc., in cases where there are no sentence topics in the first place. See for example Rizzi (1997), where it is necessary to stipulate that Topic Phrases are only projected when there is a topic present in order to account for the "anti-adjacency effects" in the analysis of topicalization in English.

47. Some speakers show an irregular pattern with respect to *experiencers* of Psych verbs (but not with other semantic roles). For these speakers, there are a number of cases where the only felicitous order is the one where the *experiencer* is the leftmost topic. It seems to me that animacy may help understand this pattern, since the *experiencer* of a psych verb is necessarily animate, but the *theme* subjects of such are verbs are typically not, and animacy is well-known to induce linear order effects in some languages (see Müller 1999). All of the speakers consulted have the same judgments for (58) below, however, where the *experiencer* is the innermost topic. More research is needed to clarify this issue, which I will leave open for the time being.

48. Example (56) shows that there is in fact a distinction between *manner* and *temporal* adverbials not considered in the Thematic Hierarchy adopted in §3.2.1. Henceforth I break up the constraint *Pole/Manner-Temporal into *Pole/Manner and *Pole/Temporal, with the former out-ranking the latter.

49. Alignment constraints in syntax have been proposed in Samek-Lodovici (1996), Costa (1998), Grimshaw & Samek-Lodovici (1998), Choi (1999), Sells (2001), among others.

50. Formally, the constraints in (61) require that the left edge of the constituent bearing the specified semantic role be aligned with the left edge of the clause (or more precisely, the Extended Projection in terms of the analysis developed here). See McCarthy & Prince (1993) and especially Sells (2001) for details.

51. Alignment constraints are gradient constraints, so they can be violated more than once depending on the number of elements that intervene between the category to be aligned and the edge of the specified domain. For simplicity, in the tableau I do not represent the gradient violations of these constraints, since they will not be relevant for our discussion. Also, for simplicity violations of STAY resulting from V-to-I movement are left out of the tableau.

NOTES TO CHAPTER FIVE

1. In this chapter I consider only the interaction between *wh*-movement and structural markedness in interrogative clauses. Word order facts are different

in relative clauses, presumably because they are uniformly CPs, and accordingly Spec-CP is always independently available as a landing site in the left periphery. See Gutiérrez-Bravo (2005a) for an analysis.

2. There are no uniform judgments across speakers of Mexican Spanish for WH-Subj-V examples with *reason* operators in matrix clauses like (3). The double interrogation mark (??) is meant to indicate that judgments from most of the speakers consulted run from slightly deviant (?), to ungrammatical. However, some speakers do accept (3b). I assume that there are two different varieties of Mexican Spanish, Mexican Spanish A and Mexican Spanish B, which are minimally different in this respect. In this chapter I only provide an analysis of the variety illustrated in (1–3), i.e. Mexican Spanish A, since *wh*-interrogatives in this variety display an interesting matrix-subordinate asymmetry. A preliminary analysis of Mexican Spanish B (where (3b) is indeed acceptable) is presented in Gutiérrez-Bravo (2002b: 282–287).

3. Glosses are my own.

4. Free translations are my own.

5. Bakovic (1998) does not state his findings in relation to preverbal subjects, but rather with respect to *inversion*, following the analysis in Torrego (1984). I avoid the use of the term inversion, since there is considerable evidence that an inversion (i.e., I-to-C) analysis of Spanish interrogatives is not adequate. I address this issue in detail in §5.3.

6. It is important to note that this phenomenon is not dependent on the specific nature of the matrix verb. In Spanish the sentential complements of verbs of illocution, such as *preguntar* 'ask,' allow CP recursion, as discussed in Plann (1992) and Suñer (1991); see also McCloskey (1992). Crucially, the pattern in (8a) is still observed in interrogative complements that do not allow CP recursion, such as the complements of *saber* 'know,' and *acordarse* 'to remember.' To control for this variable, throughout I make use of data where the matrix verb is *saber* 'know.'

7. We have good reason to think that the subject in (11a) is a topic, since it corresponds to the subject of an unaccusative verb. Hence, it would not otherwise appear in the preverbal field, as discussed in Chapter Three and §4.3.

8. One may try to find a solution to this problem in the fact that *reason* adverbials behave differently from other kinds of adverbials in some languages. For instance, Rizzi (1990) suggests that *reason wh*-operators are base-generated in [Spec, C], in contrast with other kinds of operators. There are two reasons why such an analysis is unattractive. First, this analysis would still not explain the matrix-subordinate asymmetry observed in Mexican Spanish. If we claim that (8) and (14) are possible because the *reason* operator can be base generated in a position above the position occupied by the subject or topic, we still need to explain why this is a possibility in embedded but not in matrix interrogatives. Notice that we cannot go around this problem by suggesting that only embedded clauses have a CP layer, since

wh-operators and fronted topics in matrix clauses are equally hosted in C-related projections in an exploded CP analysis. Second, such an analysis would fail to capture the fact that the pattern of Mexican Spanish simply corresponds to a point in a larger continuum, as discussed in Bakovic (1998). In other words, in Mexican Spanish preverbal subjects can only co-occur with *reason* operators (in embedded interrogatives) but as we have seen, other varieties allow this pattern with a wider variety of operators, and Suñer's data in (15) suggests that this pattern extends to preverbal topics too.

9. I will not follow Cheng with respect to this last point, though, which brings with it the conclusion that English complementizers like *whether* and *if* are not inherently interrogative (see Cheng 1991 for discussion). Although I will have relatively little to say about the typology that emerges from the OT analysis that I develop building on Cheng (1991), we will see that in such an OT analysis we are not forced to conclude that languages can only have one of the two typing mechanisms in (17).

10. This is in contrast with the *Wh*-Criterion of Rizzi (1996), for which examples like (18) are problematic. See Rizzi (1996) for discussion and a possible solution.

11. It is my sense, however, that Ackema & Neeleman's Q-MARKING analysis (where the scope of *wh*-operators is not specified in the input) is not incompatible with analyses where scope is specified in the input, as in Legendre et. al. (1995) and Legendre et. al. (1998). When contrasted with these analyses, the result would be that *wh*-movement in languages like English and Spanish is not the result of mapping the scope in the input to the surface representation (i.e., it is not a Faithfulness-to-scope issue). Crucially, it seems to me that the scope specifications in the input would still be relevant for deriving the interpretive properties of *wh*-operators. As a result, I believe that the most comprehensive analysis of *wh*-movement in languages like English and Spanish would be one that takes into account the interaction between Q-MARKING and constraints that require Faithfulness to the scope properties in the input. Here I will not attempt to develop such a proposal, though, since the interpretive properties associated with scope are not crucial for accounting the surface word order of *wh*-operators in Spanish.

12. Further notice that the distinction between *wh*-fronting derived by clause typing and *wh*-fronting derived by scope opens the possibility for an alternative to the analysis of the partial *wh*-movement facts developed in McDaniel (1989) for German and Romani. In partial *wh*-movement, a *wh*-expletive is found in a higher specifier position than the one occupied by the *wh*-operator that it is associated with. However, as noted by McDaniel, this has the consequence that the *wh*-operator in partial *wh*-movement ends up in a Spec-CP position that is [-WH], in contrast with what is observed with full *wh*-movement. In other words, a fronted *wh*-operator marks the clause as interrogative in full *wh*-movement but not

in partial *wh*-movement. Given Ackema & Neeleman's proposal, this is not entirely surprising. It is possible that in the former case the *wh*-operator simultaneously moves to take scope and to mark the clause as interrogative, whereas in the latter case it just moves to have scope over the open proposition. This is a possibility that I leave open for future investigation.

13. Alternatively, if the analysis developed in §2.1.2 is adopted, this problem does not arise in the first place. This is because in this analysis the minimal matrix clause is IP and not VP, so the subject in (23) would be in [Spec, I] and not in [Spec, V] to begin with.

14. This is under the assumption that multiple specifiers are not allowed in languages like English. Ackema & Neeleman (1998a) do not explicitly make this assumption, but it is necessary for their analysis.

15. Notice that once (25) is adopted, constructions with *wh*-in situ violate Q-Marking once for every *wh*-operator that stays in situ, which is not the case with the first definition of this constraint. See Ackema & Neeleman (1998a) for details.

16. In this I depart from analyses like Kayne (1990) where *whether* is analyzed as an XP. This assumption has no consequences for the discussion that follows.

17. Ultimately this implies that there must be two different sets of *wh*-operators, those that bear the feature [Q] and relative operators, which do not. This is indeed the case in German, as reported in McDaniel (1989:598), and it is also partly confirmed in Spanish, where there are interrogative operators like *por qué* 'why' which cannot be used in relative clauses and relative operators that cannot be used in interrogative clauses, such as *por el cúal* 'why,' *al que* '(to) whom,' *cuyo* 'whose,' etc. The important point is that nothing in principle rules out a language with partial or total homophony among the operators in both sets.

18. In Ackema & Neeleman's analysis, the appropriate Spec-head configuration can only be established with an overt head. I-to-C movement in English matrix interrogatives then becomes necessary to establish the required Spec-Head configuration between a fronted *wh*-operator and an overt head. For English subordinate interrogatives Ackema & Neeleman (1998a) propose that the Spec-head configuration is established between the fronted *wh*-operator and an overt complementizer that is part of the input. The complementizer is then deleted in order to satisfy the OT-constraint that corresponds to the Doubly Filled Comp Filter (Pesetsky 1998). Instead I follow the analysis in Grimshaw (1997), where I-to-C in English matrix interrogatives is instead the result of the high ranking of the purely structural Ob-HD constraint, and its absence in subordinate interrogatives is the result of the high-ranking Pure-EP constraint (which penalizes movement into the highest head position of a subordinate extended projection). See also §5.4.

19. As discussed in note 11, a proposal along these lines is still compatible with an analysis where the scope of *wh*-operators is specified in the input.

20. This is in contrast with Bakovic & Keer (2001), where complementizers are proposed to be part of the input in order to account for the optionality of *that* in English subordinate clauses. Although I cannot address Bakovic & Keer's analysis in detail, two observations are relevant here. First, Bakovic & Keer's proposal is devised to avoid the numerous problems that result from the analyses of optionality in Grimshaw (1997) and Pesetsky (1998). However, more recent analyses of optionality, such as Boersma & Hayes (2001), equally avoid the problems of the earlier analyses without the need to make special assumptions about the input. Second, in any event it is not immediately clear if Bakovic & Keer's analysis of *that* (and the issues of optionality that engendered it) is relevant for interrogative complementizers, since these are essentially obligatory.

21. This analysis raises the question of why a [+Q] C^0 is not inserted in matrix yes-no interrogatives. There are two (possibly overlapping) solutions to this question. The first one is to suggest that, following standard analyses, matrix questions have the option of making use of a null [Q] operator. The second one is to suggest that complementizers in matrix clauses in English are banned altogether by an independent (and high-ranked) constraint. Addressing this issue goes beyond the scope of this work. However, my analysis does predict that there should be languages where [+Q] complementizers are found in matrix yes-no interrogatives. According to Cheng (1991) Korean, Japanese, Mandarin, and a number of other languages indeed behave in this way (see Cheng 1991:21 for a full list of languages of this type).

22. In Torrego's (1984) pre-CP analysis the subject is base-generated as the NP sister of VP, and the inversion transformation adjoins the verb to S when there is a *wh*-operator in COMP. Torrego's inversion rule is further stipulated to apply only when the *wh*-operator corresponds to an argument, since adjunct *wh*-operators do not trigger "inversion" in the variety of Spanish she considers.

23. *Wh*-fronting in Bakovic's analysis is derived by a high-ranking OPERATOR-SCOPE constraint similar to the Q-SCOPE constraint of Ackema & Neeleman (1998b).

24. Bakovic also develops an analysis of the matrix-subordinate asymmetries discussed in §5.1. I refer the reader to Bakovic (1998) for details.

25. This is in contrast with both the inversion analysis in Torrego (1984), and with more contemporary analyses that reject the inversion analysis of Spanish interrogatives, such as Goodall (1991a, 1991b) and Suñer (1994).

26. Observe that, in contrast with the inversion analyses, my proposal that in Spanish *wh*-operators occupy the Pole of the clause is compatible with these facts.

27. Gloss and free translation are my own.

28. See Suñer (1994) for a similar argument that relies instead on data from sluicing.

29. In contrast, this possibility is not available with the markedness constraints developed in Bakovic (1998), since these constraints are specific to syntactic operators.

30. Notice in support of this analysis that (56b) is a possible sentence in Spanish under an echo reading. Crucially, echo questions are not true interrogatives. My analysis predicts that an input like (56) without the [Q] morpheme would have (56b) as its output (since satisfaction of the ICC would not be at stake in this case), and the existence of (56b) with a echo reading confirms this prediction.

31. In fact, some of the speakers consulted readily note that (57a) and (58) (and analogous examples) are not equivalent, and that the preverbal subject in (57a) has an "emphasis" that the post-verbal subject in (58) lacks altogether.

32. One of the speakers consulted does not accept this pattern at all. For other speakers these constructions are acceptable but generally slightly degraded, and in some cases strongly degraded (??). For other speakers still, some of these constructions are perfect and others are slightly degraded. None of the speakers in my survey finds every instance of this pattern perfect. At present, I have no explanation for this fact.

33. This might help explain why the examples in (60) are generally less than perfect.

34. The structure in (62) might seem strange given the analysis of the syntax of Mexican Spanish developed up to this point. However, there is nothing inherently exotic about this structure, which is in essence identical to the structure of English embedded interrogatives. Notice that this structure further indicates that Ob-HD is a low ranking constraint in Spanish. Otherwise, the verb in I^0 would move to C^0. This is an important point, because it provides evidence that verb raising (V-to-I) in Spanish is not the result of the high ranking of Ob-HD (cf. Bakovic 1998). Rather, it seems that V-to-I in Spanish is derived by a high-ranking constraint related to the feature content and the morphology associated with I^0, as in standard transformational accounts of this language and in the analysis of French V-to-I in Grimshaw (1997: 381–382).

35. At present I have no evidence that would allow us determine unequivocally if XP in (62) corresponds to a fully vacuous XP or to a recursion of IP. Settling this matter will not be crucial for the analysis, though.

36. Grimshaw (1997) in fact notes that PURE-EP can possibly be understood as two different constraints for subordinate clauses, one on adjunction and one on head movement, although in her analysis of English there is no reason to separate them. However, this is not the case in Spanish. Under the assumption that most Mexican Spanish embedded interrogatives are IPs, PURE-EP as defined in (64) would always be violated, since the verb always moves to I^0 in Spanish. This is why I only consider the prohibition on adjunction here.

37. With this ranking, the optimal candidate in matrix interrogatives is still the one where the fronted topic precedes the *wh*-operator, because ICC is not a constraint on linear order. The reader can verify this result by substituting the double line that separates ICC from the other constraints in tableau (56) for a single solid line indicating a strict ranking.

38. This constraint conjunction analysis might appear to be somewhat *ad hoc,* but this mostly has to do with the specifics of the formalism. If the scale of structural markedness that we are considering in OT terms could be formalized in some other way, the conjoined constraint [PURE-EP &*Pole/Reason] would simply correspond to the point in the scale at which it is better to project a vacuous XP than to abide by Economy of Structure.

39. This is somewhat obscured by the fact that candidate (73a) also violates TOPIC-FIRST, though.

Bibliography

Ackema, P. & A. Neeleman. 1998a. 'Optimal questions,' *Natural Language and Linguistic Theory* 16.443–490.

Ackema, P. & A. Neeleman. 1998b. '*WHOT*,' in P. Barbosa, D. Fox, P. Hagstrom, M. McGinnis and D. Pesetsky (eds.), *Is the Best Good Enough?* Cambridge, Mass., MIT Press. 15–33.

Ackerman, Farrell & John Moore. 1999. 'Syntagmatic and paradigmatic dimensions of causee encodings.' *Linguistics and Philosophy* 22:1–44.

Ackerman, Farrell & John Moore. 2001. *Proto-properties and grammatical encoding: A correspondence theory of argument selection.* Stanford, CSLI.

Aissen, Judith. 1999a. 'Markedness and subject choice in Optimality Theory,' *Natural Language and Linguistic Theory* 17.673–711.

Aissen, Judith. 1999b. 'External Possesor and Logical Subject in Tz'utujil,' in D. Payne & I. Barshi (eds.), *External Possession.* Amsterdam/Philadelphia, John Benjamins. 167–193.

Aissen, Judith. 2003. 'Differential Object Marking: Iconicity vs. Economy,' *Natural Language and Linguistic Theory* 21.435–483.

Alexiadou, A. & E. Anagnostopoulou. 1998. 'Parametrizing AGR; word order, V-movement and EPP-Checking.' *Natural Language and Linguistic Theory* 16: 491–539.

Alexiadou, A. y E. Anagnostopoulou. 1999 'EPP without Spec, IP,' in D. Adger, S. Pintzuk, B. Plunkett & G. Tsoulas (eds.), *Specifiers: Minimalist Approaches,* Oxford University Press, Oxford. 93–109.

Arnaiz, Alfredo R. 1998. 'An overview of the main word order characteristics of Romance,' in Siewerska, Anna, Jan Rijkhoff, & Dik Bakker (eds.), *Constituent order in the languages of Europe.* Berlin, Mouton de Gruyter. 47–73.

Asudeh, Ash. 2001. 'Linking, optionality and ambiguity in Marathi,' in P. Sells (ed.), *Formal and Empirical issues in Optimality Theoretic Syntax.* Stanford, CSLI. 257–312.

Babyonyshev, M. 1996. *Structural connections in syntax and processing: studies in Russian and Japanese.* Ph.D. dissertation, MIT.

Baker, Clyde. 1970. 'Note on the description of English questions: The role of an abstract question morpheme,' *Foundations of Language* 6.197–219.

Baker, Mark. 1995. *The Polysynthesis Parameter.* Oxford, Oxford University Press.

Bakovic, Eric. 1998. 'Optimality and inversion in Spanish,' in P. Barbosa, D. Fox, P. Hagstrom, M. McGinnis and D. Pesetsky (eds.), *Is the Best Good Enough?* Cambridge, Mass., MIT Press. 35–58.

Bakovic, E. & E. Keer. 2001. 'Optionality and ineffability,' in G. Legendre, J. Grimshaw & S. Vikner (eds.), *Optimality-Theoretic Syntax.* Cambridge, Mass., MIT Press. 97–112.

Baltin, Mark. 1982. 'A landing site for movement rules,' *Linguistic Inquiry* 13.1–38.

Barker, C. & G. K. Pullum. 1990. 'A theory of command relations,' *Linguistics and Philosophy* 13.1–34.

Battistella, Edwin. 1990. *Markedness: The Evaluative Superstructure of Language.* Albany, SUNY Press.

Battistella, Edwin. 1996. *The Logic of Markedness.* Oxford, Oxford University Press.

Bedell-García, Kathleen. 1993. *Spanish negation and the I Projection.* MA thesis, University of California, Santa Cruz.

Belletti, Adriana & Luigi Rizzi. 1988. 'Psych verbs and Theta theory,' *Natural Language and Linguistic Theory* 6.291–352.

Boersma, P. & B. Hayes. 2001. 'Empirical tests of the Gradual Learning Algorithm,' *Linguistic Inquiry* 32.45–86.

Bolinger, Dwight. 1954–55. 'Meaningful word order in Spanish,' *Boletín de Filología,* Universidad de Chile 7.45–56.

Branigan, Philip. 1992. *Subjects and complementizers.* Ph.D. dissertation, MIT.

Bresnan, Joan. 2000a. 'Explaining morphosyntactic competition,' in M. Baltin & C. Collins (eds.), *Handbook of Contemporary Syntactic Theory.* Oxford, Blackwell Publishers. 11–44.

Bresnan, Joan. 2000b. 'Optimal syntax' in J. Dekkers, F. van der Leeuw & J. de Weijer (eds.), *Optimality Theory: Phonology, Syntax and Acquisition.* Oxford, Oxford University Press. 334–385.

Brody, Michael. 1995. *Lexico-Logical Form.* Cambridge, Mass., MIT Press.

Broekhuis, Hans. 2000. 'Against feature strength,' *Natural Language and Linguistic Theory* 18.673–721.

Brucart, José María. 1987. *La elisión sintáctica en español.* Bellaterra, Publicacions de la Universitat Autònoma de Barcelona.

Brucart, José María. 1999. 'La elipsis,' in I. Bosque & V. Demonte (eds.), *Gramática Descriptiva de la lengua española.* Madrid, Espasa-Calpe. 2787–2863.

Büring, Daniel. 2001. 'Let's phrase it!,' in G. Müller & W. Sternefeld (eds.) *Competition in syntax.* Amsterdam, John Benjamins. 101–137.

Büring, D. & R. Gutiérrez-Bravo. 2001. 'Focus-related word order variation without the NSR,' in J. McCloskey (ed.), *Syntax and Semantics at Santa Cruz 3.* University of California, Santa Cruz. 41–58.

Casielles-Suárez, Eugenia. 1995. 'FOCUS PREPOSING (it is called),' in E. Benedicto, M. Romero, & S. Tomioka (eds.), *Proceedings of the Workshop on Focus.* University of Massachusetts, Amherst. 51–64.

Chafe, Wallace. 1976. 'Givenness, Contrastiveness, Definiteness, Subjects, Topics and Point of view,' in Charles N. Li (ed.), *Subject and Topic.* New York, Academic Press. 25–55.

Chafe, Wallace. 1987. 'Cognitive constraints on information flow,' in R. Tomlin (ed.) *Coherence and grounding in discourse.* Typological Studies in Language Vol. XI. Amsterdam, John Benjamins. 21–52.

Cheng, Lisa. 1991. *On the typology of Wh-questions.* Ph.D. Dissertation, MIT.

Choi, Hye-Won. 1999. *Optimizing Structure in Context.* Stanford, CSLI.

Chomsky, Noam. 1981. *Lectures on Government and Binding.* Dordrecht, Foris.

Chomsky, Noam. 1982. *Some concepts and consequences of the theory of Government and Binding.* Cambridge, Mass., MIT Press.

Chomsky, Noam. 1986. *Barriers.* Cambridge, Mass., MIT Press.

Chomsky, Noam. 1993. 'A minimalist program for linguistic theory,' in K. Hale & S. J. Keyser (eds.), *The view from Building 20.* Cambridge, Mass., MIT Press. 1–52.

Chomsky, Noam. 1995. *The Minimalist Program.* Cambridge, Mass., MIT Press.

Chomsky, Noam. 2000. 'Minimalist Inquiries: The framework,' in R. Martin, D. Michaels, & J. Uriagereka (eds.), *Step by step: Essays on minimalist syntax in honor of Howard Lasnik.* Cambridge, Mass., MIT Press.

Cinque, G. 1990. *Types of A-Bar dependencies.* Cambridge, Mass., MIT Press.

Collins, Christopher. 1997. *Local Economy.* Cambridge, Mass., MIT Press.

Contreras, Heles. 1976. *A theory of word order with special reference to Spanish.* Amsterdam, North Holland.

Contreras, Heles. 1991. 'On the position of subjects,' in S. Rothstein (ed.), *Perspectives on phrase structure: heads and licensing* (Syntax and Semantics 25). San Diego, Academic Press. 63–79.

Costa, João. 1998. *Word order variation: A constraint-based approach.* Ph.D. Diss., University of Leiden.

Costa, João. 2001. 'The emergence of unmarked word order,' in G. Legendre, J. Grimshaw & S. Vikner (eds.), *Optimality-theoretic syntax.* Cambridge, Mass., MIT Press. 171–204.

Croft, William. 1990. *Typology and Universals.* Cambridge, Cambridge University Press.

Déprez, Viviane. 1991. 'Wh-movement: adjunction and substitution,' in D. Bates, (ed.), *The proceedings of the tenth West Coast Conference on Formal Linguistics.* Stanford, CSLI, 103–114.

Diesing, Molly. 1990. 'Verb movement and the subject position in Yiddish,' *Natural Language and Linguistic Theory* 8.41–79.

Dik, Simon. 1978. *Functional Grammar.* Amsterdam, North Holland.

Dohertry, Cathal. 1993. *Clauses without 'that': The case for bare sentential complementation in English.* PhD diss., University of California, Santa Cruz.

Dowty, David. 1991. 'Thematic Proto-roles and argument selection,' *Language* 67. 547–619.

Fant, Lars. 1984. *Estructura informativa en español: estudio sintáctico y entonativo*. Stockholm, Almqvist & Wiksell.

Fernández-Soriano, Olga. 1999. 'Impersonal sentences in Spanish,' *Syntax* 2.101–140.

Fontana, Josep. 1994. 'A residual A-Bar position in Spanish,' in Duncan, E., D. Farkas & P. Spaelti (eds.), *Proceedings of WCCFL 12*. Stanford, CSLI. 233–250.

Gili y Gaya, Samuel. 1961. *Curso superior de sintaxis española*. Barcelona.

Goodall, Grant. 1991a. 'Spec of IP and Spec of CP in Spanish Wh-Questions,' in M. Mithun, G. Perissinotto & E. Raposo (eds.), *Linguistic Perspectives on the Romance Languages*. Amsterdam/Philadelphia, John Benjamins. 199–209.

Goodall, Grant. 1991b. 'On the status of Spec of IP,' in Dawn Bates (ed.), *Proceedings of the 10th West Coast Conference on Formal Linguistics*. Stanford, CSLI. 175–182.

Goodall, Grant. 2001. 'The EPP in Spanish,' in Davis, W. & S. Dubinsky (eds.), *Objects and other subjects*. Dordrecht, Kluwer. 193–223.

Grimshaw, Jane. 1990. *Argument Structure*. Cambridge, Mass., MIT Press.

Grimshaw, Jane. 1994. 'Minimal projection and clause structure,' in B. Lust, M. Suñer, & J. Whitman (eds.), *Heads, projections and learnability*. Hillsdale, New Jersey, Lawrence Earlbaum. 75–83.

Grimshaw, Jane. 1997. 'Projection, heads and optimality,' *Linguistic Inquiry* 28. 373–422.

Grimshaw, Jane. 2000. 'Locality and Extended Projection,' in P. Coopmans, M. Everaert & J. Grimshaw (eds.), *Lexical specification and insertion*. Amsterdam/Philadelphia, John Benjamins. 115–133.

Grimshaw, J. & V. Samek-Lodovici. 1998. 'Optimal Subjects and Subject Universals,' in P. Barbosa, D. Fox, P. Hagstrom, M. McGinnis and D. Pesetsky (eds.), *Is the Best Good Enough?* Cambridge, Mass., MIT Press. 193–219.

Groos, Anneke & Reineke Bok-Benema. 1986. 'The structure of the sentence in Spanish,' in Ivonne Bordelois, Heles Contreras & Karen Zagona (eds.), *Generative studies in Spanish syntax*. Dordrecht, Foris. 46–62.

Gundel, Jeanette. 1974. *The role of Topic and comment in Linguistic Theory*. Indiana University linguistic club. Bloomington, Indiana.

Gundel, Jeanette. 1999. 'On different kinds of focus,' in P. Bosch & R. Van der Sandt (eds.), *Focus: Linguistic, cognitive and computational perspectives*. Cambridge, Cambridge University Press. 293–305.

Gutiérrez-Bravo, Rodrigo. 2000. 'Subjects, left periphery and word order in Mexican Spanish.' Ms. University of California, Santa Cruz.

Gutiérrez-Bravo, Rodrigo. 2002a. 'Focus, word order variation and intonation in Spanish and English: An OT account,' in C. Wiltshire and J. Camps, (eds.), *Romance Phonology and Variation*. Amsterdam/Philadelphia, John Benjamins. 39–53.

Gutiérrez-Bravo, Rodrigo. 2002b. *Structural Markedness and Syntactic Structure.* Ph.D. Diss., University of California, Santa Cruz.

Gutiérrez-Bravo, Rodrigo. 2005a. 'Subject inversion in Spanish relative clauses,' in T. Geerts , I. van Ginneken & H. Jacobs, (eds.), *Romance Languages and Linguistic Theory 2003.* Amsterdam/Philadelphia, John Benjamins. 150–166.

Gutiérrez-Bravo, Rodrigo. 2005b. 'A reinterpretation of quirky subjects and related phenomena in Spanish,' to appear in J. P. Montrevil & C. Nishida (eds.), *New Perspectives in Romance Linguistics.* Amsterdam/Philadelphia, John Benjamins.

Halliday, M. A. K. 1967. 'Notes on transitivity and theme in English (Part 2),' *Journal of Linguistics* 3:199–244.

Harris, Alice. 1984. 'Inversion as a rule of Universal Grammar: Georgian Evidence,' in D. Perlmutter & C. Rosen (eds.), *Studies in Relational Grammar Vol. 2.* Chicago, The University of Chicago Press. 259–291.

Hatcher, Anna. G. 1956. *Theme and underlying question: Two studies of Spanish word order.* Word Supplement No. 3 (Vol. 12).

Hatcher, Anna. G. 1958. 'Se hace algo vs. Algo se hace,' *Modern Language Notes* 73. 102–107.

Haegeman, Liliane. 1991. *Introduction to Government and Binding Theory.* Oxford, Basil Blackwell.

Haegeman, Liliane. 1995. *The syntax of negation.* Cambridge, Cambridge University Press.

Haegeman, L. & R. Zanuttini. 1991. 'Negative heads and the Neg criterion,' *The Linguitic Review* 8.233–252.

Heck, Fabian & Gereon Müller. 2000. 'Successive cyclicity, long-distance superiority, and local optimization,' in R. Billerey & B. D. Lillehaugen (eds.), *Proceedings of WCCFL 19.* Somerville, Mass., Cascadilla Press. 218–231.

Henríquez Ureña, Pedro. 1939. 'Ello,' *Revista de Filología Hispánica* 1.209–229.

Hernanz, M. L. & J. M. Brucart.1987. *La Sintaxis.* Barcelona, Editorial Crítica.

Holmberg, Anders. 2000. 'Scandinavian stylistic fronting: How any category become an expletive.,' *Linguistic Inquiry* 31.445–484.

Holmberg, Anders, & Jan Rijkhoff. 1998. 'Word order in the Germanic languages,' in Siewerska, Anna, Jan Rijkhoff, & Dik Bakker (eds.), *Constituent order in the languages of Europe.* Berlin, Mouton de Gruyter. 75–104.

Holmberg, Anders & Urpo Nikanne. 2002. 'Expletives, subjects and topics in Finnish,' in P. Svenonius (ed.), *Subjects, Expletives and the EPP.* New York, Oxford University Press. 71–105.

Huybregts, R. 1996. 'Minimalism, Typology and Language Universals,' paper presented at TIN 96, Utrecht.

Jackendoff, Ray. 1972. *Semantic interpretation in generative grammar.* Cambridge: MIT Press.

Jaeggli, Oswaldo. 1982. *Topics in Romance Syntax.* Dordrecht, Foris.

Jelinek, Eloise. 1984. 'Empty categories, case and configurationality,' *Natural Language and Linguistic Theory* 2.39–76.

Jiménez, María Luisa. 1994. 'XP-preposing in Spanish,' in R. Aranovich, W. Byrne, S. Preus & M. Senturia (eds.), *Proceedings of WCCFL 13.* Stanford, CSLI. 253–268.

Jonas, D. & J. Bobaljik. 1993. 'Specs for subjects: the role of TP in Icelandic,' in J. Bobaljik & C. Philips (eds.) *Papers on Case and agreement 1, MITWPL 18,* MIT Working Papers in Linguistics, Cambridge, Mass. 59–98.

Jonas, D. & J. Bobaljik. 1996. 'Subject positions and the roles of TP,' *Linguistic Inquiry* 27.195–136

Kahane, H. & R. Kahane. 1950. 'The position of the actor expression in colloquial Mexican Spanish,' *Language* 26.236–263.

Kayne, Richard. 1990. 'Romance clitics and PRO,' NELS 20.

Keenan, E. & B. Comrie. 1977. 'Noun Phrase Accessibility and Universal Grammar,' *Linguistic Inquiry* 8.63–99.

Kiss, É. Katalin. 1998. 'Identificational focus versus information focus,' *Language* 74.245–273.

Kuhn, Jonas. 2001. 'Generation and parsing in optimality theoretic syntax,' in P. Sells (ed.), *Formal and Empirical issues in Optimality Theoretic Syntax.* Stanford, CSLI. 313–366.

Kuhn, Jonas. 2003. *Optimality-theoretic syntax: a declarative approach.* Stanford, CSLI.

Kuno, Susumo. 1972. 'Functional sentence perspective: a case study from Japanese and English,' *Linguistic Inquiry* 3.269–320.

Kuroda, S.Y. 1972. 'The categorical and the thetic judgement: evidence from Japanese syntax,' *Foundations of Language* 9.153–185.

Ladd, D. Robert. 1996. *Intonational phonology.* Cambridge, Cambridge University Press.

Ladusaw, William. 1992. 'Expressing negation,' in C. Barker & D. Dowty (eds.), *Proceedings of Salt II.* Columbus, Ohio, The Ohio State University. 237–259.

Laka, Itziar. 1990. *Negation in syntax: On the nature of functional categories and projections.* Ph.D. dissertation, MIT.

Lambrecht, Knud. 1994. *Information structure and sentence form.* Cambridge, Cambridge University Press.

Larson, Richard K. 1988. 'On the double object construction,' *Linguistic Inquiry* 19. 335–391.

Lasnik, H. & M. Saito. 1992. *Move Alpha.* Cambridge, Mass., MIT Press.

Lasnik, H. & T. Stowell. 1991. 'Weakest crossover,' *Linguistic Inquiry* 22.687–720.

Legendre, G., W. Raymond & P. Smolensky. 1993. 'An Optimality-Theoretic typology of case and grammatical voice systems,' *Proceedings of the Berkeley Linguistics Society* 19. 464–478.

Legendre, G., C. Wilson, P. Smolensky, K. Homer & W. Raymond. 1995. 'Optimality and *Wh*-extraction,' in J. Beckman, L. Walsh Dickey & S. Urbanczyk (eds.), *Papers in Optimality Theory.* University of Massachusetts Occasional Papers 18. University of Massachusetts, Amherst. 607–636.

Legendre, G., P. Smolensky & C. Wilson. 1998. 'When is less more?, in P. Barbosa, D. Fox, P. Hagstrom, M. McGinnis and D. Pesetsky (eds.), *Is the Best Good Enough?* Cambridge, Mass., MIT Press. 249–289.

López, Luis. 1999. 'VP-Ellipsis in Spanish and English and the features of Aux,' *Probus* 11.263–297.

López, L. & S. Winkler. 2000. 'Focus and topic in VP-anaphora constructions,' *Linguistics* 38.623–664.

Masullo, Pascual J. 1993. 'Two types of quirky subjects: Spanish versus Icelandic,' in Proceedings of NELS 23. GLSA, University of Massachusetts, Amherst. 303–317.

Matos, Maria Gabriela. 1994. *Construçoes de Elipse do Predicado em Portugues—SV Nulo e Despojamento,* Ph.D. diss., Faculdade de Letras de Lisboa.

McCarthy, John & Alan Prince. 1993. 'Generalized Alignment,' in G. Booij & J. van Marle (eds.), *Yearbook of Morphology.* Dordrecht, Kluwer. 79–154.

McCarthy, John & Alan Prince. 1995. 'Faithfulness and reduplicative identity,' in J. Beckman, L. Walsh Dickey & S. Urbanczyk (eds.) *Papers in Optimality Theory.* Amherst, Mass., GLSA. 249–384.

McCarthy, John. 2002. *A thematic guide to Optimality Theory.* Cambridge, Cambridge University Press.

McCloskey, James. 1992. 'Adjunction, selection and embedded verb second.' Linguistics Research Center, University of California, Santa Cruz.

McCloskey, James. 1996. 'Subjects and subject positions in Irish,' in B. Borsley, & I. Roberts (eds.), *The Syntax of Celtic Langauges.* Cambridge, Cambridge University Press. 241–283.

McCloskey, James. 1997. 'Subjecthood and subject positions,' in L. Haegeman (ed.), *Elements of grammar.* Dordrecht, Kluwer. 197–235.

McCloskey, James. 2001. 'The distribution of subject properties in Irish,' in W. Davies & S. Dubinsky (eds.), *Objects and other Subjects.* Dordrecht, Kluwer. 157–192.

McDaniel, Dana. 1989. 'Partial and multiple *wh*-movement,' *Natural Language and Linguistic Theory* 7: 565–604.

Meyer, Paula. 1972. 'Some observations on constituent order in Spanish,' in J. Casagrande & B. Saciuk (eds.), *Generative Studies in Romance Languages.* Rowley, Mass., Newbury House Publishers. 184–195.

Moore, John & David Perlmutter. 2000. 'To Be a Dative Subject,' *Natural Language and Linguistic Theory* 18.373–416.

Müller, Gereon. 1999. 'Optimality, markedness and word order,' *Linguistics* 37.777–818.

Müller, G. & W. Sternefeld. 1993. 'Improper movement and unambiguous binding,' *Linguistic Inquiry* 24.461–507.

Niño, María-Eugenia. 1993. 'VSO order in Spanish declaratives,' paper presented at the 67th annual meeting of the LSA, January 1993.

Ordóñez, Francisco. 1997. 'The inversion construction in interrogatives in Spanish and Catalan,' in J. Lema & E. Teviño (eds.), *Theoretical Analyses on Romance Languages.* Amsterdam/Philadelphia, John Benjamins. 328–350.

Ordóñez, Francisco. 1998. 'Post-verbal asymmetries in Spanish,' *Natural Language and Linguistic Theory* 16.347–385.

Ordóñez, F. & E. Treviño. 1999. 'Left dislocated subjects and the pro-drop parameter: A case study of Spanish,' *Lingua* 107.39–68.

Parodi, Teresa. 2003. 'Clitic Doubling and Clitic-Left Dislocation in Spanish and Greek as Native and as L2 Grammars' in von Heusinger, Klaus & Georg Kaiser (eds.), *Proceedings of the Workshop 'Semantic and Syntactic Aspects of Specificity in Romance Languages,'* 103–117. Fachbereich Sprachwissenschaft der Universität Konstanz, Konstanz.

Partee, B., A. ter Meulen & R. E. Wall. 1987. *Mathematical Methods in Linguistics.* Dordrecht, Kluwer.

Perlmutter, David. 1984. 'Working 1s and inversion in Italian, Japanese and Quechua,' in D. Perlmutter & C. Rosen (eds.), *Studies in Relational Grammar Vol. 2.* Chicago, The University of Chicago Press, 292–330.

Pestsky, David. 1995. *Zero syntax.* Cambridge, Mass., MIT Press.

Pesetsky, David, 1998. 'Some optimality principles of sentence pronunciation,' in P. Barbosa, D. Fox, P. Hagstrom, M. McGinnis and D. Pesetsky (eds.), *Is the Best Good Enough?* Cambridge, Mass., MIT Press. 337–384.

Pinto, M. 1994. 'Subjects in Italian: Distribution and interpretation,' in R. Bok-Bennema & C. Cremers (eds.), *Linguistics in the Netherlands.* Amsterdam, John Benjamins.

Plann, Susan. 1982. 'Indirect questions in Spanish,' *Linguistic Inquiry* 13.297–312.

Pollock, Jean Yves. 1989. 'Verb movement, universal grammar, and the structure of IP,' *Linguistic Inquiry* 20.365–424.

Prince, Alan. & Paul. Smolensky. 2004 (1993). *Optimality Theory: Constraint interaction in generative grammar.* Oxford, Blackwell.

Prince, Ellen F. 1981. 'Topicalization, Focus-Movement and Yiddish movement.' *Proceedings of BLS 1981.* 249–264.

Prince, Ellen F. 1984. 'Topicalization and left-dislocation: a functional analysis,' in S. J. White & V. Teller (eds.) *Discourses in reading and Linguistics.* Annals of the New York Academy of Sciences. 213–225.

Radford, Andrew. 1997. *Syntactic Theory and the Structure of English: A Minimalist Approach.* Cambridge, Cambridge University Press.

Reinhart, Tanya. 1976. *The syntactic domain of anaphora.* Ph.D. dissertation, MIT.

Reinhart, Tanya. 1981. 'Definite NP anaphora and C-Command domains,' *Linguistic Inquiry* 12.605–635.

Reinhart, Tanya. 1982. *Pragmatics and linguistics: an analysis of sentence topics.* Bloomington, Indiana, Indiana University Linguistics Club.

Rizzi, Luigi. 1982. *Issues in Italian Syntax.* Dordrecht, Foris.

Rizzi, Luigi. 1990. *Relativized Minimality.* Cambridge, Mass., MIT Press.

Rizzi, Luigi. 1996. 'Residual verb second and the *Wh*-Criterion,' in A. Belletti & L. Rizzi (eds.), *Parameters and Functional Heads.* Oxford, Oxford University Press. 63–90.

Rizzi, Luigi. 1997. The fine structure of the left periphery,' in L. Haegeman (ed.), *Elements of grammar.* Dordrecht, Kluwer. 281–337.

Roberts, Michael. 2000. *Information structure, Proto-roles and argument inversion.* MA Thesis, University of California, Santa Cruz.

Rochemont, Michael. 1986. *Focus in Generative Grammar.* Amsterdam, John Benjamins.

Rochemont, Michael. 1989. 'Topic islands and the subjacency parameter,' *Canadian Journal of Linguistics* 34.145–170.

Rudin, Catherine. 1988. 'On multiple questions and multiple *wh*-fronting,' *Natural Language and Linguistic Theory* 6.445–501.

Saito, M. 1989. 'Scrambling as semantically vacuous A'-movement,' in M. Baltin & A. Kroch (eds.), *Alternative conceptions of phrase structure.* Chicago, University of Chicago Press. 182–200.

Samek-Lodovici, Vieri. 1996. *Constraints on subjects: An Optimality Theoretic Analysis.* Ph.D. dissertation, Rutgers University.

Sánchez-López, Cristina. 1999. 'La negación,' in I. Bosque & V. Demonte (eds.), *Gramática Descriptiva de la lengua española.* Madrid, Espasa-Calpe. 2561–2634.

Santorini, Beatrice. 1992. 'Variation and change in Yiddish subordinate clause word order,' *Natural Language and Linguistic Theory* 10.595–640.

Schuyler, Tamara. 2001. 'Wh-Movement out of the site of VP ellipsis,' in J. McCloskey (ed.), *Syntax and Semantics at Santa Cruz 3.* University of California, Santa Cruz. 1–20.

Schwarzschild, Roger. 1999. 'GIVENness, AvoidF and other constraints on the placement of accent,' *Natural Language Semantics* 7.141–177.

Selkirk, Elisabeth. 1984. *Phonology and Syntax: the relation between sound and structure.* Cambridge, Mass., MIT Press.

Selkirk, Elisabeth. 1995. 'Sentence prosody: Intonation, Stress and Phrasing,' in J. Goldsmith (ed.) *The Handbook of Phonological Theory.* Oxford, Blackwell.

Sells, Peter. 2001. *Structure, Alignment and Optimality in Swedish.* Stanford, CSLI.

Sells, P., J. Rickford & T. Wasow. 1996. 'An optimality theoretic approach to variation in negative inversion in AAVE,' *Natural Language and Linguistic Theory* 14.591–627.

Sharma, Deviani. 2001. 'Case clitics and person hierarchy effects,' in P. Sells (ed.), *Formal and Empirical issues in Optimality Theoretic Syntax.* Stanford, CSLI. 225–256.

Sigurðsson, Ármann Halldór. 2004. 'Icelandic Non-Nominative Subjects: Facts and Implications.' *Non-Nominative Subjects* ed. by P. Bhaskarao and K. V. Subarao, Vol. 2, 137–159. Amestrdam/Philadelphia: John Benjamins.

Silva-Corvalán Carmen. 1983. 'On the interaction of Word Order and Intonation: Some OV Constructions in Spanish,' in Flora Klein-Andreu (ed.), *Discourse Perspectives on Syntax,* New York, Academic Press. 117–140.

Smolensky, Paul. 1995. 'On the internal structure of the constraint component CON of UG,' handout of talk, UCLA.

Speas, Margaret. 1990. *Phrase Structure in Natural Language.* Dordrecht, Kluwer.

Suñer, Margarita. 1988. 'The role of agreement in Clitic-Doubled constructions,' *Natural Language and Linguistic Theory* 6: 391–434.

Suñer, Margarita. 1991. 'Indirect questions and the structure of CP: Some consequences,' in H. Campos & F. Martínez-Gil (eds.), *Current studies in Spanish Linguistics.* Washington, DC, Georgetown University Press. 238–312.

Suñer, Margarita. 1994. 'V-movement and the licensing of argumental *wh*-phrases in Spanish,' *Natural Language and Linguistic Theory* 12.335–372.

Suñer, Margarita. 1995. 'Negative elements, island effects and resumptive *no,*' *The Linguistic Review* 12.233–273.

Szendröi, Kriszta. 2001. *Focus and the syntax-phonology interface.* Ph.D. diss., University College London.

Terzi, Arhonto. 1999. 'Clitic combinations, their hosts and their ordering,' *Natural Language and Linguistic Theory* 17.85–121.

Thompson, Sandra. 1987. 'The passive in English: a discourse perspective,' in Channon, Robert & Linda Shockey (eds.), *In Honor of Ilse Lehiste.* Dordrecht, Foris. 497–511.

Tomlin, Russell. 1985. 'Interaction of Subject, Theme and Agent,' in With, Jessica (ed.), *Beyond the sentence: Discourse and sentential form.* Ann Arbor, Karoma Publishers. 61–80.

Toribio, A. Jaqueline. 1994. 'Dialectal Variation in the Licensing of Null Referential and Expletive Subjects,' in C. Parodi, C. Quicoli, M. Saltarelli & M. L. Zubizarreta (eds.), *Aspects of Romance Linguistics,* Georgetown University Press, Washington D.C. 409–432.

Toribio, A. Jaqueline. 2000. 'Setting parametric limits on dialectal variation in Spanish,' *Lingua* 110.315–341.

Torrego, Esther. 1984. 'On inversion in Spanish and some of its effects,' *Linguistic Inquiry* 15.103–129.

Treviño, Esthela. 1992. 'Subjects in Spanish causative constructions.' in P. Hirschbüler & K. Koerner (eds.), *Romance Languages and Modern Linguistic Theory.* Amsterdam/Philadelphia, John Benjamins. 309–324.

Truckenbrodt, Hubert. 1999. 'On the relation between syntactic phrases and phonological phrases,' *Linguistic Inquiry* 30.219–255.

Uribe-Etxebarria, Miriam. 1992. 'On the structural positions of the subjects in Spanish, their nature and their consequences for quantification,' in J. Lakarra & J. Ortiz de Urbina (eds.), *Syntactic Theory and Basque Syntax.* Supplements of the ASJU, Donostia, San Sebastián. 447–491.

Vallduví, Enric. 1992. *The Informational component.* New York/London. Garland.

Vennemann, Theo. 1972. 'On the theory of syllabic phonology,' *Linguistische Berichte* 18.1–18.

Vennemann, Theo. 1988. *Preference laws for syllable structure.* Berlin, Mouton de Gruyter.

Williams, Edwin. 1981. 'Argument structure and morphology', *The Linguistic Review* 1.81–114.

Williams, Edwin. 1986. 'A reassignment of the functions of LF', *Linguistic Inquiry* 17.265–299.

Zaenen, A., J. Maling, & H. Thráisson. 1985. 'Case and grammatical functions: The Icelandic passive,' *Natural Language and Linguistic Theory* 3.441–483.

Zagona, Karen. 2002. *The Syntax of Spanish.* Cambridge, Cambridge University Press.

Zanuttini, Raffaella. 1997a. 'Negation and verb movement,' in L. Haegeman (ed.), *The New Comparative syntax.* Singapore, Longman. 214–245.

Zanuttini, Raffaella. 1997b. *Negation and Clausal Structure.* Oxford, Oxford University Press.

Zec, Draga. 1988. *Sonority constraints on prosodic structure.* Ph.D. dissertation, Stanford University.

Zec, Draga. 1994. 'Sonority constraints on syllable structure,' *Phonology* 12. 85–129.

Zubizarreta, María Luisa. 1998. *Prosody, focus and word order.* Cambridge, Mass., MIT Press.

Zubizarreta, María Luisa. 1999. 'Tema y foco,' in I. Bosque & V. Demonte (eds.), *Gramática descriptiva de la lengua española.* Madrid, Espasa-Calpe. 4216–4244.

Zwart, Jan-Wouter. 1997. *Morphosyntax of verb movement.* Dordrecht, Kluwer.

Index